To Brighten Each Day

To Brighten Each Day

Daily Thoughts for Inspired Living

J. Winston Pearce

BROADMAN PRESS
Nashville, Tennessee

4252-20
ISBN: 0-8054-5220-6

Unless otherwise indicated, Scripture quotations are from the King James Version
Bible. From *The Bible: a New Translation* by James A. R. Moffatt. Copyright ©
1935 by Harper and Row, Publishers, Inc. Used by permission. Subsequent
quotations are marked Moffatt. From *The Modern Language Bible, The New
Berkeley Version.* Copyright 1945, 1959, © 1969 by Zondervan Publishing House.
Used by permission. Subsequent quotations are marked MLB. From HOLY BIBLE
New International Version, copyright © 1978, New York Bible Society. Used by
permission. Subsequent quotations are marked NIV. From J. B. Phillips, *The New
Testament in Modern English,* Revised Edition © J. B. Phillips 1958, 1960, 1972.
Reprinted with permission of Macmillan Publishing Company, Inc. Subsequent
quotations are marked Phillips. From the Revised Standard Version of the Bible,
copyrighted 1946, 1952, © 1971, 1973. Subsequent quotations are marked RSV.

Dewey Decimal Classification: 242.2
Subject heading: DEVOTIONS, DAILY

Library of Congress Catalog Card Number: 83-70001
Printed in the United States of America

To
Allan and Beth,
Alex, Jackie, and Peter
my five
"Grand Children"

Introduction

The naming of books and babies frequently presents problems. Of course, each carries the "family name" that may be a handicap to the baby and the book! It is the "given names" that cause parents and authors the most trouble. The names are important and frequently the names do not fit.

Considerable time and thought were given to the naming of the present volume. For a time I thought an appropriate title would be, "Something Old, Something New, Something Borrowed. . . . " The reason for focusing upon such a title is the nature of the material in the book. In the main, but not entirely, the substance of the book comes from books I have written; there is the emphasis upon the "Old." Then, there is material which has not been used before, the "New." Much of the writing is "Borrowed," in that I have drawn heavily upon a lifetime of wide reading, varied types of reading: history, fiction, drama, poetry, especially religious writings. And, the "twice-told" tale has not been excluded.

The fact that many of the daily pieces have been drawn from my former writings explains the wide difference in the types of material found in the present volume. Some of the pieces are strictly expository. Many more are of a devotional, inspirational, or biblical nature. But quite a few of the writings are not *religious*, in the usually accepted understanding of the word. These pieces fall in the general understanding of "life experiences"; some lean heavily upon the fields of reading and writing. Some go with the hope that a smile, or even a hearty chuckle, may result.

Each page gives a suggested Bible reading for the day, with special emphasis upon a verse or words chosen from a verse. Many, though not all, of the readings have a "Thought for the Day," a line or lines of a poem, a hymn, a thought-provoking quotation, a brief prayer, or an anecdote that will, I trust, brighten the reader's day and possibly serve as a conversation bit to pass along during the day.

It was this purpose that caused us to settle on the title, *To Brighten Each Day.* The author, editor, and publisher send the volume forth with the earnest hope that the title is appropriate.

The indexes should prove helpful, especially since there is no table of contents. First, there is the "Index of Names," with numerous names of persons quoted or considered. Second, there is a limited index of "Special Days." This will make the material in the book readily accessible to the minister, teacher, or family for special seasons. And finally, there is the "Topics Index." It is rather full, cross-referenced, with many entries. Again, a careful look at this should make the particular discussion, story, illustration, example available when needed.

And, now, a word of deep and sincere gratitude to two groups. One, to that host of writers who have clarified my mind, stimulated my spirit, and warmed the cockles of my heart with their books for so many years. What they have done for my life is reflected in the many references to them and to their writings which you will find in this book. Two, my unbounded thanks to that wonderful group of editors at Broadman who have been my friends. They have been warm and encouraging; they have been helpful and professional in their constructive disciplines and in their creative criticism. They have been my Moses and Joshua. Again and again, when I have been deep in "the house of bondage" to some troublesome manuscript, they have given direction and guidance all the way across my "Jordans" and have seen me safely into that "goodly land," that land which only a writer, whose work has been published, can know!

J. WINSTON PEARCE
Campbell University
Buies Creek, N.C.

On Making Covenants

Now it is in mine heart to make a covenant with the Lord (v. 10).

This is the New Year season, a time for looking back, a time for facing forward. It is a time for the confession of failures experienced in the past year; it is a time for commitments for the year ahead. It is a time for covenant-making. Never underestimate the value of covenants, covenants made with one's better self, with others, and most of all, covenants made with God.

These covenants serve as monuments, memorials. Life begins with ideals; youth sees to that. "We hope, we aspire, we resolve, we trust when morning calls us to life and light." Yes, but go on to the next line, "But our hearts grow weary, and, ere the night, our lives are trailing the sordid dust." The attrition of the days, the months, and the years take their toll.

Robert Robinson was converted through the preaching of George Whitefield. When Robinson was twenty, he heard John Wesley; it was the preaching of Wesley that led him to become a preacher. Two years later, when he was twenty-two and pastor at Norwich, Robinson wrote the hymn, "Come Thou Fount of Every Blessing/Tune my heart to sing thy grace." Years later, when trials and discouragement had done their stint to his faith, a woman reproved him for his waywardness and read to him the words of his own hymn, not knowing the author. Robinson replied, "Madam, I am the poor, unhappy man who composed it; and I would give a thousand worlds, if I had them, to enjoy the feelings I knew then."

It is often at this point that covenants do their work. We come upon our covenant as a lover might come upon a dear keepsake. The covenant says: This is how you felt; this is what you said; this is what you covenanted. And, now? What about it? Renew vows!

"In the Beginning"

Born, not of blood . . . nor of the will of man, but of God (v. 13).

Folk sayings and words of philosophers alike have recognized the value of a good beginning: "A bad beginning makes a bad ending" . . . "In the beginning is my end" . . . "The beginning is the most important part of the work" . . . And a writer of verse cries, "I wish there were some place called the land of beginning again."

There is the story of a traveler asking for directions. The would-be-guide made several attempts at telling the traveler how to get where he wanted to go. Each time the directions were reversed. The bridge was out if he took one route; he faced a detour if he went another way; another way led to a dead end. Finally the guide said, "Mister, if I were going to that place, I just wouldn't start from here." Where you begin is important.

Now, ask yourself some important questions: Was Christ in the beginning of your home—first date, betrothal, wedding, honeymoon, setting up your new home? Was Christ, "the Word," present when you took your first job? Was the task performed under his guidance and as unto him? Was he in the plans for your family, your children? Is Christ in the beginning of your stewardship?

What of habits? They can be good or bad; they can bless or damn, pull down or lift up. If Christ is in the beginning of establishing habits, how will that affect the matter of drinking, smoking, Sunday observance, types of reading, places of amusement, topics, and manner of conversation?

"The Word" was in the beginning of the world. Was he, is he, in the beginnings of your many worlds?

> Do you believe in doing what comes naturally? Or do you believe in doing what naturally comes from beginning all things in the presence of "the Word"?

Unfinished Business

All that Jesus began to do and teach (v. 1).

The Scripture passage for today points up "all that Jesus began to do and teach." It is a simple statement of fact, easily understood. However, in the light of history and the Christian faith, it is more than a mere statement of fact. For Jesus "began" what was to go on, and on, and on. What he began could not be accomplished in one brief lifetime; it could not be limited to one small, conquered country, among one people called "The Jews." He began something that would go on until every knee shall bow and every tongue confess that he is Lord. We, too, are constantly faced with "unfinished business."

To speak of "unfinished business" is to think of the good and the bad, of the desirable and the undesirable. If you say of a person, "That man never finishes anything he begins," it is an uncomplimentary thing to say, not a good recommendation. Jesus said if a man was going to war he ought to evaluate forces to see if he could finish what he was beginning. No matter how many men a baseball team gets on first base, it is crossing home plate that counts for runs.

Yet, if we never begin anything that we cannot finish, we shall leave unattempted the great things in life. The poet, Robert Browning, stated:

> This low man seeks a little thing to do,
>   Sees it and does it;
> This high man, with a great thing to pursue,
>   Dies ere he knows it.

We cannot *finish* our education, our character, our homes, our Christian faith. It is all "unfinished business." As the author of Hebrews said, "Let us go on."

Not for Sale

For your sakes he became poor (v. 9b).

There is the old saying, "Beggars can't be choosers." Christ came to make you rich! Consider again that breathtaking word of the apostle's, "For you know the grace of our Lord Jesus Christ, that, though he was rich, yet for your sakes he became poor, that ye through his poverty might be rich." But "beggars can't be choosers." Whether one is rich in honor or in stocks and bonds, in name or mansion, one must accept as a beggar that which God in Christ offers. That is, one must accept it as a gift. Rich people do not like to do this. They are accustomed to "paying their own way." They do not like to be obligated to anyone. Christ is not a sharp trader; he is a bounteous giver.

There is a delightful story about Colonel Theodore Roosevelt during the Spanish-American War. Colonel Roosevelt's troops were in desperate need of medical supplies. The supplies were near. Clara Barton, founder of the American Red Cross, was in charge of these supplies. Roosevelt sent word to Miss Barton that he would like to make a purchase of the medical materials. Back came the word that the supplies were not for sale. "Teddy" was disturbed. He cared for his men, and the supplies were essential to the welfare of his troops. He went to see Miss Barton in person. "What can I do to secure these supplies?" he asked. Back came the answer, accompanied by a smile, "Why, Colonel, just by asking for them." Roosevelt saw her point, smiled, and said, "Then, Miss Barton, I sincerely request these supplies for my troops." And the supplies were given.

The medicine was not for sale; it was for the asking. Roosevelt could not pay; he could accept. The gift of salvation is from God's great heart of love. The supplies are adequate for all. The acceptance of these "supplies" as a free gift from the heart of God is the world's only hope.

> Jesus paid it all,
> All to him I owe;
> Sin had left a crimson stain,
> He wash'd it white as snow.
>
> —ELVINA M. HALL

Read John 12:20-26   **January 5**
You Die to Live

If it die, it bringeth forth much fruit (v. 24c).

The seed has to fall into the ground and die, if it does not, it will abide alone. When I was a small boy, my father gave a neighbor some peanuts for planting purposes. Now, "Aunt Ryor" was fond of peanuts; they were her favorite food, morning, noon, or night. Several weeks later my father saw "Aunt Ryor" and asked how the peanuts were coming along in her garden. She hesitated, smiled, and said, "Mr. Pearce, to tell you the truth, I never planted those peanuts. I got to thinking about the moles and the crows; I knew I might lose those peanuts; so, I just sat down and ate them." She never allowed the peanuts to "fall into the ground and die"; therefore, the peanuts had to abide alone. Life is like that. The cross proves it.

The way of the cross says the first shall be last and the last shall be first. This does not mean, of course, that men will lose their true spiritual stature. Those who are now first in service, love, and humility will, because of those qualities, always be in the front ranks of the kingdom. But as Jesus faced the cross, the reversal of worldly values was brought out again and again. Pharisees were put last and publicans first. Samaritans were put first and Levites were put last. A Roman centurion was praised and religious leaders were condemned.

Some years ago there was a balloting for greatness. Elmer Davis, renowned radio commentator, had this to say: "Who during the reign of Tiberius would have said that a carpenter from Nazareth was the greatest man in the world? Maybe the greatest man in the world today is Joe Blotz—who does his job, pays his taxes, tries not to chisel on his fellow citizens, makes an honest endeavor to find out what it is all about."

> I must needs go home by the way of the cross,
> There's no other way but this.
>
> —JESSIE B. POUNDS

11

January 6   Read Matthew 24:36-44
On Finding It the Day Before

Therefore be ye also ready (v. 44a).

The *Charlotte Observer* reported on the driver of a small compact car's run-in with the driver of a big truck. The driver of the truck cut in front of the small car without giving a signal. A little farther along both had to stop for a red light. The driver of the small car got out, took a big tire wrench, marched back to the truck, and smashed its rearview mirror. He looked at the driver and announced, "As long as you don't use it, you don't need it"; then he turned and went back to his car and drove off. The truck driver's reaction? He would not sign a complaint.

Hal Luccock once told of a group of children on a "treasure hunt" in Vermont. It was a typical game; the teams were sent out to find a list of "impossible" things; they were to be back at the starting place by a certain time. One of the things they were to find and bring back was a snake. Now, as Dr. Luccock says, a snake is a rather difficult thing to find when you are looking for it. But one of the teams came back with a snake. True, it was a dead snake, but there was nothing in the rules which said it had to be a live snake. So, the team with the snake was declared the winner. Then one of the losers asked one of the winners, "How in the world did you find that snake?" The winner replied, "I saw it yesterday." Dr. Luccock then scored his point; he said that the Bible will not yield to hasty searching; we must see our treasures in its pages "yesterday."

A Window on the Mountain

His windows being open toward Jerusalem, he kneeled and prayed (v. 10b).

A minister was sent to pastor a little church in the White Mountains of New Hampshire. Shortly after he arrived, an old farmhouse, the home of an old man and his wife, burned. The home was near the little church. The new pastor watched the home burn and tried to give comfort to the aged couple. The next morning, before the foundation sills had stopped smoking, the minister was at work raising funds to rebuild for the old couple.

The people of the mountain area responded loyally, and the new house was soon rising over the ashes of the old one. It became apparent that the generosity of friends and neighbors had not only assured a new house but that there would be sufficient funds to do something extra.

The pastor went to the old lady and said, "What would you like for us to put in the house that was not in the old one—something you have always wanted but could not have? He thought the request would be for an extra bathroom or an extra cupboard or clothes closet, but the old woman replied, "I have stood over that sink and washed dishes for thirty-five years. Always I have had to look at the blank kitchen wall; yet, all the time I have known that that kitchen wall hid the most beautiful view in the White Mountains. I wish you would put a window in the wall, so I could see the mountain."

The window was put in and for a dozen years the lady looked out her new window up to her beautiful mountains, and, as she said, "Since my husband died, *beyond* the mountains."

> As one looks on a face through a window,
>   through life I have looked upon God.
> Because I have loved life,
>   I shall have no sorrow to die.
>
> —AMELIA BURR

Still Husband and Wife

For this cause shall a man leave his father and mother (v. 31).

The book bearing the title, *A Window On the Mountain,* was a joint effort between my wife and me. Not so much in the writing, though she did do three chapters; but the book was a joint effort primarily because it grew out of joint experiences and discussions. This is the only way the book could be a joint effort, really, for as is frequently the case, my wife and I do not use the same style and approach in describing mutual experiences. Our friends have observed this and have often commented on it.

While we each do a great deal of public speaking, we can seldom use each other's notes and material. Indeed, in more than forty years that we have been husband and wife, I can think of only once when either of us has been able to make use of an address the other had prepared. That once was enough!

We were both scheduled to speak on the same program. My wife was to speak first. As we drove to the engagement, we talked about the theme of the meeting. The wife asked and I told her of the approach and the outline that I intended to use. She was kind and said it sounded like a very good approach to her.

The reader may imagine, but certainly not experience, my consternation when that woman, preceding me on the program, got up and gave my speech—point by point! And, we are still husband and wife! Long-suffering? That's me.

> To have and to hold from this day forward, for better, for worse, for richer, for poorer, in sickness, and in health, to love and to cherish, till death do part us.
>
> —BOOK OF COMMON PRAYER

The Ability to Read

Blessed is he that readeth (v. 3*a*).

Aparticular blessing is promised those who read the Word of God. Think of the Gospels. We read of the teaching and preaching of Jesus that "without a parable spake he not unto them." That is, Jesus used stories, pictures, to hang on the walls of the mind. And how well he did it! No wonder people would listen all day, forgetting about food and drink! That they would crowd the streets and the seashore until there was no time for rest and sleep.

Late in his life, Professor William Lyon Phelps, beloved teacher of English literature at Yale University, wrote:

> The art of living can be cultivated; the more we stock our minds with interesting thoughts, the richer we are. And these riches remain; they cannot be lost. They add to the happiness and to the excitement of daily living. In my life of professional teaching, I never endeavored to make young men more efficient; I tried to make them more interesting. If one is interested, one is usually interesting. The business of the teacher is not to supply information, it is to raise a thirst. I like to hang pictures on the walls of the mind, I like to make it possible for a man to live with himself, so that he will not be bored with himself.

Think of that, stocking the mind with interesting thoughts, hanging pictures on the walls of the mind, not efficiency but thirst, living with the self and not becoming bored! One of the best ways to do that, of course, and no one knew it better than Professor Phelps, is through reading, reading the right kind of material.

James Russell Lowell wrote:

> Have you ever rightly considered what the mere ability to read means? That it is the key which admits us to the whole world of thought and imagination; to the company of the saint, and the sage, of the wisest and the wittest moments? That it enables us to see with the keenest eyes, hear with the keenest ears, and listen to the sweetest voices of all time?"

Read Nehemiah 8:1-3
"Mr. Pointer" and "Mr. Beaner"

The ears of all the people were attentive unto the book of the law (v. 3b).

Often we go to church in about the same attitude that we go to a concert or a picture show. We go to be entertained, as spectators. If the performance pleases us, we applaud; if it does not please us, we criticize. If the service is interesting, we are alert; if the service is dull, we drowse and nod. We evaluate the service in terms of our neighbor; we regret that he or she is not present to hear an especially sharp arrow shot by the preacher on behalf of some besetting sin of the neighbor!

Records in an old church in Ohio reveal that this is not a new problem, however. There it was realized that the responsibility did not all rest with the preacher; the congregation had to stay alert and receptive. To ensure this, according to Theodore Heimarck, they appointed two special officers: "Mr. Pointer" and "Mr. Beaner."

Now the duty of "Mr. Pointer" was to stand near the preacher during the sermon. As the preacher made a certain point that was especially pertinent for a particular individual in the congregation, "Mr. Pointer" would level a finger and cry out, "You, there, Bill Jones, that applies especially to you!"

"Mr. Beaner" was given a chair in a prominent place in the choir loft. From this position he surveyed, with hawk-like eyes, the congregation. If he saw a head begin to gently sway and bob from lack of attention or drowsiness, he would raise his beanshooter to his lips—he was always a crack shot—and zing, the sleeping individual was reinstated to the ranks of the attentive. Now, there's a job to warm the cockles of the heart of any young or older boy.

Worship is not passive, it is active; worship requires active participation on the part of the worshiper.

Coming in and Going Out

The place whereon thou standest is holy ground (v. 5b).

Before we spend all our time trying to improve the world, let us spend a little time trying to improve ourselves. We need to know and obey a few local ordinances before we try to rewrite the constitution of the world. We frequently try to keep everyone else's vineyard, but our own vineyards we do not keep. The fact that we do not know our own children is scarcely the best recommendation for instructing the families of the world about their children. And, above all, let us give thought to our own relationship with Christ before we set out to convert the world to him. Look to your local loyalty.

Once a person has seen to local loyalties the task is not complete; the task is just beginning. There are social causes, community, national, and world causes that claim his "ounce of courage." Many years ago Edmund Burke wrote, "All that is needed for the success of evil is that good people do nothing." It is still true.

At midway of this century, E. M. House wrote a book called, *Saints in Politics.* It is the dramatic story of a small group of British politicians at the turn of the century: Thomas Babington, Henry Thornton, William Wilberforce, and others. These were religious men, ardently evangelical in their faith. Their personal religion was the fountain spring of their social concern. They were, as Wilberforce himself said, " . . . true Christians who knew what it was to practice saintliness in daily living and by whom the minutest detail of actions were considered with reference to eternity." The author affirms that there is scarcely a moral, social, political, or religious reform of nineteenth-century England that cannot be traced to the influences of these men. Local loyalties to come into; social and political causes that call us out.

The world is my parish.

—JOHN WESLEY

A Lonely Hunter

He began to be in want (v. 14b).

"**M**y heart," wrote William Sharp, "is a lonely hunter that hunts on a lonely hill." Carson McCullers thought enough of that haunting confession to make it the title of her popular novel. Motion picture executives thought enough of the novel to make it into a disturbing picture.

"The heart is a lonely hunter that hunts on a lonely hill." Right! It is and it does. The best-loved short story in the world, the parable of the prodigal son, emphasizes the truth. Man is a hunter; all men are hunters; all men have always been hunters. They have not all hunted in the same way, for the same game, on the same "hills" but man is, and always has been, a hunter. Columbus hunts for a sea route; Galileo hunts for a planet; the biologist hunts for a death-dealing germ; the astronaut hunts for the moon. All persons hunt for happiness and for God.

This is one of the basic truths of the story of the prodigal son. He was a hunter. He wanted something he did not have, something that could not be found, he thought, where he was, doing what he was doing. He determined to "go hunting." Restless, rebellious, selfish! He was determined to live his own life, in his own way, on his own chosen "hills," seeking new "friends" and new social values. The "establishment," the "power structure," the "old morality," as he had known them, were left behind. Carl Sandburg wrote, "God must have wanted man to be a changer. Else God wouldn't have put that awful unrest in him." The following lines were a part of the epitaph that Robert Louis Stevenson wrote for himself:

This be the verse ye grave for me:
Here he lies where he longed to be;
Home is the sailor, home from the sea,
And the hunter home from the hill.

On Building Coffins

Whatsoever a man soweth, that shall he also reap (v. 7b).

There is a story about the Roman Emperor Julian, known as the Apostate Emperor. In childhood Julian had a friend by the name of Agathon. After boyhood their ways parted; Agathon became a Christian; Julian became the Roman emperor who persecuted Christians. One day Agathon and Julian met. The emperor said, "Tell me, Agathon, what has become of your carpenter of Nazareth?" Pointing across the street where the multitudes were entering the pagan temple, he continued, "Has your carpenter any work these days? Are there still some small jobs coming his way?" Agathon, the Christian, looked at his boyhood friend and said, "Yes, Julian, the carpenter of Nazareth is very busy these days. He is nailing together a coffin to put your empire in."

History tells the story. Julian's reign lasted less than two years. He was slain in battle with the Persians. And tradition has it that as he fell, mortally wounded, he cried, "Galilean, thou hast conquered!" Tradition? Possibly. But hear this, "Be not deceived; God is not mocked: for whatsoever a man soweth, that shall he also reap." Someone has said that a free translation of that might read, "Don't kid yourself; you can't get away with it!" And, that is not just tradition!

Of course, the matter of time is involved. We must not expect God to balance his book every Saturday night, nor to balance our's weekly. And, that points up one of the major differences between the people of faith and the people of no faith. The people who have no faith have to be concerned with time, it is all they have to work with. But the people of faith in God are not bound by clocks and calendars and the hourglass. They have eternity for the balancing of the books. No faith? Listen:

> But at my back I always hear
> Time's winged chariot hurrying near;
> And yonder all before us lie
> Deserts of vast eternity.
>
> —ANDREW MARVELL

"You'll Never Get It All Out"

Teaching them to observe all things whatsoever I have commanded you (v. 20a).

The word *discipline* means student, pupil, or learner. When Jesus said, "Go . . . and make disciples" (v. 19, RSV), he was instructing his followers to enroll people in his school, let them come to school to him, let them learn of his teachings. Jesus said that learners were to be enrolled; he did not say geniuses, the top 3 percent of the graduating class, or young, or old, or rich, or poor, it is "learners" who are to be enrolled.

This school of Christ is one from which one never graduates. No matter how brilliant, how diligent, you never learn all there is to know about Christ. The little girl said, after her first day in school, "Mother, is there as much that I do not know as there is that I do know?" There is always more to learn. This has been one of the phases of the school of Christ that has attracted discerning minds. They wanted to give themselves to something that they would never be able to master. Suppose you were given a gold mine with the understanding that you would never get all the gold out of it, no matter how much you mined, no matter how long you dug—there would always be more gold than you could get out of the mine.

It is interesting to note that the more one knows of Christ and his teaching, the more humble one is about that knowledge. The saint who has lived with Christ and been a student of his word for a half century feels that he is still in the nursery school of the Savior. It is always, more beyond. This "Teaching them . . . all things." Where does it stop? Only when we "know as we are fully known."

> The greatest thing the disciples got from the teaching was not a doctrine but an influence. To the last hour of their lives the big thing was that they had been with him.

—JOHN MARQUIS

Hearing and Doing

As we therefore have opportunity, let us do good unto all men (v. 10a).

There are those who are forever studying but never doing; always learning but never putting into practice what they learn. There is something disturbing about a person who stays in the same Sunday School class for twenty-five years, regular in attendance but never puts into practice anything that is learned. As the lepers went, in keeping with the instruction of Jesus, they were healed. In the kingdom there is a place for on-the-job training.

At a summer Bible conference a friend of mine called to another and said, "Come on, Blank, let's go hear what this man has to say in his second hour." "Blank" responded, "I am just trying to make up my mind about that. I have been asking myself, seriously, if I was going to do anything about what he told us in the first hour. If I am not, there's no use hearing him again."

Gandhi, the great Indian leader, stood before 15,000 of his countrymen and made one of the shortest speeches in history. He said, "I owe, and India owes, more to one who never set his foot in it than to anyone else; that is Jesus Christ." In the fall of 1927, at a YMCA meeting in Ceylon he said, "If I had to face only the Sermon on the Mount and my own interpretation of it, I would not hesitate to say, 'O yes, I am a Christian.' He then added, "You of the West take Jesus apologetically at this point, while I take him seriously and literally."

To tell that experience is not to approve of Gandhi's position. It takes more than the Sermon on the Mount and the ethics of Jesus to make one a Christian. We regret the great Indian leader never understood, never accepted the gospel, the whole gospel of the Son of God. However, we can and should be rebuked that in those parts of the teachings of Jesus that he did accept, he took more seriously than Christians often do.

Magnifying the Church

The Lord added to their number day by day (v. 47b, RSV).

The New Testament is full of the glory of the church. Charles Edward Jefferson said that there are only two objects in the Scriptures that are of supreme importance—one is the Lord Jesus and the other is his church. The Gospels do not have much to say about the church; it is in formation. The Acts of the Apostles tells about the planting and the spreading of the churches. It is in Paul's letters that we come to the most glowing accounts of the churches. This man Paul, who once had done everything in his power to stamp out the cause of Christ, pauperizes the language as he tries to do justice to his love and admiration for the church.

We have pictures of the churches, poetry about the churches, novels, learned theological treatises about the churches. We sing about the churches.

Years ago E. Norfleet Gardner published a small volume of sermons about the church, *Magnifying the Church.* The listings of the subjects of the sermons, which had been used previously in the Church Training program of the churches, whets one's appetite: A Divine Institution, The Herald of Salvation, The Mother of Benevolence, The Home Base of World Evangelism, The Church's Part in Rebuilding the World, The Ally of the Churches, The Champion of Justice, A Lighthouse of Truth, The Cradle of Freedom, A Fellowship for Worship, The Stronghold of Righteousness, A Builder of Character, and The Church and Its Minister. The subjects show something of the scope of usefulness of the churches.

I will build my church; and the gates of hell shall not prevail against it (Matt. 16:18).

"He Remembered Two Things"

By the grace of God I am what I am (v. 10a).

During the War Between the States, a system was in operation whereby a man called into service could pay another man to take his place. The second man could be paid, employed to sacrifice, and possibly die as a substitute. In ways that are higher and deeper and broader and longer than that, Christ sacrificed for us, fought our battles, died on the cross in our place. He did this because he cared, because he loved us so much. He did it because no one else could do it—here the analogy of the war substitute breaks down entirely. Again, the act of his taking our place is free and voluntary. It is without money and without price. This is not to say that the result of his sacrifice will not lead to deep dedication and high service. However, such service is a result of Jesus' action rather than a payment that initiates the action.

The redeeming grace of Christ wrought its marvelous work in the life of John Newton, the sinning seaman who became the preacher, poet, and saint. Before he died, Newton's mind and tongue were hesitant about doing their accustomed work. However, when friends would call, he would sometimes manage to bear his witness. He would say haltingly, "My memory is almost gone, but I do remember two things—that I am a great sinner and Christ is a great Savior."

Those two great truths burned themselves into the heart of Newton. They made him a saint and a blessing. Those two truths are necessary. When they are known and realized, they may not make poets and preachers of all men, as they did of Newton; but the experimental knowledge of these two great truths will make a saint out of any man— in the New Testament meaning of that word. Newton's words:

> Amazing grace! how sweet the sound,
> That saved a wretch like me!
> I once was lost, but now am found,
> Was blind but now I see!

"A Hand to Help"

"My help cometh from the Lord, which made heaven and earth" (v. 2).

The ancient word, the ever-true word, the only word that ever has been or ever will be, totally adequate is: "Believe on the Lord Jesus Christ, and thou shalt be saved" (Acts 16:31). This is not to say that one has no faith in education, scientific achievement, a decent standard of living, military preparedness, the United Nations, or other efforts of human betterment. What it does mean is this: "Except the Lord build the house, they labour in vain that build it: except the Lord keep the city, the watchman waketh but in vain" (Ps. 127:1).

During the early days of World War II, J. B. Priestly had the courage to say that the English people "got a bit sick of having the front of their minds tickled." He thought they wanted something deeper. Has the time come when we can see that "he who would save his life will lose it?"

> Still as of old
>   Men by themselves are priced—
> For thirty pieces Judas sold
>   himself, not Christ.
>
> —HESTER H. CHOLMONDELEY

The apostle Paul says that it is a faithful saying "that Christ Jesus came into the world to save sinners." We are all sinners. Only Christ can save us now; only Christ could save our fathers yesterday; only Christ will be able to save our children tomorrow. It is in Christ that our faith must be centered.

In *Les Miserables,* the little girl, Cosette, went into a dark wood to bring water from a spring. She was frightened as she heard a heavy step behind her; she thought someone was there to seize her. But just then a strong arm reached down and lifted her heavy burden, the big bucket of water. A friend fell in step with her, not an enemy to hurt, but a friend to help. So, it is when Christ becomes the center of our faith.

"I Give Myself"

They . . . first gave their own selves to the Lord (v. 5*b*).

Few persons have written as beautifully as Franz Werfel about the spiritual crises in persons' lives. In his *The Forty Days of Musa Dagh,* a man by the name of Bagradian remains in his troubled land after his fellow countrymen have been evacuated. As the ships sail away, Bagradian stands on his son's grave. A shot is fired from ambush, and he falls, grasping the cross that marks the grave. The father dies with the son's cross draped across his heart—mute testimony that a soul must have another's cross, pain, across its own heart before it can triumph. "There's a cross for ev'ryone and there's a cross for me."

Those who are familiar with the heroic stories of the missionary enterprise may know that in 1835, a young people's missionary meeting was being held in the First Baptist Church of Richmond, Virginia. When the plates were passed a young man, a student at the University of Richmond, dropped a piece of paper in the plate with these words on it: "I give myself, J. Lewis Shuck." He was the first Baptist missionary to go to China from the state of Virginia. In China he labored faithfully, along with his wife, Henrietta Hall Shuck.

One of the grave dangers of a lesson like this is that we recount the crosses that others bear, be grateful for their dedication, be moved and thank God for them, but leave the matter there. We say that we are not great and brave and that no one knows, or will know, about us. The answer to that is easy. God sees and knows and cares and calls. Every Christian is called to bear his own cross.

> All through life I see a cross—
>   Where sons of God yield up their breath;
> There is no gain except by loss;
>   There is no life except by death;
>   There is no vision but by faith.
>
> —Walter Chalmers Smith

The Tiger and the Dog

There shall they rehearse the righteous acts of the Lord (v. 11b).

Jesus taught his disciples that "the field is the world" (Matt. 13:38). It is exciting to see an individual who embraces the world in his knowledge.

I remember a college history professor who had never traveled beyond the bounds of the United States, yet, he was a citizen of the world and very much at home in the solar system. China, Greece, Rome, Persia, the islands of the sea, Europe, and South America were as much within his ken as if he had been a naturalized citizen of each. Peoples, movements, governments, wars, cultures, literature, language, religion, and philosophy were all familiar to him. He had traveled, and he had seen.

He knew just where some emperor, king, or dictator had called in a tiger to chase a dog, only to learn to his sorrow, after it was too late, that the tiger was far more dangerous than the dog! He had stocked his mind with interesting thoughts; he had hung valuable pictures on the walls of his mind; therefore, he was an interested and an interesting individual. He was a citizen of the world.

Evelyn Underhill said that people spent their lives for the most part conjugating three verbs: to want, to have, and to do. She said that it was easy to forget that none of these verbs has any ultimate significance, except as they are transcended by and included in the fundamental verb "to be."

Teach us, Father God, to ever be aware of our heritage and lineage, made in thy image and given dominion in the world. Teach us that the world is our field of stewardship. Amen.

My Ready Answer

I know that my redeemer liveth (v. 25a).

On being asked the secret of his happiness Robert Browning is reported to have said, "I am very sure of God." In "Paracelsus," one of his earliest poems, Browning says:

> I profess no other share
> In the selection of my lot, than this
> My ready answer to the will of God
> Who summons me to be his organ.

Sure of God, sure of God's summons, sure of God's will, sure of God's purpose, that he is "his organ." No wonder the poet was happy. At Browning's funeral a friend, listening to the long, slow funeral dirge, remembering the happy, vibrant life Browning had lived, said that he would have given much for a trumpeter to have stepped on the stage and let forth with a loud and glad blast!

What are you sure of? Of whom are you sure? If someone taps you on the shoulder and says, "Quick, tell me what you are sure of," what do you say? What is our mission and purpose in life? Do we give ourselves with glad, free abandon to his will and purpose?

Such questions are relevant for every age. They apply to every person, not just to pastor and missionary. They apply to all, regardless of age, sex, profession, or living conditions. The questions apply to all of life, not just the "great affairs of life," conversion, choice of vocation, and selection of spouse. It is now the early morning hour. We have the hours before us. How shall we spend them—invest them or waste them? Where shall we go? What shall we do? With whom shall we talk? What shall we read? What shall we remember, recall? What shall be our priorities today?

> The Master hath come, and He calls us to follow
> The track of the footprints He leaves on our way;
> Far over the mountain and through the deep hollow,
> The path leads us on to the mansions of day.

> —SARAH DOUDNEY

Never Too Old

Now therefore give me this mountain (v. 12a).

We think it is the youth who respond to the call of God. And, there is truth in our supposition. But it is not the whole truth. Search the Bible; the response is almost totally from adults.

Noah was a builder. For the first five hundred years of his life it looked as if he were a "chip off the old block." He was the grandson of Methuselah. Then God called Noah to build a boat; the most famous boat ever built, the ark.

Abraham is one of the most revered persons in all the tides of time. Three great religions look to him in gratitude: Judaism, Christianity, and Muhammadanism. He was a mature and wealthy man when God called him.

Moses is easily one of the greatest men. It has been said that he spent forty years thinking he was somebody; forty years thinking he was nobody; then God called him and Moses spent the next forty years knowing that he was the servant of God.

Jonah was a preacher. The late Hersey Davis of Southern Seminary thought he was the greatest preacher in the Old Testament. Jonah was a mature, well-established man when God called him.

Paul was a missionary, probably the greatest; he "turned the world upside down." Thirteen New Testament books, we think, were written by him. Check the great revival of Christianity over the past two thousand years; the spark came from Paul! God called him when he was a mature man. You are never too old to hear God's call.

> He forces no man, each must choose his way,
> And as he chooses so the end will be.

—JOHN OXENHAM

"God's Signature"

Yea, I have loved thee with an everlasting love (v. 3b).

A magnet is a valuable instrument; that is to say, it is a valuable instrument for working with elements that have an affinity for it. A magnet is valueless for working with wood shavings; these will not cleave to the magnet. But drag the magnet through iron filings and immediately these will rush to join the magnet. There is kinship. Christ affirmed that when he was lifted up he would draw all men unto himself. He would become a magnet that attracts like to like. Christ does not attract the beasts of the fields, nor the animals of the forest, nor the fish of the sea; he attracts persons who are made in the image of God.

There is a little poem that tells of man's creation. It says that in the dim time of beginning God made man. God scattered through man's mind "the starry stuff" and then God called on all creation to behold what he had made. But God was not satisfied. He said that he would have to leave man incomplete, leave him torn between the "no and the yes," would leave him restless until man found his rest in God. In substance, the poem says what Augustine affirmed, that God so made man that he remains restless until he finds his rest in God.

This places a serious responsibility upon man. No man can come unto the Father except the Spirit draw him, but no one is forced to follow the leadership of the Spirit. The church covenant says, "led by the Spirit"—led, not driven; led, not commanded; led, not herded.

> All people that on earth do dwell,
>   Sing to the Lord with cheerful voice;
> Him serve with fear, His praise forthtell;
>   Come ye before Him and rejoice.
>
> The Lord, ye know, is God indeed,
>   Without our aid He did us make;
> We are His folk, He doth us feed,
>   And for His sheep He doth us take.
>
> —WILLIAM KETHE

The Continuing Incarnation

Christ in you, the hope of glory (v. 27b).

The incarnation is a theological term; it means the coming of the divine into the human in the form of Jesus of Nazareth. "The Word became flesh and dwelt among us" (John 1:14, RSV). God had been with his people, among his people, before his people, along beside, but never, as Richard LaRue Swain says, are we told that he was *within* his people. Then, one night in Bethlehem, God came in human flesh, put it on, and wore it like a royal garment! That is the incarnation!

What we are prone to forget is that having come into human life, God never left it. In that first "coming" he came in a unique way, a way never to be repeated, for "in him all the fulness of God was pleased to dwell" (Col. 1:19, RSV). But the incarnation continues through the ministry of the Holy Spirit, "Christ in you, the hope of glory."

Christ dwelt within the body of Jesus of Nazareth once. His desire now is to live, through the Holy Spirit, in the life of his churches, his followers. The body of Jesus of Nazareth once did the bidding of the Son of God. Now, we are that body and he wants to do his work through us. That is the deep meaning of the lovely Christmas hymn, "O come to us, abide with us, Our Lord Immanuel."

The Italian author, Luigi Pirandello, wrote an interesting play with a novel plot. He called the play *Six Characters in Search of an Author.* A group of players meet to rehearse a new play; suddenly they are interrupted by six characters. The manager asks what they want. The characters say that they are interesting characters but they have been sidetracked. What can the manager do for them? He can let the characters live in him!

Christ became what we are in order to make us what he is.

—IRENAEUS

If the Book Were Lost

I have found the book of the law in the house of the Lord (v. 8b).

It is a make-believe story. One morning England awoke to learn that she had no Bible; she had lost it. More than that she had lost its total influence in the life of the people and the work of their hands. It was an awful situation! England's literature could not be understood; Shakespeare was unintelligible; Ruskin made no sense; Browning was in rags and tatters; Milton was a crossword puzzle. People could scarcely carry on a conversation; pledges, treaties, and covenants meant nothing. The daily papers, the news magazines could not be understood; their great music was no more; their art museums were stripped.

But, the Bible is much more than this. The Bible is concerned with redemption. And, apart from the Bible, we know little about redemption. The Bible is not the source of redemption. Redemption is in and through a person, not a book, any book, not even the Bible. But it is in and through the Bible that we learn of that person, Jesus Christ.

Are we interested in the churches? The message of the churches is in and through the Bible. Does the word of God come to us through preaching? indeed; but it is in and through the Bible that all worthy preaching finds its base. Are we blessed by the beautiful ordinances of the church, baptism and the Lord's Supper? Where do we learn about these ordinances? Do we believe in the effectiveness of prayer? We learn of prayer, why and how to pray from and through the Bible. The children's song is worthy of the adults' attention:

> Holy Bible, Book divine;
> Precious treasure, thou art mine.

> —JOHN BURTON, SR.

31

"Bring Me That Book!"

So they read in the book in the law of God distinctly (v. 8a).

Bishop Oldham has given an account of an experience of his in India. It was night, moonlight. Before him sat a large group of men, only men—proof that the Bible was unknown. The missionary spoke long and earnestly. Finally, when he stopped, the leader of the tribe, an old man with a long beard, the son of a king, hobbled to him, looked up into his face and said:

"Young man, you are a young man; you have spoken words of wisdom tonight. Where did you learn that?" Bishop Oldham said, "I did not learn it by my wisdom or my knowledge; I found it in a book." Said the old man, "Do you mean to say that the things you have said to us tonight are in a book?" "Yes, Father, I mean just that." "Tell me, is that book written in my language; you have spoken in my language; is the book in my language?" "Yes," said the missionary. The old man drew himself straight and pointed a finger at the missionary and said, "Then bring me that book."

Going quickly to his tent, Bishop Oldham came back with two copies of the Bible in the language of the people. He handed one copy to the old man and kept the other in his own hands.

The old man spoke again, "You say that these words you have been speaking to us tonight are in this book?" "Yes." "And how long has this book been written?" "Thousands of years," said the missionary. Queried the old man, "Have you people had this book all that time?" "Yes," said the bishop. "Then," said the old man, "I am an old man. My friends and people have died without this book. Why haven't you brought it to me before?" And, our answer?

A Batch of Old Love Letters

Is there any word from the Lord: and Jeremiah said, There is (v. 17b).

It sounds authentic, but I cannot vouch for it. The minister was spending the night in a home. Before going to bed he was asked to read from the Bible and pray. Some difficulty was experienced in finding the Bible. When the minister opened it, a pair of reading glasses fell out. The wife exclaimed before she could check herself, "Oh, there are my specs! I lost them four years ago and haven't been able to find them anywhere!"

Is an "honest confession good for the soul"? I have heard that it is. Then here goes: I have never found it easy to find extended periods of time to read the Bible. I have "used" the Bible, "studied" it, but to find time to read it leisurely, as John Ruskin once advised a group of young people, so as "to be present as if in the body at each recorded event in the life of the Redeemer," is another matter. What a difference that makes!

Henry Ward Beecher, great American preacher of a past era, once said, "I never knew my mother. She died when I was four years of age. She joined the angels that she might be with me forever. But one day," he wrote, "I was poring over a lot of letters that my mother had written to my father, and I found the letters that she had written from the first day that she met him until their love was one. And," he continued, "I found the letter that she wrote the first time she gave her love completely to my father, and I held the letter in my hand, and then, I understood my mother."

That says it! That is close to a parable. The Bible gives to us a batch of love letters; there we find where, and when, a loving Father God first gave his Son for our redemption. Now, we can begin to understand this God of ours!

Talk About God

But they that wait upon the Lord shall renew their strength (v. 31a).

It is said that a young minister once went to Bishop Stubbs of Oxford for advice about preaching. What did the bishop recommend? Said the older man, "My son, preach about God and preach about twenty minutes." Wise *and* bitter medicine!

Yet, unless a minister's preaching begins with God and ends with God, he has no worthy beginning, and he might as well end in less than twenty minutes. Let all preaching be rooted and grounded in the God and Father of our Lord Jesus Christ.

During the Second World War, when the children were being evacuated from London, one little girl was heard to pray, "Dear God, please protect mummie and daddy from those terrible German bombs, and, dear God, do take care of yourself, 'cause if anything happens to you, we're all sunk!" Right? Right!

And yet, weak and sinful creatures that we are, we give so little thought to the One who is great and holy! We become infatuated over time and place and position. We want to know the right people, go to the right places, wear the right clothes, drive the right cars, until we merit the remark Mark Twain once got from his young daughter. The humorist had received an invitation to visit the Kaiser in Germany. The daughter was quite impressed. She exclaimed: "Why, Daddy, if this keeps up, you will know everybody but God!"

> O world, thou chooseth not the better part!
> It is not wisdom to be only wise,
> And on the inward vision close the eyes,
> But it is wisdom to believe the heart.
>
> . . . .
>
> Our knowledge is a torch of smoky pine
> That lights the pathway but one step ahead
> Across a void of mystery and dread.
> Bid, then, the tender light of faith to shine
> By which alone the mortal heart is led
> Unto the thinking of the thought divine.[1]

—GEORGE SANTAYANA

Can God Do Anything He Wants to Do?

And he did not many mighty works there because of their unbelief (v. 58).

Can God do anything? It is an old question but one that persists. It seems the answer would have to be in the negative, to the best of our understanding. For, it is not merely a matter of getting something done, good though it may be, but getting it done in a certain way for a certain purpose. God cannot deny himself; he cannot be untrue to himself. Consider a domestic example.

When our first child was fifteen months old, we moved into a new home, a home in which all the bedrooms were on the second floor. What would we do about Patricia and those stairs? Put a gate at the bottom and another at the top? Someone would certainly leave the gate open. Lead her up and down the stairs? Of course, that could not be done indefinitely. We decided to risk the danger from the beginning. It was a harrowing experience. Her mother would be hanging over the railing above, watching; I would be at the bottom ready to pick up the pieces! The problem was not just to get the child from the bottom to the top of the stairs; or top to the bottom of the stairs. That would have been easy; pick the child up and carry her. We wanted her to learn to go up and down the stairs, and stairs of life, on her own.

Apparently, God is faced with something of the same problem. He wants certain things done, done under certain conditions, to attain certain goals for certain results. Now, God always insists that his children do their own homework, climb the stairs of life, play the game of life, by the rules. He will help, encourage, love, die, but he will not *force* his children to be good; though, that is what he wants for each of us.

Without God we cannot; without us God will not.

"On Letting 'Em Have It"

By one man sin entered into the world, and death by sin (v. 12).

At the close of a Sunday morning hour of worship when I had preached on forgiveness of sin, a fine Christian layman came and said, "Pastor, I feel like a dog!" Next in line, came one who, to be easy and kind, was not as careful of his Christian way and walk as the former man. But this one said, in a jocular vein, "Preacher, you sure let 'em have it this morning."

Probably one reason for such an attitude as the second man revealed is our limited view of sin. So often we think only of the sins of the flesh: adultery, drunkenness, dope, lust, murder. These must not be neglected but it is far from a complete list. There are the sins of the spirit: envy, jealousy, pride, selfishness, anger, an unwilling spirit of forgiveness. And, according to Jesus, these may be even worse than sins of the flesh. Consider his attitude and judgment upon the scribes and Pharisees as opposed to the woman taken in adultery. Or, again, think of the sins of omission. The right things we fail to do as well as the wrong things we do. When Johnny was asked by the teacher for a definition of the sins of omission, he said, "Well, Teacher, 'dems 'de sins I oughter commit and don't." No. But to "him that knoweth to do good and doeth it not, to him it is a sin."

And, again, there are the social sins for which we are, at least, partially responsible. As members of groups we enter into, are a part of, customs, habits, policies that we would never be guilty of as individuals. Yet, we are a part of the whole. It may well be that there is no way for us to avoid this entirely, but if we understand there is a place for the cry, "God be merciful to me a sinner" (Luke 18:13).

The greatest security against sin is to be shocked at its presence.

—THOMAS CARLYLE

"Too Late to Start Now!"

Sow to yourselves in righteousness, reap in mercy (v. 12a).

A friend of mine liked to tell about the old mountaineer who claimed to be an Episcopalian. Someone questioned him: "Who is your bishop?" "I don't know no bishop," he replied.

"What diocese are you a member of?" "Never heard of no diocese," replied the mountaineer.

"What is your parish?" persisted the questioner. "Well now, Sonny, I don't rightly know nothing about no parish, neither."

"Now, how can you claim to be an Episcopalian if you know nothing about a bishop, diocese, or parish?" "Well, I jes' tell you, 'bout a year ago I went to a meetin' and they said hit was an Episcolopian meetin' and I heard de preacher say, 'We done dem things we ought notter done; and we left undone dem things we orter done'; and I said, right thar, 'Well, I'm a Episcolopian.' "

That could have been an Episcopalian meeting. It could just as well have been a Baptist meeting, a Methodist, Presbyterian, or any one of a much longer list of denominations. For at this point we are all and each "tarred with the same brush."

And, yet, to acknowledge that is something in our favor. Let us never boast of our virtue, it is as "filthy rags." If there be any virtue, any righteousness, it is through Christ, not because of anything we have achieved.

A professor friend of mine told about the father of Gilbert Chesterton's coming home from church and announcing that he had been elected a vestryman in the Anglican Church. His wife cried out, "Oh, Edward, don't take it. We'll have to be respectable! We've never been respectable! Let's not start it now." Of course, she was thinking of the stiffness, the formality, proper clothes, high hats, and long tails.

Read Exodus 6:2-7

Unbelievable!

I will take you to me for a people (v. 7a).

All boys and girls who have been regular in Sunday School attendance and attention know the means God used to bring deliverance to the children of Israel.

Some years ago a story made the rounds about a father quizzing his son about the morning's Sunday School lesson. The boy told his father that the lesson was about the Hebrews crossing the Red Sea. The son took some liberties with the story. He said the Israelites came to the Red Sea; they looked back and saw the Egyptians coming in tanks and trucks. Moses called the Seabees; they threw down a pontoon bridge. All the Israelites got safely over and then the Egyptians tried to cross. Moses gave the word; some of his bombers took to the air; the bridge was blasted to bits and the Egyptians were all drowned. The father was not too familiar with his Bible but he did question parts of the boy's story. He wanted to know if the boy had told the story exactly as the teacher had told it. "No," admitted the boy, "but, Dad, you never would believe the story the way she told it!"

The modern mind may have difficulty in believing the miracles. Actually, the problem is not so much with the miracles as with our view of the God of miracles. How big is God? What kind of God is he? What is his nature, his spirit? Does he see and hear and will he come to deliver his people? Is he great enough to command nature to cooperate with him for the welfare of his children? If our God is big enough the miracles will seem small enough. William A. Ogden's old song states it beautifully:

> 'Tis the grandest theme thro' the ages rung;
> 'Tis the grandest theme for a mortal tongue;
> 'Tis the grandest theme that the world e'er sung:
> Our God is able to deliver thee.
>
> —WILLIAM A. OGDEN

No Silence, Please

God hath not given us the spirit of fear (v. 7a).

We are silent when we should bear our verbal witness, because we claim that living a consistent Christian life is sufficient witness in itself. This claim is not true. Of course one should witness with a consistent life. But more is needed. A life of example alone cannot tell of Christ's life, death, resurrection, and intercession; it cannot tell of the wooing of the Holy Spirit; it cannot tell of the necessity of belief in the heart or of confession from the lips.

Again, we are often made to keep silent from an honest belief that we have little or nothing to share with others. The disciples, when faced with the instruction to feed the multitude, looked at their five loaves and two fishes and asked, "What are they among so many?" (John 9:6). We feel that way. We have not enough faith, we feel, for our own existence. Yet, we have learned in sharing our supply has been multiplied. And, too, we are silent in our witness for fear that we shall be rebuffed. It is a possibility. But how seldom it has been so. When there has been love and sincerity, there was usually courtesy, if refusal.

John Kenyon, a warm friend and distant cousin of Elizabeth Barrett (later Mrs. Robert Browning), once remarked that he thought the scriptural tone of her poetry was injurious to its popularity. Hear her reply:

> Certainly I would rather be a pagan whose religion was actual, earnest and continual—than be a Christian who, from whatever motive, shrank from hearing or uttering the name of Christ out of a "church." I am no fanatic, but I like truth and earnestness in all things, and I cannot choose but that such a Christian shows but ill beside such a pagan. What pagan poet ever thought of casting his gods out of his poetry? . . . And if I shrank from naming the name of my God lest it should not meet the sympathy of some readers, or lest it should offend the delicacies of other readers, or lest, generally, it should be unfit for the purposes of poetry, in what more forceful manner than by that act can I secure myself unanswerable shame?

"And Goat's Hair"

And blue, and purple, and scarlet, and fine linen, and goats' hair (v. 4).

The people of Israel were to provide the means for the building of the place of worship. All of the people were given an opportunity to share in the preparation of the place of worship. The "everyone" is emphasized. The need was great, the needs were varied. There were those who could give their gold and silver and bronze and blue and purple and scarlet and fine linen. Then comes some interesting words, "and goats' hair."

It was as though God said through Moses: "There will be need for the precious metals and rare fabrics; those who can contribute these may do so. However, there are some too poor to possess these. I know and accept their state. However, there is something that each can give; each can give it; God needs it; God will accept it. It is goats' hair. There is not a one of you who is so poor that he does not possess this humble product. It will be needed in the building of my place of worship no less than gold and silver will be needed. Remember, you are to give what you have, not what you do not have."

There was one requirement which all—rich and poor, small and great, women and men—had to meet. They had to want to give. Every gift was to be a free, voluntary contribution. Moses could emphasize the need; he could point up the advantages; he could spotlight God's will and word, but Moses could not, dare not, force the people to give. In the building of the place of worship, the heart had to speak.

One day David Sandstrom apologized to his Jewish neighbor for rushing through the neighbor's yard on his way to church. The neighbor reminded Sandstrom of an old rabbinical saying to the effect that one should always run to church and walk home. Eager voluntariness is a befitting element in worship.

When the Vision Came

The Lord appeared to Solomon the second time (v. 2a).

God appeared to Solomon at Gibeon; the king was young then. Now, God appears to him at Jerusalem. During those long intervening years there had been no special revelation. At the beginning of Solomon's reign and now at the completion of a major ambition, God spoke in special ways.

Are we surprised that God did not come to Solomon more often? It is easy to think that the great and chosen characters of the Bible had the blessings of God's revealed presence constantly; no, not so. It is a compliment to a child when the parent trusts him to carry out a responsibility once the duty has been made known.

Gossip, the Scottish preacher, once stated that he had known only two special revelations of God. One was as the preacher was going into his pulpit on a certain day. God met him there and asked if he felt that his preparation had been the best he could make it. The preacher thought about that and answered that he thought, under the circumstances, he had done his best. The Lord accepted that and let him go into the pulpit where he spoke to the people.

The second revelation came late one evening, after a hard day, he was bone tired. He paused at the foot of a long stairway, looked up, and decided that he would not make the call. As he turned to go, a Form passed him on the stairs. The preacher heard a voice say, "Well, if you won't go, then I must go myself." The preacher knew very well who it was. He bounded up the stairs after the Form and he and Christ made the call together.

How frequently does God have to appear to us? Can he trust us to do his will, carry out his mission, once we understand?

"No Sudden Fall"

Watch therefore (v. 13a).

During a first-aid course a group of Girl Scouts were asked, "What would you do if the child swallowed the house key?" One girl said, "I would climb in through the window!" On the basis of the parable suggested for today's lesson, such a course would be doubtful. It is never safe to count on extemporizing conduct.

The only way we can meet certain emergencies is to be prepared; there are certain matters that cannot be handled on the spur of the moment. Knowledge is one of these. I have been a teacher; I was convinced that some of my students thought they could extemporize for my examinations. Recently a cartoon carried the picture of two teenagers. One was saying, "I'm practicing thought control. I haven't thought of anything for the last twenty minutes."

Failure to prepare is often seen in the realm of health. A person "burns the candle at both ends." The person seems indestructible. Loss of sleep and rest, heavy drinking, chain smoking, improper foods, he goes "all the way," then illness. The doctors say, "He has no resistance"; it seems that he has "no reserves"; there is "no fight left in him." He is unprepared.

It is doubtful that any person falls to temptation suddenly. The moral fibers of the soul are gradually weakened, or never allowed to develop. Samson did not fall before the wiles of Delilah the day she gave him a haircut; he had been falling all the days he flirted with her and her tricks.

Lord, let us be prepared, so that emergencies may become doors of opportunity and be thought of as given privileges. Amen.

Always Going Home

This one thing I do (v. 13b).

Paul believed that excess baggage can hinder Christian growth. No excess baggage on the trip of life. "This one thing I do" gets down to basics.

The story is told that one day as Dr. Albert Schweitzer was getting ready to attend a funeral, he brought out an old green necktie. It was faded with age, and the cockroaches had been chewing on it. The nurses told the great doctor that he could not wear such a tie on such an occasion. Dr. Schweitzer said that it was the only necktie he owned; it had been his only tie for thirty-two years. He said that his father had owned two ties, but that one was constantly getting lost; so, he had decided one tie was enough. The nurses told him there were men in America who had as many as one hundred neckties. The old doctor thought about that and then the nurses heard him murmur, "One hundred ties and only one neck!"

To relieve life of excess baggage does not require the wearing of the same tie for thirty-two years. It does not mean that the person who determines to do "this one thing" must enter a monastery or a nunnery, become a preacher or a missionary, or choose some other church-related vocation. That choosing is God's business, not ours. To do "this one thing" does mean that the person determines that whatever he does, it will be for the glory of God through Christ and for the good of God's children.

It was said of Francis of Assisi that he "took the queerest and most zigzag cuts through the woods, but he was always going home."

Arms Around the World

For the love of Christ constraineth us (v. 14a).

To accept Christ as the foundation of your life is to experience the "second birth." It is "being born from above," "born of the Spirit." Birth is not all, should not be all. Yet, birth is important. Unless you get the child born, all of your dreams, ideals, and ambitions are of little value. Get the baby born! Then there is much to do. If the figure means anything, it must say that a baby is a baby; there is much growing and developing to be done. But, first, spiritual birth. The foundation is Christ.

That foundation is adequate to support every worthy structure. It is adequate in personal relationships and in social conduct and institutions. Writing of his conversion experience, John Bunyan said that he was so taken with the love of God that he could have spoken to the crows that sat on the plowed fields! Before John Wesley found this sure foundation he went to Georgia to convert the Indians, but he cried, "Who shall convert me?" Writing of Wesley's conversion, Lecky, the historian, said that it was a national epoch when Wesley's "heart was strangely warmed."

John Newton, who wrote the hymn "How Sweet the Name of Jesus Sounds," said that he was "a wild thing" on the coast of Africa, but that the Lord Christ caught and tamed him. He said that since then people had come to see him as they came to see lions in a zoo, and that if anyone doubted God's ability to convert the heathen they should look at him, John Newton! The foundation is adequate.

> How sweet the name of Jesus sounds
>   In a believer's ear!
> It soothes his sorrows, heals his wounds,
>   And drives away his fears.

The Hour Within Thy Hand

This is your hour (v. 53*b*).

Do you recall the wise word of Moses in his farewell address to the children of Israel? They must have been wondering about the future, especially since they would not have Moses to lead them. Ahead was untried leadership, walled cities, and battles to be fought. Moses said, "As thy days, so shall thy strength be" (Deut. 33:25). As if to say, "Do not worry about the years; leave the years to God; you deal with the days and for those God has promised adequate strength."

But that day and hour are within thy hand. For these you are responsible, not alone or solely, of course. Jesus said to Judas, "This is your hour, and the power of darkness." Judas could have made it an hour of loyalty and courage.

To an amazing extent we do control these present experiences and events. Even a person who is blindfolded and on the way to the gallows or electric chair can determine how he will meet the experience, cowardly or courageously.

There are things that we cannot do in the immediate present, of course. If we center on these restrictions, life can be frightening   old age, for example. Of course, there are things that we cannot do in the present hour but there are things that we can do. How the present hour is lived—in mood, spirit, enthusiasm, faith, hope, and love—is exceedingly important. The present hours just might be our very best!

At the main entrance to Johns Hopkins Hospital in Baltimore is a sundial. I have stopped to look at that legend scores of times:

> The only hour within thy hand
> Is the hour on which the shadow stands.

No Proviso in the Contract

Thou shalt not tempt the Lord thy God (v. 7b).

The temptation to leap from the pinnacle of the Temple was not only an effort to put God on the spot; it was an effort to put a proviso in the contract. The tempter was trying to get Jesus to put a conditional stipulation in the obedience agreement. See how it works, "I am your Son; I am come to do your will and work. I am willing to do all that, provided; I will serve you, provided; I will witness for you, provided—provided you protect me from danger. You must not let me get a broken leg in foolish leaps; you must not let me have an accident on the highway whether due to my carelessness, poor judgement, or the other person's intoxication, unsafe condition of the road, mechanical failure of the car, or etc. You must not allow my body to become a lodging place for cancer germs, a TB microbe, a defective heart, etc."

One of the great temptations of life is to try to force God to play favorites. When we become followers of Christ, we may think that the laws affecting ordinary human beings should not apply to us. Gravity, bacteria, catastrophe should not treat the nonbeliever and the Christian the same way. If the non-Christian jumps from the pinnacles of the temple of law and order, he must pay the consequences. Not so for us, the Christians.

It is so very easy to insist on provisos! How hard it is to leave the small print in the contract entirely up to God. We are so conditioned by the thinking of the secular world that it is difficult for us to shift gears when we deal with God.

> Courage, brother! do not stumble,
>   Though thy path be dark as night;
> There's a star to guide the humble;
>   Trust in God and do the right.

—NORMAN MACLEOD

Tempus Fugit

He placed at the east of the garden of Eden Cherubims (v. 24b).

Thomas Wolfe believed that you could not go back in time and experience. He was right about that; my wife and I proved it. We spent our honeymoon at Chimney Rock, high in the mountains of western North Carolina. The cottage was a dream; spruce, laurel, and rhododendron enclosing it; down below there was a lake; above were the everlasting hills! Within the cottage a few well-chosen, rustic pictures, flagstone walk, hollyhocks about the door. We had ten glorious days there!

Following that honeymoon, there were five years when we lived with the memory of those days. Then, we were able to return. We arrived late in the afternoon, went to "Big John's" place and asked if he had a vacant cottage. "Yes, just one." "We'll take it; how do we get to it?" Right, same cottage!

We drove up the little mountain road; parked in front of "our" honeymoon cottage. It was all there, lovely cottage, beautiful setting, flagstone walk, lake below, mountains above, the whippoorwill's call from deep in the trees. But, but something was missing. There seemed a crack in the fortress of memory and through that crack something had escaped. After a little we closed the door, locked it, and drove down the mountain, paid "Big John" for the use of the cottage, and drove into Asheville to spend the night at a hotel. "You can't go home again."

Why? I'm not sure about that. Perhaps it is that cherubim with his sword, flaming and turning, to keep us from going back to our earlier Edens.

47

A Gamble, a Nuisance, and Discipleship

Rightly dividing the word of truth (v. 15b).

Dr. LaRue Swain related a story about a father who had three sons. The first son said, "Take me into business with you." The father knew his son's unreliable nature. He said, "My son, I am sorry but I cannot do that now." The son was not surprised, and not particularily disappointed. He was not sure he wanted to take on the responsibility that such an involvement entailed.

The second son came to his father with the same request. "Father, make me the purchasing agent in your business." The father was aware of the selfish disposition of his son, and so he said, "Son, I cannot do that now." This son was not willing to take no for an answer. He continued to ask and to plead; though, he never sought to improve his own condition.

Finally the third son came with his request. His petition was also denied. However, unlike the first two sons, he was eager to justify his request. "Father," he said, "you know what is best for the company, and what is best for me, I trust your wisdom. But this matter is of such importance to me I wonder if you would be willing to talk with me about the matter. It may be that with your help I could study and train and qualify myself to where you could grant my request." The father was pleased with his son's desire and willingness to prepare. He and the third son became very close; they were often seen together. The father shared his concerns with the son; told him about the business. The son worked hard, observed closely. In a very short time, passersby saw a new sign over the door of the business, "A. B. Mansell & Son."

That, says Dr. Swain, represents three kinds of prayer—a gamble, a nagging nuisance, and serious discipleship.

Wait for the Final Whistle

Take Mark, and bring him with thee: for he is profitable to me (v. 11b).

Paul said, "Take Mark, and bring him with thee: for he is profitable to me for the ministry." Mark had failed; Paul had once rejected him, but the final whistle hadn't blown for Mark. He had made good, and Paul was glad to have him back on the team. It is one of the thrilling things of life.

Some of the most thrilling chapters in biography lie at the point of the "final whistle." All who are familiar with the life of Abraham Lincoln know about his poor beginnings and his wonderful ending. He failed in business when he was twenty-two; he was defeated the next year when he ran for the legislature; he failed in business a second time the next year. When he was twenty-nine, he suffered a nervous breakdown. Two years later he was defeated as the Speaker in the legislature. Two years later he was defeated as State Elector. When he was thirty-four, he was defeated for Land Officer; the same year he was defeated as he ran for Congress. He ran for Congress twice more, and was defeated each time. Later he was defeated when he ran for the Senate. He was defeated when he ran for the vice-presidential nomination. He ran again for the senate and was defeated again. But, in 1860 he was elected President; then, what did his failures matter!

The *Reader's Digest* once carried an interesting article on a boy who was refused admittance to a boys' school because of his poor grades, his disposition in general, and his attitude toward persons and subjects in particular. When every member of the admittance board had voted against admitting the boy, the principal informed them that they had been studying a transcript of the grades of Winston Churchill when he was at Harrow.

You just have to wait for the final whistle before you count a person out.

God's greatest victories are won on the battlefields that have seen our biggest defeats.

This Is How It Was

The heavens were opened, and I saw visions of God (v. 1b).

James Archibald Campbell, the founding father of the institution that is now Campbell University, was born on January 13, 1862. That is only a little over a hundred years ago; there are people living who are nearly that old. However, that is calendar measurement and the calendar is not always the best instrument for measuring events. By events Campbell was born a thousand years ago! Consider:

When Campbell was born, every third person in North Carolina was a slave. On January 6, 1862, just seven days before Campbell's birth, the following announcement appeared in the *Fayetteville Observer*: "Sale of Negroes—The following sale of Negroes took place in this city yesterday. The sale was conducted by J. J. Moore, auctioneer, and considering the times, the prices realized were very good:

> Bett, 65 years old, $800
> Ida, 60 years old, $400
> Caroline, 11 years old, $475
> Lemuel, 32 years old, $550
> Louisa, 18 years old, $660
> Lizzie, 17 years old, $535
> Wiley, 80 years old, $1"

The day young Campbell was born the following announcement appeared in the *New York Times*:

> William Lloyd Garrison,
> The Pioneer of the Antislavery movement
>   will deliver a lecture upon
> "The Abolitionists and Their Relationship to the War"
> At the Cooper Institute
> On Tuesday Evening, January 14.

Remember Dickens's words: "It was the best of times, it was the worst of times"? Of course, we have to remember that God seems to send his favorites where they are most needed, and when. That means that his Son, and his sons, will come when the sky is dark and the earth runs with evil. For, the task of his Son, and of his sons, is to change persons and circumstances, change both for the good.

Hand on Shoulder

And Enoch walked with God (v. 24a).

Enoch walked with God." I am not sure of all that is involved in that statement. It certainly means Enoch and God were in agreement, for "can two walk together, except they be agreed?" (Amos 3:3). It means that Enoch lived his life in keeping with the will and purpose of God. It probably means that Enoch and God enjoyed being with each other, that they found pleasure in each other's company. Just think of that!

There is a meaningful story about a young lawyer going to see Baron Rothschild, the powerful London merchant and financier. The young lawyer was having a difficult time getting established in his profession, no work was coming his way. He knew the quickest and surest way to success was to have the approval and influence of Rothschild. In desperation he managed to get past the line of secretaries and receptionists and threw himself into the presence of the old baron. In a stream of tumbling words he told his story—his need for support and approval; his willingness to work and to sacrifice. The young man's story touched the old man. Putting his arm about the young man's shoulder Rothschild suggested that they walk together. Together, in step, in conversation, in agreement, they walked the length of the stock exchange and back to Rothschild's office door. There they shook hands and the young man was sent on his way.

Disappointed! No letter of recommendation, no calls of recommendation to possible clients, not one contract arranged, only a friendly stroll and a good-bye handshake. But when the young man reached his office calls were coming in asking for his services. And, before the day was over he had been assured of all the work that he could do. Why? They had seen him walking with the prince of merchants and bankers. That was enough recommendation. The young man had to be dependable, trustworthy, and capable, or Baron Rothschild would not have walked with him.

"The Power's On!"

"Put on the whole armour of God" (v. 11a).

G. Ernest Thomas told of an incident taking place in a village in the state of Washington. The village was far out, away from the advantages of electricity; the residents never expected to have electricity in their homes and businesses. Then the news began to spread. A dam was being built fifty miles away and the dam would guarantee that there would be power, electric power, in the village. The homes were wired and all was in readiness months before the power was turned on.

One evening the power came on unexpectedly. In a home at the far end of the main street the switches had been left open. Suddenly every room in the house was ablaze with light; there was shock and excitement. The man ran out into the streets shouting to his neighbors: "The power's on! The power's on!" Good news and it could not be kept; there was no desire to keep it to himself; there was enough power for all. The use that others made of the power in no way lessened the resources available to him; besides, the power belonged to all; they had prepared for it, waiting for its coming. "Ye shall receive power" (Acts 1:8) was the promise.

The poet Wordsworth once said that a great person was one who did what had never been done before and which once it had been done became a standard below which a man dared not be content. What we become aware of, as we read the New Testament with understanding, is that these early followers of Jesus hooked up to a great power. That power made them into new persons. They came to a new understanding of goodness and godliness. Goodness for them was not something that they got through negatives, what they did not do, a refraining from this and that, it was a passion, a warfare, a love affair, a new power.

Christ is the only transforming power there is and we strive in vain without him whether we are building a life or a country.

—ROSALIE MILLS APPLEBY

"Country and Brilliant"

Therefore shall Zion for your sake be plowed as a field (v. 12a).

R udyard Kipling wrote that a toad beneath the harrow knows exactly where each tooth of the harrow goes; the sparrow above the road can preach contentment to the toad. There was none of this detachment or theory about Micah's preaching. He knew exactly where the wrong, the pain, and the hurt were.

My twelve-year-old daughter (then) once commented on the message of a theological professor. She said, "Daddy, I like that man; he's brilliant enough to have something to say and he's country enough to get it across." Micah was brilliant and he was "country." His message came across "loud and clear." He was involved. However, involvement is not a characteristic of our day. We tend to stand on the sidelines and observe.

Jesus did not demand that his followers memorize a creed or swallow a dogma. He wanted involvement and that is what he got from his disciples. It was what Peter exemplified in his declaration, "Thou art the Christ the Son of the living God" (Matt. 16:16). Jesus said, "You did not learn this on your own; my Father revealed it to you" (Matt. 16:17, author). That is involvement.

Micah spoke out against the leaders of his day for not being of and for the people. These leaders did to the people and took from the people in a way that would have been impossible had they been involved.

The prophet said that he came where the people were, that he sat where they sat, he had sat there for seven days before he spoke. He came to the people, saw and felt and heard, then he spoke. In the parable of the good Samaritan Jesus said, he "came where he was: and when he saw him, he had compassion on him." Involvement.

There is nothing so kingly as kindness.

—ALICE CARY

Clear Image of the Past

Thou shalt remember all the way the Lord thy God led thee (v. 2a).

"Nothing is so powerful," it has been said, "as an idea whose time has come." Have you known personally, through history or biography, men and women who came too early? They were ahead of their time; they spoke words and propounded ideas that seemed premature. A few years, a few decades, a century later the ideas would have a familiar ring, but coming when they did they were out of place. Or, you have known those who came too late, the parade had passed them by; earlier their ideas and words were relevant, not now.

I used to visit in a great hospital on a ward called "Osler." The ward was named for the great surgeon, William Osler. This man was wise as well as skilled. He once wrote, "The load of tomorrow added to that of yesterday, carried today, makes the strongest falter. We must learn to shut off the future as tightly as the past." If we were only wise enough to know when the time has come! God did, it was "in the fullness of time" that God sent forth his Son.

Osler's advice against carrying the load of yesterday upon the back of today does not mean that we should not be conscious of the promises of yesterday. To do that is to become, as Elton Trueblood said, "a cut-flower" society.

Jan Struther wrote in her fine book, *Mrs. Miniver,* "In the convex driving mirror she could see, dwindling rapidly, the patch of road where they had stood; and she wondered why it had never occurred to her before that you cannot successfully navigate the future unless you keep always framed beside it a small clear image of the past."

Father God, plan our lives for us better than we can plan them ourselves, and don't let us get in your way. Amen.

Time to Dust It Off

But as for you, ye thought evil against me; but God (v. 20a).

A few years ago Vaughn Shoemaker produced a Pulitzer Prize-winning cartoon. It showed an old man with a broom and a feather duster. He was approaching an unoccupied pulpit, a closed Bible, and an altar from which you could see cobwebs running in every direction. The caption of the cartoon read, "Time to Dust It Off." Still current and timely.

But, that idea can be applied to history. The "average man" needs to "dust off" his idea of history. Do you believe that God is there, that he is concerned, that he has anything to say or do with it? Do you suppose he is interested in the individual but not in the great social and political currents of the world?

There is a widespread belief that man controls history. Winston Churchill once sent a message to men who were unloading tonnage at a strategic spot, "Tell them from me they are unloading history." Well, now, God uses persons to "unload history." But, we cannot determine its outcome.

Once Franz Werfel, the brilliant author, wrote, "The world has forgotten in its preoccupation with Left and Right that there is an Above and Below." This is exactly what we forget when we believe that we can control history.

If the key to history is man's control of it, then we are at the mercy of every Genghis Khan, Alexander, Napoleon, Hitler, or any other little strutting dictator. These have had their brief hour of glory upon the stage. But neither the best nor the worst of men know enough, nor do they have enough goodness to be trusted with the control of the world; that is God's domain!

History = "His-Story"

"Resting on Certainties"

He shall not be afraid of evil tidings: his heart is fixed (v. 7).

Michael Faraday, the English chemist and physicist, was once asked, "What are your speculations?" He replied, "Speculations? I have no speculations. I am resting on certainties." So, the ancients of which the psalmist writes, rested on certainties. They were not afraid of evil tidings, their hearts were fixed; they trusted in the Lord.

Faith operates from within. The results of faith can be seen, but faith cannot be seen. The actions of faith can be observed; the faith that is responsible for the action is invisible. The best things in life are often hidden. Whoever saw a mother's love? Who has seen a martyr's faith? Whoever looked upon God; we have been told that no man ever saw God.

But faith pleases God. "Without faith it is impossible to please him" (Heb. 11:6). Our youth groups sing,

> Turn your eyes upon Jesus,
> Look full into his wonderful face.

> —HELEN H. LEMMEL

It is through faith that it is done.

John A. Redhead tells about a little boy and the movie, *Snow White and the Seven Dwarfs*. The old witch in the story was so mean and so real that the parents took the small children out before the witch came on the scene. One little boy, playing with older boys, boasted that he was going to see the movie. The older boys chided the little fellow, telling him that he was so small he would have to leave before the old witch came in; and so he would not even see all the movie. The little boy told them he was going, too! And when the old witch came out he was not even going to look at her; he would look at his daddy and he wouldn't be afraid! Don't push the story too far, but it does pay to turn our eyes upon Jesus.

Not Writing but Translating

For ye are bought with a price (v. 20).

In the suggested passage for today's reading is stated a marvelous truth. Paul lists all the terrible sins and then he says, "And such were some of you" (v. 11). He was writing to the church members. So, the gospel was preached to the most wicked; the gospel was adequate to redeem the most wicked and, now, Paul could call them "saints."

There is the well-known story of Oliver Cromwell telling the artist who was painting his portrait to "put in warts and all." There are passages in the Bible that embarrass us to read in public, we would like to leave out those "warts." But, the Bible puts in "warts and all."

I once studied with Dr. Goodspeed, the great New Testament scholar. One day in class he told us about a letter that he had received from an angry woman who took him to task for using the word *slave* in his translation of the New Testament. He told us how he had answered the letter. "My dear lady," he wrote, "I am not writing the New Testament; I am only translating it."

In the first century Celsus, in a debate with Origen, one of the early church fathers, said:

Those who summon people to other mysteries make this preliminary proclamation: "Whosoever has pure hands and a wise tongue. . . . Whoever is pure from defilement, who lives righteously may come. . . . But hear what folk these Christians call: 'Whoever is a sinner,' they say, 'whosoever is unwise . . . whosoever is a wretch, the kingdom of God will receive him.' Origen replied, "Even if a Christian does call those whom the robber would call, he does so with a different motive, that he may bind up their wounds by the gospel, and pour medicine of the gospel upon the soul festering with evil, like the wine, olive oil and emollient, and the other medicinal aids which relieve the soul."

"The Diamond Shield"

Faith, hope, love, these three; but the greatest of these is love (v. 13).

In a beautiful little volume, now long out of print, Samuel Judson Porter told the legend of the diamond shield. During the Crusades, Ubald and his companion knights were sent to rescue Rinaldo from his exile in the Land of the Enchantress. Before they started they were given a diamond shield. This shield had a double purpose; it was to give them safety; and, it was to be a kind of magic mirror to aid them in the recovery of their fellow knight. They were charged to take the diamond shield and hold it before the young man's face three times.

The first time he would see his own face. There he would read the story of his debasement, the deplorable plight into which he had fallen, and be stirred to a holy desire for escape. The second time he looked into the magic mirror he would see carved on the shield the heroic deeds of his ancestors, and be inspired to emulate their example. The third time he looked he would see a vision of the future, get a glimpse of the victory calling him to a life of new adventure. So, looking at the diamond shield Rinaldo would see an unworthy present from which to flee, a worthy past toward which to aspire, and a glorious future to beckon and challenge. The young man was awakened by the revelations of the shield; he quit the land of the Enchantress; he returned to the camp of the Crusades and led the attack for the deliverance of Jerusalem.

In making his application Dr. Porter said that love is the "diamond shield." Paul's hymn of Christian love in 1 Corinthians 13 is a magic mirror. Here one is given to see the present, past, and future. Love is the "more excellent way" (1 Cor. 12:31).

> O love of God most full,
>   O love of God most free,
> Come, warm my heart, come, fill my soul,
>   Come lead me unto thee.

> —Oscar Clute

He Didn't Like General Washington

Who art thou to judge another man's servant? (v. 4a).

The people who love, serve, and, when need be, sacrifice for their country have a right to criticize her. It has been said that men should behave toward their country as women behave toward the men they love, they will do anything, make any sacrifice, but they will not stop criticizing them!

It is the constant and chronic critic who never does anything for his country to make it better (except pay taxes and he does that only because he is afraid not to) whose criticism has a false ring.

Dr. Ralph Sockman once told a story of a visitor to a fine old ancestral home in Connecticut. The owner was the last of the family line. She was proud of the house and took great delight in showing the different relics. Noticing an unusually old rifle over the mantel, the visitor asked permission to take it down and examine it. The hostess said that she was afraid it would be unwise to handle the rifle, for it was loaded, primed, and ready to fire. It had been so since the days of her great-grandfather. He wanted it to be ready when he needed it to "strike a blow for freedom." The visitor observed that her grandfather must have died before the Revolutionary War, since the gun had never been fired. "No," said the great-granddaughter, "he lived to a ripe old age and died in 1802, but he just never had any confidence in General Washington."

Ultimately the love of country has to come down to the individual. What have you done since nine o'clock yesterday morning to make America a better country! And, the words of Jesus, "Not every one that saith Lord, Lord" (Matt. 7:21), but the person who does the will of our Father God.

He serves his party best who serves his country best.

—RUTHERFORD B. HAYES

On Describing the Man

A good man obtaineth favor of the Lord (v. 2a).

J. A. Campbell, the preacher and teacher, was six feet tall. He had sandy-red hair and mustache, both carefully trimmed. His eyes were blue, sharp, and gentle. They mirrored his emotions, quickly changing from one mood to another, from smiles to tears, from deep conviction to lighthearted banter, from compassion to righteous indignation, from happy human relations to moving spiritual communion, from strict academics to an overriding religious concern that swept everything in its strong thrust.

He blushed like a modest maiden. His coloring would forecast his own speech, radioing ahead to announce that something humorous was coming. In this way we were able to anticipate his humor before it was put into words. The blush would begin at his shirt collar, move up across his cheeks, emphasizing the light crow's feet at the corner of his blue eyes, mount into his temples, and invade his tawny hair. By this time he would be speaking the words, the anticipation of which had brought the glow to his countenance.

He kept a large 500-gallon gasoline tank from which he serviced his car. On one occasion as he was ready to pay the man who had filled the tank, looking at the statement filled out by the man, Dr. Campbell exclaimed, "Ah, man, you have ruined my tank!" "Why, how is that, Professor Campbell?" "Well," said Dr. Campbell, with that ruddy glow beginning to move up his neck, "that tank will hold only 500 gallons and I see you have gone and forced 505 gallons into it!" The man began to sputter and stutter, "Ah, uh, well, maybe, Professor Campbell, I just miscounted. I guess it was only 500 gallons I put in your tank."

> The art of biography
> Is different from geography.
> Geography is about maps,
> Biography is about chaps.
>
> —EDMUND BENTLEY

"Mark the Earth with a Cross"

God forbid that I should glory save in the cross (v. 14a).

Remember the old legend that said it was never safe to die until you had taken a stick and marked on the earth the sign of the cross? Legend and superstition? Of course. And, yet, as is so often the case, it is a legend based upon a great truth. Because it is not safe to live or die until we have marked the earth, our work, our lives, our influence, with the spirit of the cross of Jesus.

Take the matter of evil, evil in our personal lives. Do we dare mark that with the cross? There was time when this disturbed us, when conscience put up a howl about it, when we even shed tears over it, went to the "lonesome valley" about it, spent time trying to eradicate it from our lives. We did what Robert Louis Stevenson once called, "Hewing Agag to pieces." But now, all that seems old-fashioned, completely out of date and style. Everyone acts this way now—why worry about it!

Maurice Maeterlink once pictured God sitting on the side of a green hill, smiling at man's offenses as one might smile at a puppy playing on a rug before an open fire. That is repulsive! If we have any theological upbringing, any memory of "an old rugged cross," it is utterly revolting. Yet, I challenge my own heart and I challenge yours. Before we completely banish that awful picture from our minds, let us have the courage and honesty to do a little soul searching. What do we care about a selfish spirit? How disturbed are we over outbursts of temper? How conscience-stricken are we over prejudice? When were we deeply concerned because of greed, covetousness, and lust? When did an agonizing cry arise from our souls, begging God to remove an unforgiving spirit? When did we ever cry, "O sinful man that I am"?

You cannot repent too soon, because you do not know how soon it will be too late.

—THOMAS FULLER

Where Do You Plant Your Foot?

But if not, be known unto thee, O King, that we will not serve thy gods (v. 18a).

In today's text Daniel and his three friends stood their ground against idolatry. Earlier the prophet Elijah had to make a choice. He could believe the reality of the fire falling from heaven and consuming the altar, or he could believe his fear when he was fleeing from Jezebel; he could not live by both. John the Baptist could believe his insight when he cried, "Behold the Lamb of God that taketh away the sin of the world." Or he might have relied on his doubts which asked, "Art thou he who should come, or look we for another?" He could not stake his life on both. Neither can you or I.

Surely, it is the point of wisdom to believe our best hours, to act upon the insights, the resolutions formed, the covenants made when life was at its clearest. After he had completed his "Dream of Gerontius," Sir Edward Elgar wrote a friend, saying that it was the best work he had ever done. He also wrote that for the rest he ate and drank and slept and loved and hated "like other men." Then he wrote, " . . . but this I saw and knew; this, if anything of mine, is worth your memory." Now, would it not have been wise for Sir Edward to have lived by that, not the hours when he was "like other men"?

Remember the scene in *Jane Eyre,* when Rochester is pleading with Jane to go away with him. They love each other; she has dreamed of a love like this, but:

> I care for myself. The more solitary, the more friendless, the more unstained I am, the more I will respect myself. I will keep the law given by God; sanctioned by men. I will hold the principles received by me when I was sane and not mad as I am now. Laws and principles are not for the time when there are no temptations; they are for such moments as this; when body and souls rise in mutiny against their rigor. Stringent they are; inviolate they shall be. If at my individual conscience I could break them, what would be their worth? So I have always believed and if I cannot believe it now, it is because I am insane; with my veins running fire, and my heart beating faster than I can count its throbs. *Here I plant my foot.*

"On the Value of Discipline"

All my bones shall say, Lord, who is like unto thee . . . ? (v. 10a).

How is it that God "gives songs in the night"? Is it that only those who have been in the darkroom of life can experience the development of the grace of God within the heart? That it is only in weakness that we are made strong? That it is only in illness that we are willing to accept the services of the Great Physician? Is Rabindarath Tagore's parable pertinent, that only the taut violin string is really *free*, and that it is through the tautness and the freeness that music is heard?

I once found it necessary to discipline my young son—once?! He was instructed to remain indoors; he could not go out; his friends could not come in; the telephone, radio, and television were "off limits." He was in isolation for the day. Then, I left for the office. Throughout the day I thought of my boy and his punishment. I decided that the punishment was a little severe and that, when I returned home in the afternoon, I would release him from the restrictions. For I knew he was grieved, penitent, and filled with self-pity. However, he met me at the door with a cheerful greeting and with no sign of unhappiness.

Explanation? I had overlooked the hidden resources of his mother! She had seen to it that the discipline imposed had been strictly carried out, every part of it. Beyond that her deep love and rare inventiveness had come into full play. She and Perry had talked and laughed and shared experiences and secrets and planned! It had been one of the richest days of the boy's life; he and his mother had enjoyed themselves immensely, and he was eager to have the experience repeated—I was not going to give him that joy! A parable? Close to it. Only through the fact that the boy was "in isolation" did he have time for his mother. So, frequently, only through "isolation" of pain, disappointment, illness, and failure, do we have time for the presence and grace of a loving God.

Rest for the Weary

There remaineth therefore a rest for the people of God (v. 9).

There is an old German epitaph which says, "When thou callest me, Lord Christ, I will arise. But first let me rest a little for I am weary." And there was the poor woman who responded to her pastor's words of comfort in an unexpected way. He said, "Yes, sister, I know you are tired and long for rest, but one day the gentle hand of Jesus will be laid upon your brow, and then you will find rest." The woman replied hastily, "You know something, pastor, I'll just bet the resurrection will be the next day!"

Rest and comfort come to God's people in different ways. One may find rest in having his workload reduced, or he may find rest in having his strength doubled. One may find rest in taking a few hours off from her task each day; or she may find rest in having her health restored. One may find rest in having the child sleep through the night; she may find rest in taking a vacation.

I remember a man who was always tired and whose strength seemed constantly depleted. We never saw him when he was not complaining. He spent his Sundays at home, usually in bed. Then he was prevailed upon, against his will, to assume leadership in a certain phase of his church. It was a place of responsibility which required more hours of attention and work on Sunday than he put in on the job during the week. Result? It has been observed before. New life came to the man—his eyes were sharp, enthusiasm ran high, he gained weight, his employes found him easier to work for, his work prospered, and for a quarter of a century he gave untiring and magnificent service to Christ and his church.

> To rest is not quitting the busy career,
> To rest is fitting life to its sphere.
>
> —ANONYMOUS

"On Keeping the Faith"

I am now ready to be offered (v. 6).

From 1898 until his death in 1934, J. A. Campbell was pastor of the Baptist church at Buies Creek. The church was on the edge of the campus of the school that bore the Campbell name, for all those years when he was pastor of the church, he was also president of the school. He was as concerned that Christ be honored in his classrooms as that he be worshiped in the sanctuary. In the church by the school he baptized the converts, many of whom were students in his school. It pained him for any student to graduate from his school without having made a public profession of faith in Jesus Christ as Lord and Master of his life. The year before he died, Dr. Campbell wrote:

> During these nearly forty years it has been the pastor's privilege to baptize his own three children and one grandson and 1,350 others. 1,354 in all. Many of this number have gone on to glory, while hundreds of others are marching toward the Holy City with song of victory in their hearts, praises for the King on their lips.
>
> From this church the gospel has been sounded out to the ends of the earth. From this treasury the orphans have been clothed and fed. The aged minister has been comforted. The sick and the suffering in hospitals have been visited. Many struggling young men and women have found mental and spiritual equipment for service. Many here have found light for the valley of shadow.
>
> Here we have brought our dead to bear them to their last resting place, while our tears have mingled with the tears of those whose hearts were broken, whose homes were left lonely, and here, ere long, they will bring our lifeless bodies and then bear them out to await the Saviour's coming.
>
> Thank God afresh for His church placed here, for folk who love it and keep it holy unto the Lord. Thank God anew for our young men and women who worship here and upon whom we and our Saviour must depend to make this church go and grow and glow. Let us preserve for them a great spiritual church, in which Jesus shall live and dominate our community life.

The first sermon that J. A. Campbell preached had as its text, "Ye shall know the truth, and the truth shall make you free" (John 8:32). With that message he set the tone for his entire ministry.

"Deeper Than That"

They shall dwell safely, and none shall make them afraid (v. 28b).

When Nansen, the Norwegian explorer of the Arctic, was taking soundings to learn the depth of the Arctic Ocean, his measuring line was too short. He recorded the depth he had sounded and wrote in his diary, "Deeper than that." The next day he extended his line, but it was still not long enough to reach the bottom; he entered in his journal, "Deeper than that." The next day he took all the line he had on the boat, strung it together, and dropped it overboard. Again it would not reach bottom. "Deeper than that."

Love is like that, the love of God, at least. And that is what Ezekiel is trying to say to his people. They had been disobedient—God's love was "deeper than that." They had rebelled; his love was "deeper than that." They had been carried into exile, homes had been destroyed, they were sinners. There was no good thing in them—it was "deeper than that!" No measuring line could measure the length and the breadth and the height and the depth of God's love!

Jacob Braude tells a story about the repairs which were being made on a great building. On one side of the structure workmen were removing large quantities of brick and mortar that had crumbled. Why had one side of the building decayed while the rest was in safe condition? The foreman explained that old records revealed when the building was constructed fifty years earlier, there came a day when the laborers at the brickyard had trouble among themselves. Fifty years later the failure to work together was written in crumbling brick. Write over every disagreement within the home and community, "The love of God is deeper than that!"

"One Is Your Master, Christ"

But seek ye first the kingdom of God (v. 33a).

The Methodist seminary in Frankfurt, Germany, was bombed during World War II. Dormitories were badly damaged, but this was not where restoration began. Classrooms were destroyed; teaching is the main business of a school, but they did not start to rebuild at that point. The library was a mass of ruins. What can you do in a theological seminary without books? They did not start the rebuilding there. First they restored the arch over the chancel of the chapel. The inscription on the arch: "One is your Master, Christ." That is the place to begin. Let the young ministers go out sure of that fact and they will go out as good ministers. That is not all they need to know, but they need to know that first.

I saw this fact become an experience in the life of a lovely young woman. A fine Christian was teaching in the church where I had the privilege of serving as pastor. One evening he was speaking on what it meant to "receive Christ." He looked at one of the young women and said, "Have you received him?" She hesitated for just a moment and said, "No, I have not." The group became electric! The leader went on teaching. In a bit, looking at the girl, he asked, "Would you like to receive him?" Another pause, "Yes, I would." Some more teaching, then back to the girl as if there had been nothing between her response to his last question, "Will you receive him?" No hesitation this time, "Yes, I will." A few evenings later I baptized her; later I performed the marriage ceremony for her; later still I led in a dedication service for her and her husband at the birth of their child. Still later, I had the memorial service for the husband. And just recently I conducted the funeral service for the "young woman," not so young now; it started forty years ago, when she received Christ into her heart and life.

"If Any Be Mislead"

If ye shall ask any thing in my name, I will do it (v. 14).

> He is a path, if any be misled;
> He is a robe, if any naked be;
> If any chance to hunger, He is bread;
>   If any be a bondman, he is free;
>   If any be but weak, how strong is he!
> To dead men, life he is, to sick men, health;
> To blind men, sight, and to the needy, wealth;
>   A pleasure without loss, a treasure with stealth.

—GILES FLETCHER

We receive Christ as Savior and Lord because of who he will be and what he will do throughout all eternity. He is at the Father's right hand; the Father has given into his hands the kingdoms and the powers. The Father has given him a name that is above every name. At that name every knee shall bow; at that name every tongue shall confess that he is Lord and Christ. It is to him the saints shall offer service.

He is no stranger to our earth. He visited our planet once in the form of man; in the form of Spirit he has never left our earth. Therefore, we must never despise this earth and the sons of men who dwell upon it. Our Lord thought well of both; we must not feel differently!

We believe in his name and our sins are forgiven; we live in his name and our lives are pleasing to God; we pray in his name and devils are cast out; we die in his name and we stand unafraid before the judgment.

> There is a name I love to hear,
>   I love to sing its worth;
> It sounds like music in mine ear,
>   The sweetest name on earth.

—FREDERICK WHITFIELD

"Roses in December"

Even so we also should walk in newness of life (v. 4b).

In certain parts of India a part of the baptismal service is for the candidate to place his own hand on top of his head and say, "Woe is me if I preach not the gospel." In a significant way, this is one of the true meanings of the service of baptism. It says that from henceforth, for the person being baptized, Christ is to dwell within his life and that as the Father sent Christ into the world to represent God's love even so the candidate is to go into the world to represent the love of God. Baptism has no saving merit. One is baptized because one has been saved, not in order to be saved.

The service of baptism is time for the entire church to recommit itself to Christ and his cause. It has been said that "God gave us memory that we might have roses in December." Often the baptismal service has caused "roses" to bloom in December hearts. For even as every beautifully performed marriage ceremony should be a time of recommitment for every couple present, even so, in baptism all should be reminded of former vows. The Christian is reminded of what Christ has done for him, and also reminded of his own failures and sins. One, too, should be reminded of that "great cloud of witnesses," many now residing in the realms of glory, who have walked these watery ways and now encourage one to live at one's best. The service of baptism should remind us, too, of the future, that "far off event" when we "shall know as we are known." For the service should remind us that since Christ lives we too shall live. As the poet Whittier has it, "Life is ever lord of Death/And love can never lose its own."

> O happy day that fixed my choice
>   On thee, my Savior and my God!
> Well may this glowing heart rejoice,
>   And tell its raptures all abroad.
>
> Happy day, happy day,
>   When Jesus washed my sins away!
> He taught me how to watch and pray,
>   And live rejoicing ev'ry day;
> Happy day, happy day,
>   When Jesus washed my sins away!
>
> —PHILIP DODDRIDGE

"It Is Good to Be Glad"

That they might have my joy fulfilled in them (v. 13b).

George Buttrick said that the early Christians possessed six things that many church members of the present day do not have:

1. They had a transforming, communicable experience of the living Christ.
2. They had a passion to pass this experience on to others.
3. They had an unbreakable fellowship with other members of the church.
4. They had a love for men which was not dependent on being loved, or liked, or flattered; a love not in terms of sentimental feeling but of unbreakable good will and high desire.
5. They had an inward security or peace not dependent on the number of things there are to do in a day.
6. They had a deep sense of joy not dependent on being happy; for joy is not the opposite of unhappiness, but the opposite of unbelief, and the word *joy* is too great and grand to be confused with the superficial thing called happiness. It was joy and peace that Jesus said he left men in his will.[2]

No wonder those early Christians could sing at the open graves of their loved ones, smile at their executioners when tied to the stakes and thrown in dungeons, and shout their songs of victory when thrown into the arenas to be torn by the wild beasts.

They could say "Rejoice in the Lord alway: and again I say, Rejoice" (Phil. 4:4). Robert Browning, Christian poet, was close to the heart of this when he wrote, "Desire joy and thank God for it. Renounce it, if need be, for others' sake. That's joy beyond joy!"

It is a comely fashion to be glad;
Joy is the grace we say to God.

Always By His Side

The soul of Jonathan was knit with the soul of David (v. 1b).

On the first morning of school, the school that was to become Campbell University, the young schoolman's frugal Scottish nature revealed itself. He had a roll book that he had used at a former school; there were a few unused pages left in it. So, he used it rather than beginning with a new book. There were sixteen names listed. Of course, the name of Cornelia Pearson was one of the sixteen students. It was fitting that she be with him on the first day; she also shared in the responsibilities of the school that first day, looking after the younger children. From that day until the day when J. A. Campbell died in 1934, she was by his side. Together they would pray, plan, direct, teach, and administer.

Harvey Holleman's name was on the list of the sixteen; he was the first boarding student. He would become an outstanding businessman and would always remain loyal to the founder of the school, to the son who would succeed the founder as head of the school, and to the institution in general. E. B. Johnson's name was on the list. His father was sheriff of the county. When the son arrived on that first morning, he gave a small purse and a note to the teacher, saying: "Papa sent these to you, Mr. Campbell." The young teacher opened the note and read:

> Dear Bro. Somehow I got it into my old head that you might need a little money to pay your running expenses. Take the purse and the money and credit me with the ten dollars on the tuition, and the Lord bless you in your work. Yours truly,
>
> —JAMES A. JOHNSON

I heard J. A. Campbell tell of that experience; always his eyes would moisten and he would say, "I put my arm about the boy and said, 'God bless you and your father, son.'" Then he would continue, "I had neither purse nor money and here were both, with the assurance that someone cared."

"The Galilean Accent"

Your accent betrays you (v. 73b, Moffatt).

When Christ was arrested in the garden of Gethsemane and taken to the courtyard, Peter followed, shrinking in the shadows. It was a cold night; there was an open fire in the courtyard where the soldiers and bystanders were warming themselves. Peter joined the group.

A young woman looked at him, looked away; her eyes came back to Peter and she said, "You were with Jesus of Galilee." Peter denied the charge, saying, "I don't know what you are talking about." A little later Peter moved on to the porch, another of the young women saw him and the challenge was issued the second time: "That fellow was with Jesus of Nazareth," she said. This time Peter lapsed back into the language of the seas, ripping out an oath he said: "I don't even know the man!" After a little while another person in the crowd, looking closely at Peter, said, "To be sure you are one of them, too. Why, *your accent betrays you!*" (author's italics).

There is a startling incident in the twelfth chapter of Judges that gives the origin of a word. The Gileadites and the Ephraimites were at war with each other. The Ephraimites were infiltrating the ranks of the Gileadites, but, in order to do so, they had to pass a "Checkpoint Charlie." So, when one of the infiltrators would come to the crossing he was asked, "Are you an Ephraimite?" He, of course, would deny it. Then the guard would order: "Say, 'Shibboleth'; the Ephraimite would say, 'Sibboleth,' for he couldn't form the letters "sh." Then the Gileadites would take the would-be intruder and slay him. So, we are informed that 42,000 Ephraimites were detected and slain. What a price to pay for an accent? And, for the word, *Shibboleth.*

Yes, the way we talk, act, react, what we love and hate, where we go, and where we refuse to go; the color and tone of life, *accents!*

"Old Mother Hubbard"

But Jesus said unto them, They need not depart; give ye them to eat (v. 16).

The Scripture passage offers three points of reference. First, there is the hungry, confused crowd. They are young and old, they are wise and foolish, they are intelligent and uninformed, and they are in need. It is an easily recognizable situation. The need is worldwide, but is it local, too. People are out of work; they have lost and are losing the accumulations of a lifetime. But the need is more than just physical; there are mental and emotional needs. People are frustrated. Basically, the greatest need is spiritual. People are lost and without hope in the world.

Second, there are the disciples. These men who have been with Jesus, who have heard him preach and teach, have been present when he prayed and healed. These disciples are the men of the hour; they will know what to do; they will take care of the situation. And, what was the disciples' solution? "Send [them] away." That is the disciples' solution. Well, they are in a desert place; the crowd is large; it is late in the day; the people have been thoughtless in coming out without provisions. There are always good arguments for 'sending the people away.' There are always reasons for not meeting the physical, emotional, and spiritual needs of the people.

Third, there is the compassionate and adequate Christ. When the disciples make their brilliant suggestion that the people be sent away, he says, "They need not depart; give ye them to eat." Obviously the disciples cannot do that! They cannot feed that crowd, that multitude—of course not! But they do feed the crowd; that is, the disciples plus Jesus feed them. Come, now, let us gather the five loaves and the two fishes—then let us depend upon Jesus.

Four Things to Do

Watch ye, stand fast in the faith, quit you like men, be strong (v. 13).

> Four things a man must learn to do
> If he would make his record true:
> To think without confusion clearly;
> To love his fellowmen sincerely;
> To act from honest motives purely;
> To trust in God and Heaven securely.
>
> —HENRY VAN DYKE

Thinking is hard business! It is one of the most expensive products on the market. There are different kinds of thinking. We need to think creatively. In this age of science and technology such thinking is essential. We need straight thinking, or our economic and political systems are in trouble. We need courageous thinking; our judicial system, morals, and ethics are dependent upon it. We need pure and honest thinking. Isaiah declared that the people "did not know," they did not consider.

Love your fellowmen sincerely. There are different kinds of love, too. There is romantic love, maternal love, filial love, the love of a mate. We are commanded to love neighbor as self. And, Jesus said, "Love ye one another; as I have loved you" (John 14:34). What a goal!

Act from honest motives purely. I guess Van Dyke was saying two things. One, act! Two, act from honest motives. Now the Christian religion is interested in more than conduct; it is interested in the source of conduct. Why do you act as you do?

Trust in God and heaven securely. We all act on faith; we cannot live without that. We eat in restaurants not knowing the cooks; we drive on highways, not knowing the other drivers; we take medicine, not being sure of the druggist. But, to trust in God! Strange that we sometimes have more trust in a baker or a grocer.

Ashamed of Your Best

I know not this man of whom you speak (v. 71).

A t the heart and the center of the passage for our thought today is that business of Peter being ashamed of Jesus. He said, "I know not this man." In one sense, of course, Peter was telling the truth. He did not *really know Jesus,* if so, he would never have denied him. Still, that is not the point here; in the sense that Peter meant his statement to be taken, Peter lied. Jesus had called Peter and Peter had responded. Peter was one of the inner group: he was on the mount of transfiguration, he heard Jesus preach, saw him heal, heard him pray, lent him his boat, and declared that Jesus was the "Son of the living God."

"I know not this man." It has been said when Peter spoke those words he was denying and being ashamed of the best thing that ever happened to him. Frequently we are ashamed of our best. Sir Walter Scott wanted to be a poet so much that when he began to write the wonderful Waverley novels he was ashamed. He would not even sign his name to them, the best thing Scott ever wrote. Beatrix Potter gave to the world that wonderful tale, *Peter Rabbit,* of Flopsy, Mopsy, and Mr. McGregor. That story has delighted millions, adults as well as children. But Beatrix Potter became ashamed of it. She married a wealthy landowner and became very "respectable," pompous, and formal. It is said that she became quite an expert at shooting rabbits. Or, again, think of Sir Arthur Conan Doyle, who became ashamed of Sherlock Holmes, the best thing he ever created.

In the Coptic Church, a branch of the ancient church in Egypt and the Near East, Pontius Pilate is regarded as a saint. Their basis: he said of Jesus, "I find no fault in him." But, Pilate did not back up his evaluation; he allowed them to crucify Jesus. We, too, can, and do say, "I find no fault in him." Then what?

The Good in Going to Church

Howbeit, he entered not into the temple of the Lord (v. 2b).

These verses say three things, each so clearly that he "who runs may read." The first thing the verses say is that Jotham was a good man. Fine! We like that. We need good men in government, business, school, home, and church. We can agree with the poet that we are all blind until we see that nothing is worth the making if it does not make the man. But, it does take more than moral and ethical goodness to please God. Many atheists have been morally and ethically straight. To please God there must be whole soul commitment to him and his way of life.

Second, the verses say that Jotham did not go to church. It does not say why he did not go, only that he did not. He may have found the services uninteresting, the preachers dull, the choir uninspiring, the leaders and deacons, dishonest. But, he did not go to church, and he should have gone. He needed the church; the church needed him; it was God's house and God promises to meet his people there in a special way because the church is a special place.

The third point the verses make is this, "And the people did yet corruptly." Those words coming in such close proximity to the word about Jotham not going to church, surely implies that there is a connection between the two. He was a good man, but he did not go to church. It is possible for enough religious morality and influence to be carried to a son or a daughter that some straightness of walk results, but what about children and children's children? Can you not hear it: "The king is a good man, he does not worship." "My dad is the best man I know, he never goes to church; why should I?" "Why do you love God?" asked the teacher. The little girl thought about that and said, "Teacher, I guess it just runs in our family."

Religion in Silver Slippers

Unto you it is given in behalf of Christ . . . to suffer for his sake (v. 29).

Christian and Hopeful, characters in Bunyan's *The Pilgrim's Progress,* overtook one who was going before them whose name was "By-ends." In their conversation By-ends described the people in the town of "Fair-speech" from which he had come.

"'Tis true," he said, "we somewhat differ in religion from those of the stricter sort, yet but in two small points: first, we never strive against the wind and tide. Secondly, we are always most zealous when religion goes in his silver slippers, we love much to walk with him in the street, if the sun shines and the people applaud it."

To this Christian replied, "If you go with us, you must go against wind and tide. . . . You must also own religion in his rags, as well as when . . . he walketh the streets with applause."

Then By-ends makes his decision, "I shall never desert my old principles, since they are harmless and profitable." So, Christian and Hopeful parted company with him, and he was joined by three other companions who rejoiced in the names of Mr. Hold-the-World, Mr. Money-love, and Mr. Save-all, all of whom were for "religion in what, and so far as the times, and my safety will bear it."

No wonder *The Pilgrim's Progress* stood next to the Bible in sales for centuries! We know Mr. By-ends don't we? There have been times when he was a close relative of ours. We, too, have loved the company of religion when he wore silver slippers, and when he was applauded in the streets.

Roads of the Loving Heart

He stedfastly set his face to go to Jerusalem (v. 51b).

Ray Freeman Jenny has said that there are four roads down which the Christian must walk. In keeping with an episode in the life of Robert Louis Stevenson, let's call them "the roads of the loving heart."

Health was gone for Stevenson and he sought the South Sea island of Samoa. When he arrived he made friends with Mataafa who laid claim to the throne but the authorities had imprisoned the man, along with other tribal chiefs. Stevenson was ill but he visited his friends in prison, doing what he could to make their lot lighter. Later when these prisoners were released they wanted to show their gratitude to Stevenson. What could they do? Well, he had made a roadway to their prison, they would make a roadway to his home, through the brush.

It was a difficult undertaking; it was hard work; there were no modern implements. The Samoans do not like to work. It is beneath the dignity of the chiefs to work. Yet, Stevenson was a man who had come to them in their need. So, they endured the hardship, they despised the humiliation, and they built a road and gave it to Stevenson. They called it, "The Road of the Loving Heart."

What about those "roads" that the Christian travels? First, the Damascus road, the road of conversion, the road of the loving heart that leads to salvation. Second, the Jericho road of usefulness. The good Samaritan went where the wounded was and helped him. Three, the Jerusalem road of commitment. The focal verse for today says it, "He [Jesus] stedfastly set his face to go to Jerusalem." Fourth, the Emmaus road of fellowship. Jesus drew near and went with them. These are "The Roads of the Loving Heart."

Ulcers?

That which cometh upon me daily, the care of all the churches (v. 28b).

Modern life moves at an exceedingly fast pace; tension and pressure are almost unavoidable. We are told that even dogs are getting ulcers. The heavy traffic, the problem of getting across the street, is just too much for "Fido." Still, children of God should have built-in "stabilizers." The surprising thing should not be that dogs get ulcers, but that human beings do. (Lest I be misunderstood; I have had an ulcer!)

We assume that dogs have no knowledge of a Heavenly Father such as should be common knowledge to every Christian. Could the problem be a matter of polytheism, many gods? And could it be that these gods have a good-sized civil war going on within the lives of many, as Chad Walsh would put it?

Who pointed out the fact that we cannot get through the day, to say nothing of the night, without our pills? We have pills for everything. There is a pill to make you relax and one to make you sleep and another to keep you awake and one to keep you from eating too much and another when you have eaten too much and another when you have not eaten enough and one to take when you have eaten onions and garlic—that is just too much responsibility to place on a pill!

No wonder the little boy was confused about his Sunday School lesson. He told his mother that they had studied about "Moses and his pills." That didn't sound quite right to the mother; she called the teacher. The teacher told the mother that the lesson had been on "Moses and the Tablets of the Law."

Perhaps what we need is the old prescription: "They that wait upon the Lord shall renew their strength" (Isa. 40:31).

How Would You Sing It?

The lines have fallen unto me in pleasant places [whereof I am glad] (v. 6).

In Archbishop William Temple's biography there is a revealing incident; it says much about the bishop as well as the people to whom he was speaking. He had led in a service of dedication for two thousand young men and women.

At the close of the service Dr. Temple asked that the group sing Isaac Watts's great hymn, "When I Survey the Wondrous Cross." Before the last verse Dr. Temple stopped the singing and said, "I want you to read over this last verse before you sing it. These are tremendous words.

"If you mean them with all your heart, sing them as loud as you can. If you don't mean them at all, keep silent. If you mean them a little and want to mean them more, sing them very softly."

There was complete silence as every eye scanned the page for the tremendous words:

> Were the whole real of nature mine,
>   That were a present far too small;
> Love so amazing, so divine,
>   Demands my soul, my life, my all.

—Isaac Watts

The organist touched the keys; then, two thousand voices *whispered* the words. It was a never-to-be-forgotten experience. It is said that when Bernard of Clairvaux came to a village to proclaim the love of God that mothers hid their sons and wives protected their husbands from the power of the message. That effect came from the message and the messenger. If the two are properly allied, something approaching such a result might be experienced more frequently. How would you sing Watts's hymn?

One Foot in Heaven

By the coming of our Lord Jesus Christ (v. 1b).

There are many wonderful truths connected with the doctrine of the second coming of Christ. One that is very dear is this: the soul of man and the love of God, once joined through redemption, shall never know separation. If a person lives in Christ, he shall die in Christ and belong to God in Christ forever. A relationship is set up over which sin and death and the grave have no control.

Hiram Pease loved to show his friends the epitaph he had composed for himself. It read,

> Under the sod and under the trees
> Lies the body of Hiram A. Pease.
> He is not here, only his pod
> He has shucked out his soul and gone home to God.

This faith crops up in unexpected places and in unusual ways. The day after Dick Shepherd, beloved pastor of St. Martin's in the Field, died, a London newspaper had an inspired photograph. It showed the pulpit in the great church where the radiant soul had so often preached. A beam of light shone on the reading desk; the Bible was open. In the margin of the picture the editor of that great daily paper had put the words, "Here endeth the first lesson."

On the morning after the death of John Foster Dulles, the much-traveled American secretary of state, many newspapers carried a cartoon showing Dulles boarding a giant plane, as he had so often done in life. Under the picture were the words, "His Last Flight."

That is the faith of the men who proclaimed the eternal union of a believing soul and its God. And, in such faith, we, too, can say, "Even so, come Lord Jesus."

Only a Sinner Saved by Grace

The just shall live by faith (v. 11b).

Paul became concerned when rites and ceremonies were not properly placed. He knew it was possible for rites and ceremonies to separate one from true morality, separate one from Christ, the one and only true source of salvation.

To substitute or add to simple faith in Christ any rite or ceremony as necessary to salvation was, Paul knew, untrue to fact, a false interpretation of the Scriptures, the making of the death of Christ of no avail, and the severing of men from the full, flowing grace of God!

We need to be careful at this point. Paul was not against ceremonies and ordinances and organizations in the churches. Paul taught that there was a place for baptism, the Lord's Supper, and faithful attendance upon organized public worship. But, to make any of these things *necessary to salvation* was in the sight of Paul, a denial of the mission and death of Christ. Let us, then, "Stand fast therefore in the liberty wherewith Christ hath made us free, and be not entangled again with the yoke of bondage," or as Phillips states it, "Plant your feet firmly therefore with the freedom that Christ has won for us, and do not let yourselves be caught again in the shackles of slavery" (Gal. 5:1). Of course, the old gospel song says it, too.

> Naught have I gotten but what I received;
> Grace hath bestowed it since I have believed;
> Boasting excluded, pride I abase;
> I'm only a sinner saved by grace!

> —JAMES M. GRAY

How Syrup Is Made

I have finished my course, I have kept the faith (v. 7*b*).

The first full day's work I ever did was at an old-fashioned cane mill. I sat on a stool and fed the cane into turning cylinders that crushed the juice from the stalks; the turning and crushing were produced by a mule pulling a long beam round and round in a circle. I was a small boy, and for the first few minutes the job was exciting. Then I discovered that I had to sit on the same stool, in the same place, feed stalks of cane into the same cylinders, while the same mule pulled the same beam round and round in the same circle. Neither the mule nor I seemed to be going anywhere fast! I was not greatly concerned about the mule; I was sorry for myself. Still, minute after slowly passing minute, hour after each crawling hour, throughout that slowly dying day, the sweet juice was pouring from the crushed stalks of cane into the containers that would turn it into delicious table syrup.

Life is frequently like that. Round and round and round we go; we, nor life, seem to be getting anywhere fast. The monotony is boring. Yet, these are the experiences which frequently produce the sweetness of life. It calls for staying power. "Lord God," prayed Sir Francis Drake, "when thou givest to thy servants to endeavor any great matter, grant us also to know that it is not the beginning but the continuing of the same until it is thoroughly finished which yieldeth the true glory."

One hundred steps from the top of Mt. Washington there is a marker showing the spot where a woman climber lay down and died. One hundred more steps and she would have found food and shelter, but this she did not know. Exhausted by the storm, blinded by the snows, she gave up the fight one hundred steps before reaching safety. Said the Duke of Wellington, "Hard pounding this, gentlemen; let's see who will pound the longest." Paul wrote, "I have finished the course." Great testimony!

A Suitcase Full of Books

Bring with thee . . . the books, but especially the parchments (v. 13).

Spiritual growth calls for discipline, diligence, concentration, and study. Paul cautioned Timothy to study that he might show himself "approved unto God" (v. 15). And, this study is required of all, not just the young students. Paul requested that Timothy bring his books to him.

Training in godliness means guarding the gift that we have and stirring it up until it blazes. It is the picture of guarding a precious treasure or of stirring up the coals of a fire until the fire blazes. No one of us even approaches our potential.

Our papers carried the story of a mother lifting an automobile off her son. Could she do that? No, of course not. But, she did! Have you seen how easy it is for a person under hypnosis to do impossible tasks? Did you ever see a student bogged down in his work, flunking every subject, unable to grasp any of the subject matter and, then, "come alive" and take off like a rocket? I serve in a university community; I know these students; you never know what will happen!

No area of life has greater potential for growth and development than the spiritual area. Every minister and counselor knows this. Did you ever hear corn grow? I have. I have lain in a corn row on a hot July night and listened to the rippling, rustling, popping of the blades of corn, as they sought their freedom through growth. But that example does not compare with the experiences that I have observed in the lives of the young men and women whom I have known.

Dr. Merton Rice, Methodist minister, always took a suitcase of books on his travels. One day in Buffalo a porter asked Dr. Rice if he had lead in the case! "No, it is books." "My, my, you mus' be pow'ful ig'nant!" No, just powerfully wise.

A Bowl of Red Roses

For to me to live is Christ, and to die is gain (v. 21).

One of the outstanding things about this letter to the Philippians is its inclusiveness. "We are continually thanking God for you all." That is more than an indication that Paul was a "Southerner" who took his "you alls" with him wherever he went! This is the final and emphatic *all*. Paul says that he is remembering before God, that is, praying for, every single one of them. If God can keep account of the hairs on the heads of his children, Paul should be able to remember in prayer, individually, the members of the church at Philippi. And you?

In 1923 Edmund Morel visited all the European capitals. Morel was an extremist in politics, a member of the left wing Labor party, but he enjoyed a strong friendship with Stanley Baldwin, then prime minister of Britain.

When Morel returned from his trip, he called on Baldwin and poured into the prime minister's anxious ears the sorry tale of rags, revolt, intrigue, and hunger. It was a dark picture, casting a dark shadow over the heart of each man. Then Baldwin lifted his head and asked, "Morel, do you like roses?" "Like them?" said Morel, "I love them!" Lifting a large bowl of beautiful red roses from the desk and shoving them toward Morel, the prime minister said, "Bury your face in this loveliness and thank God!"

That is what the apostle Paul did in his letter to the Philippians. He had no desire to shut out the sin and ugliness of paganism on the part of the masses or the weakness and failures on the part of the followers of Christ, but he buried a grateful face in the church of Christ and thanked God!

The Great Are Not Free

Wist ye not that I must be about my Father's business? (v. 49b).

His words were, "I must be in my Father's house." Here is the imperative of surrender. We dislike the word *must*. We like the words *freedom* and *liberty*. We respond to Robert Frost's lines, "Something there is that does not like a wall."

"I must be about my Father's business." Who said he did? Who was forcing the boy Jesus to that? Love, duty, service, sacrifice were a few of the taskmasters of his life whispering their imperial musts.

It was love that whispered, "I must be in my Father's house." It was duty that affirmed, "I must be about my Father's business." It was purpose that rang out, "I must work the works of him who sent me." It was compassion that sounded in the words, "He must needs go through Samaria." It was the voice of sacrifice that affirmed, "The Son of man must be lifted up." It was the peal of victory that sounded forth, "The third day the Son of man must rise again." This imperial "must" is used in no less than thirty times in the New Testament in relation to Jesus and his mission.

It is reported that once when the present Queen Elizabeth was a small child, she became angry, stamped her little foot, and shouted, "I am a princess, and so I can do whatever I want to do." Her father, the king, replied gently, but firmly, and a bit sadly, "No, my dear. It is just because you are a princess that you cannot do as you please." The greater one is, the more "musts" there is in his or her life.

"A Man on the Cross"

And I, if I be lifted up from the earth, will draw all men unto me (v. 32).

The Chicago Temple is a Methodist Church in the heart of the Windy City's financial center. Often, when walking through the Loop, I have looked up at the church's steeple. There atop the tall steeple is a cross, said to be the highest in the world. Charles M. Crow tells of a traffic jam that occurred at the base of the building some years ago. Thousands of people stopped and were gazing up at the cross. Why? It had been there many years; most people never gave it a glance. Now it was stopping traffic. Difference? Now there was a man on it. A workman was repairing the cross, and Chicago stopped to see. "Even so must the Son of man be lifted up." "And I, if I be lifted up . . . will draw all men unto me."

Dr. Leslie Weatherhead, long-time minister of City Temple, London once wrote:

> I well remember conducting a mission at the University of Leeds. After each session there was an opportunity for private conversations. A girl who was about to take her final degree examinations said something like this: "When I get back home, I know that the hardest thing in my religious life will be to stick with the services in our little village chapel. . . . So," she added, "I shall simply go up to the hills or into the woods. I shall more easily find God there . . . " Of course, I told her that would never do as a rule. God ceases too soon to be real when we evade men, especially fellow-seekers, and seek Him selfishly for ourselves; and I reminded her of Him who was in the synagogue on the Sabbath day "as His custom was." I reminded her that he must have had to listen to some pretty poor stuff from those old Rabbis; but that if others lifted their heads during the prayers and saw His face, they would come again; that in any case when He was there, it would be easier to pray; that she had something to give in a service as well as to get; and that her minister would break his heart if she deserted him instead of helping him to make the service what they both wanted it to become. Since that date, the spiritual life of that little village church has been transformed and renewed, and it has overflowed into another village. The girl not only attended regularly but started a group which has become the spiritual powerhouse of the neighborhood.[3]

Someone has to be on a cross!

To Help the Unemployed

Man shall not live by bread alone (v. 4b).

When God wants a man to make a plow, the man does not honor God by insisting that he be allowed to make a sermon. But this does not alter the fact that a sermon which is used of God to bring men into a saving relationship with him is more important than a plow that helps man to grow more or better ears of corn, for life is more than bread. It was a new and a higher service to which Jesus was now dedicating himself. He would be preaching the gospel to the poor, proclaiming release to the captives, the recovery of sight to the blind; he would be setting at liberty those who were oppressed; and he would be proclaiming the acceptable year of the Lord. The Spirit of the Lord was coming upon him for that purpose.

One of the church fathers said, "The kingdom of Heaven, O man, requires no other price than yourself; the value of it is yourself; give yourself for it, and you shall have it." Let us say it reverently; this was true for Christ no less than for his followers. He could gain the kingdom of God on no other grounds. This, surely, should be enough to banish any pink-tea dreams that the kingdom can be gained in our day.

Gilbert K. Chesterton, that thorny thistle in the side of his own church, as well as the churches of all persuasions, saw that many people feel the kingdom of God can be gained through criticism and complaint alone; that once a group has pronounced judgment upon other groups for what they have done or have not done, they have thereby qualified themselves for the kingdom. So Chesterton wrote,

> The Christian Social Union here
> Was very much annoyed;
> It seems there is some duty
> Which we never should avoid,
> And so they sing a lot of hymns
> To help the Unemployed.[4]

Light Gives Life

A light to lighten the Gentiles, and the glory of thy people Israel (v. 32).

Inscribed on the Eddystone lighthouse on the English coast are the words, "To give light is to give life." In order to be the life of the world, Christ had to be "the light of the world." That Light was the light from heaven. That is why it could not be put out. John came "as a burning and shining light," and men were willing to rejoice in the light that John gave them for a season. The light, the truth, the testimony that Christ brought was greater. He was the Light that the world could not put out.

It seemed a small light. One man, a working man, a carpenter by trade, one who had grown up among them, one whose brothers and sisters they knew, one who came from a town and community of no repute and a country that was held in bondage by military power, yet, he was "the true Light, which lighteth every man that cometh into the world."

In his biography of St. Francis of Assisi, Chesterton says, "While it was yet twilight a figure appeared silently and suddenly on a little hill above the city, dark against the fading darkness. For it was the end of a long and stern night, a night of vigil, not unvisited by stars. He stood with his hands lifted . . . and about him was a burst of birds singing; and behind him was the break of day."

So, to some lesser degree, it has been with every "St. Francis" who has followed the light that lighteth every man.

> The whole world was lost in the darkness of sin,
>   The Light of the world is Jesus;
> Like sunshine at noon-day His glory shone in,
>   The Light of the world is Jesus.
>
> —PHILIP P. BLISS

But Without Chains

Except for chains (v. 29b, RSV)

For two years Paul had been a prisoner in Caesarea. Then a new governor, Festus, took office. Immediately Paul's old enemies came forth to accuse him before the new governor. But, their testimony did not agree and the governor could see no cause for severe punishment. But to stay in the good graces of the Jews, Paul's enemies, Festus asked Paul if he was willing to go to Jerusalem to be judged. Paul said that he was not willing to go. He was standing before Caesar's judgment seat where he ought to be judged. He had done nothing wrong, as the governor knew. He was a Roman citizen; he appealed to Caesar.

A few days later Herod Agrippa, King of Idumea, and Bernice, his beautiful but wicked sister, came to pay their respects to the new governor. The governor told them about Paul. They wanted to see and hear this man whose fame had spread far and wide. So, Paul was brought before the group and told that he was free to speak for himself. So, Paul stands before the king and the governor, those who have power to bind or to release, and, he is given an opportunity to plead his own case.

Paul completely ignored his own situation, though his very life was at stake. He preached to them an impassioned sermon, pressing for decision on the part of the king and the governor! He cried, "King Agrippa, do you believe the prophets? I know that you do!" Agrippa said, "Much more of this, Paul, and you will be making me a Christian!" Ah, what a scene! What a preacher! That is the second time the word *Christian* has been applied to a follower of Jesus. Is that what being a Christian means? David said:

Neither will I offer burnt offering unto the Lord my God of that which doth cost me nothing (2 Sam. 24:24).

Called "Christians"

The disciples were called Christians first in Antioch (v. 26).

Why? Why were the disciples called Christians? Because that was their main business and concern. Here was a group of people who were following Christ. They talked Christ; they preached Christ; they prayed to Christ; they met in Christ's name. As one man was given the name "Carpenter" because he built houses, so, the disciples were Christians because they lived Christ.

It did not mean that they did not do other things. They were bakers, carpenters, smiths, weavers, farmers, and candlestick makers, but all this was secondary. Their main business was Christ, so the appropriateness of their name.

Immediately the implications are clear and disturbing. A Christian is one whose main business is Christ! No matter what one's other involvements may be, no matter what the profession at which one makes a living, one makes a life out of following, living, and affirming Jesus Christ. So much so, that if friends and enemies are going to identify one with a main concern one has to be identified with Christ.

Disturbing! If only those are to be called "Christians" who receive the name on the above basis, there will be quite a thinning of church rolls.

Not only personally, but think of institutions and nations. America is called a Christian nation; we know what is meant; the term is legitimate under those terms. However, if you take the above requirements, what about these "Christian" hospitals, "Christian" schools, aye, these "Christian" churches? How many would merit the title, "Christian"?

The religion of Jesus begins with the verb "follow" and ends with the verb "go."

—AUTHOR UNKNOWN

He Never Forgot

They laid hold upon one Simon . . . and on him they laid the cross (v. 26a).

We are a forgetful people and great events are soon treated lightly. However, Arthur John Gossip thinks there was one person involved in the crucifixion who never forgot. It was this man Simon who was forced to carry the cross for Jesus. Gossip sees it all very clearly in his imagination.

Simon came into the city from the country just as the mob was moving toward Calvary. Just then Jesus stumbled and fell beneath the cross. The soldier in charge looked about for help, saw Simon, and ordered him to carry the cross. Simon protested, but the soldier was accustomed to being obeyed; so, Simon carried the cross.

Then Dr. Gossip sees several possibilities. One, Simon was angry, bitter, resentful, and determined to get even with Rome, in general, and that soldier, in particular; Simon would never forgive. Or, two, if Simon became a Christian, and there are indications that he did, he would remember the incident in a different spirit, but no less vividly. Caught up in some sin, Simon would cry, "Holy God, must I forever wound him whom I adore? Was it not enough that I should assist in his crucifixion? Must I forever go on wounding him?"

Or, on another day when Simon was challenged to make some deep sacrifice for the cause of Christ, he would cry out: "Blessed be this privilege! Once more I am permitted to make his task a little easier. Once in the long ago, by God's grace, I was allowed to make the hill of Calvary a little less severe; now, again, the privilege is mine. Most gladly will I perform this deed in his name!" And, so, by acts great and small, Simon kept the great event of the crucifixion fresh in his mind and heart. And you?

A Practical Dreamer

Where there is no vision, the people perish (v. 18a).

In *The Portrait of a Practical Dreamer,* Elizabeth Yates tells the inspiring story of Howard Thurman. As a young black, Howard Thurman had a hard time in Daytona, Florida, where he grew up. He completed the seventh grade in school; it was as far as he could go. No black had ever gone beyond that in Daytona. His life was severely restricted. He could not, for example, leave the Negro settlement and cross the river at night without a letter of authorization signed by a white man.

On May 25, 1963 Dr. Thurman returned to Daytona, Florida, to give the Baccalaureate Address at Bethune-Cookman College. He was a world citizen now. Educational institutions throughout the land had honored themselves by bestowing upon him honorary degrees. He was minister-at-large of Boston University; Dean of Rankin Chapel, Howard University. He was cofounder of the Church for the Fellowship of All People, San Francisco; Fellow, National Council of Religion in Higher Education, author of books and articles in learned journals, contributor to *The Interpreter's Bible,* friend and confidant of the great.

Daytona was glad to do him honor; the day was designated "Howard Thurman Day." The mayor met him, read a proclamation that made Howard Thurman an honorary citizen of the city. A key to the city was presented to him. The car that carried him, his family, and the mayor was followed by a motorcade of city officials, four marching bands followed; the streets were lined with crowds: watching, waving, cheering.

Following a reception, Dr. Thurman visited the old doctor, now retired, who had befriended him years before, who had given him a pair of shoes, saying, "Learn to wear them, Howard, for you have a long way to go." At the old doctor's request, Dr. Thurman knelt by the chair and prayed.

Your sons and your daughters shall prophesy, your old men shall dream dreams, and your young men shall see visions (Joel 2:28).

On Guinea Pigs

Greater love hath no man than this (v. 13a).

The story is true. I verified it in alumni records, medical library, and dusty files. Dr. Claude Barlow, a graduate of the Johns Hopkins Medical School, went out to China to work in the field of medicine and hygiene. There came a dreadful plague; the people were dying at a fearful rate. Dr. Barlow had little laboratory equipment and no assistants. Understandably, the United States would not allow a patient to be brought across international borders. Dr. Barlow kept careful records on scores of patients. Then, he took a boat for America. In his possession were two small vials of the deadly germs. Just before his ship docked he drank the contents of those two vials.

He went immediately to Johns Hopkins and placed himself in the care of his old professors, telling them what he had done, turned over to them his notebooks and journals in which he had written all that he had been able to learn of the dread disease. He said to his former teachers, "Here I am; this is what I have done; here, in these books is all that I have been able to learn about the disease. Do what you can. Save my life if possible; but, regardless of my life, find a cure for the people of China." Fortunately they were able to do both.

Surprised at that example of unselfish heroism? Jesus would say, "Why are you surprised? Did I not tell you that man is a wonderful creature and thoroughly capable of rising to such heights? Otherwise, would I have paid him such compliments: 'You are the salt of the earth.' 'You are the light of the world.' 'You are my witnesses.' The things that I do shall you do, and greater."

> *"Let thy work appear unto thy servants, and thy glory unto their children.*
> *And let the beauty of the Lord our God be upon us: and establish thou the work of our hands upon us; yea, the work of our hands establish thou it," through Jesus Christ our Lord. Amen.*

"I Failed Him—He Still Trusted Me!"

Thou shalt be called Cephas, which [means], A stone (v. 42b).

A rthur John Gossip of Scotland observed if it were possible to approach the New Testament for the first time, with no former knowledge of it, never having heard of Jesus, the predominant impression would be of the faith and confidence Jesus had in those whose lives had been touched by his Spirit—not their faith in him (that of course) but his faith in them. Cephas, Peter of our text, was a prime case in point.

Dr. Gossip was at one time a chaplain in the military. He told about a young man whom he knew in the service. This man made a serious blunder and for it he was court-martialed and punished. The only comment the officer in charge made was that this young man was too good a person to lose. The commanding officer said that since the fault had been paid for, the case was forgotten so far as he was concerned, and he never intended to mention it again, either to the young man or to anyone else.

The officer was as good as his word. He slipped back into the easy ways of confidence and goodwill. Finally, the boy, who expected the storm to break at any minute, asked what it all meant. Whereupon his chaplain told him of his commanding officer's position: the deed had been paid for, the boy was too valuable to lose, it was his desire that everyone help the boy insofar as they could. The young man was silent for a moment, then turned quickly and left the chaplain.

A few weeks later the soldier was placed in a position of serious danger and responsibility, the same type of situation in which he had failed before. This time, however, he conducted himself with such courage and distinction that he won a promotion and other honors as well. He explained his actions to the chaplain: "What else could I do? I failed him, and he still trusted me!"

The only way to make a man trustworthy is to trust him.

—GEORGE WILLIAM RUSSELL

Heaven's Gates and the Gypsies

Thou art not far from the kingdom of God (v. 34c).

The world is filled with religious gypsies! They seek to camp just outside the kingdom—not far outside, but still outside. They want the benefits of kingdom living for themselves and their families: morals, ethics, laws, institutions, customs. These "religious gypsies" would not think of conducting their business, of raising their families, away from the influences of the kingdom and the churches. They do appreciate what "salt" means to society; they do want the "light" that comes from Christian living, want its advantages; though they do not care to enter into the production line of that kind of life and influence.

During my childhood I became acquainted with the customs of roving Gypsies: bright-colored clothes, rakish bandannas for their heads, wagons, pots and pans, camp fires, songs, fortune-telling. Romantic!

They liked to camp just outside the city limits—not inside, just outside. Inside would have called for an ordered life, sanitary laws would have been imposed, there would have been taxes. But just outside they had the "best of two worlds." No restrictions but closeness to ply their trade, telling fortunes.

> Heaven's gates were open wide,
> But still the Gypsies camped outside

Jesus once said to a person, "Thou art not far from the kingdom." Not far, close, near, on the border, but still, not in—and, "A miss is as good as a mile." Think about that: a plane almost clears the treetops on takeoff—not quite, but almost, and, "A miss is as good as a mile." A man has almost enough character to withstand the pressure, the competition, the temptations, not quite, but almost, and, "A miss is as good as a mile." For, remember, not to be finally in is to be ultimately out.

"With Me All the Time"

The Lord stood with me, and strengthened me (v. 17a).

A small boy was ill. The boy's father was told that an operation was necessary. The father was asked to inform the boy, which he did. The boy said, "All right, Dad, I'll go to the hospital and have the operation if you'll go and stay with me." "Sure, Son, I'll take you, stay with you through the operation, and come to see you every day you are in the hospital." "No," said the boy, "that is not what I want; I want you to stay with me at the hospital as long as I am there." That was a difficult matter. Finally, the father arranged his work so that he could do just what the boy asked.

The operation was performed, a major operation. In about six hours the boy opened his eyes; there was his father. The boy slept, again he opened his eyes; there was his father. The boy said, "Dad, I wish every day was like this." "Son," said the father, "you are in the hospital and have had surgery; you wouldn't want every day to be like this." "Yes," said the boy, "but, you've been with me all the time."

My boyhood pastor was driving past a deacon's home, out in the country. Seeing the deacon on top of a barn, the pastor stopped for a visit. After greeting the deacon, the pastor saw the deacon's son, playing in the shadow of the barn. The boy had a small toy hammer, some rusty nails; he was trying to drive the rusty nails in the hard clay. Preacher: "What are you doing, son?" Boy: "Me and my daddy's building a barn." The pastor smiled, not much help with a toy hammer, crooked, rusty nails, hard clay. But, the preacher was aware that something had happened on the barn. The boy's father had heard what his son said. The big hammer paused in mid-air; the father smiled; then, with a few mighty strokes, the big nail was driven to its head!

Father God, give us thy presence and we shall bravely face the operations of life. Give us faith to believe that even though our hammers be small and nails be crooked, that somehow, by thy grace, we can say with assurance, "My Father and I are building a kingdom." Amen.

"Raincoats and Smiles"

And Abraham journeyed (v. 9a).

The following fable appeared in one of our daily papers recently. Two men had been condemned to fight the lions. As they discussed their situation, one said that he understood the lions attacked by biting with their teeth and tearing with their claws. The other man replied that such might be the case, but there was a chance that the lions might attack by spitting on their victims. He then explained that he had a new raincoat which was guaranteed to protect up to 97 percent against spit. He persuaded his companion to hand over his money in exchange for the raincoat. The next day the two men entered the arena wearing broad smiles—one because he was protected by his new raincoat, the other because he was rich. The lions were waiting. "What fools these mortals be!"

Now, by contrast, the story of an itinerant missionary in Canada. On one of his visits to a settlement he taught a little invalid boy the verse, "The Lord is my shepherd." In saying the verse, the boy clasped one finger for each word. Thus he always held his fourth finger as he said the word "my." Two years later when the missionary came back to the home, the little invalid boy was not there. The mother said, "He died on a cold winter night. We found him in the morning with his left hand clasped around the fourth finger of his right hand." Carefully the missionary explained, "Your son was unafraid because he could say of the Lord, 'He is *my* shepherd.'"

> Lord, give me such a faith as this;
> And then what-e'er may come,
> I'll know while here, the hallowed bliss
> Of my eternal home
>
> —WILLIAM H. BATHURST

"Raise the Stone"

The salutation of Paul with my own hand (v. 17).

The art of letter writing seems to be passing. If it is understandable it is no less regrettable. We have modern inventions for communication, fast transportation, the average person's handwriting is hard to read. The student brought a paper back to his professor and said, "Professor, would you please tell me what this is that you have written on my paper?" The professor glared at the student and said, "It asks you to write more legibly."

Could it be that shallow living has something to do with the diminishing art of letter writing? Could it be that our lives are so shallow that we have few things worth writing down? Or, are our relationships too casual and superficial?

It has been suggested that we are poor letter writers because we have no great sorrow that has been sanctified. Most of the great letter writers have known great sorrow. The letters of Charles Lamb have been described as being "like white-caps on the bosom of a great sorrow." The letters of Robert Louis Stevenson are like precious pearls, but pearls formed, as all pure pearls are formed, by suffering lodged in a sensitive heart. Or, the letters of Jane Carlyle, the wife of Thomas Carlyle, are as incense offered on an altar of sacrifice and devotion that was never appreciated by her husband until after her death. Again, think of the letters of Elizabeth Barrett Browning.

How we wish we might discover a batch of letters written by Jesus to his friends—to Mary, Martha, Mary Magdalene, to John, Peter, or to Nicodemus. On the basis of the discovery of supposed words of Jesus, Van Dyke wrote, in *The Toiling of Felix*, "Raise the stone and thou shalt find me; cleave the wood and there am I."

"Church on the Brink of Hell"

Other foundation can no man lay than . . . Jesus Christ (v. 11).

The church was in Corinth, and Corinth was getting into the church! There is the problem. Disharmony in a church is always a problem. We do not lose our individual differences or shed our personalities as we enter the church door. Paul knew that nothing short of the transforming grace of God could eradicate the problem. That is why he "used a steamroller to crack a nut." The "nuts" were so hard that only the "steamroller" of the gospel could crack them.

There is a Presbyterian church in Jerusalem which clings to the side of a mountain overlooking the valley of Gehenna. Gehenna was the place where Jerusalem burned its trash and garbage. Gehenna was the name Jesus used for hell. So, naturally, this church became known as "the church on the brink of hell."

The church at Corinth was not so much on the "brink of hell," as in the midst of a Roman "hell." Yet, Paul called it "The church of God which is at Corinth." "The church of God"—a little group of people, sharing the life of God, inspired by the Spirit of God, doing the work of God. Corinth was worldly, ignorant of God, and hostile to the will and purposes of God.

"The past," said Guiceiardini, "throws light on the future, because the world was ever of the same make, and all that is or will be in another day has already been, and the same thing returns only with different names and colors. It is not everyone who knows them under the new face, but the wise know them."

It has been said that the church is like the ark. With all the animals, Noah couldn't have stood the stink on the inside but for the storm on the outside!

"Just When You Need Him Most"

When Abram was ninety years old and nine, the Lord appeared to [him] (v. 1a).

When Abram left Haran, he was seventy-five years old. When God renewed the covenant with him, he was ninety-nine. There had been three special revelations, encounters, between this man and his God. One came at Bethel as he entered the land, one after his generous attitude toward Lot and, the third after his conflict with the Eastern kings. We are prone to believe that this man's life was crowded with special revelations. Not so. The special revelations were few and far apart. Abram, like us, had to walk by faith and not by sight. God appeared to Abram, "Just when he needed him most."

In each appearance the particular characteristic of God that Abram needed most was revealed. After the war with the kings, God said, "Fear not, Abram; I am thy shield, and thy exceeding great reward,"— don't be afraid. In the fourth appearance, God said, "I am the Almighty God"—Power—never doubt my ability to fulfill promises that I make.

God's further word might be interpreted: "I am changing your name; you will not be known as Abram anymore but as *Abraham*, a father of multitudes. You are ninety-nine years old, but remember, the one who is making the promise is Almighty God."

It is good to know that in a day and world of change, God is dependable; in a time of broken promises, God keeps his word.

> I'll go where you want me to go, dear Lord,
>   O'er mountain or plain or sea;
> I'll say what you want me to say, dear Lord,
>   I'll be what you want me to be.

—MARY BROWN

Beyond the Power of Words

Because I live, ye shall live also (v. 19b).

The resurrection means at least four things for the Christian: First, it is a guarantee that sin is doomed; God and good win; Satan loses. Second, it is a guarantee of the importance of this life in the here and now. It was in the "flesh" that Christ came. Third, it guarantees the reality of everlasting life. And fourth, it guarantees that this everlasting life will be lived in fellowship with Jesus Christ.

In his fine autobiography, *River of Years,* Joseph Fort Newton wrote about the death of his father. The author was just a boy at the time. Clinging to the hand of his mother, he looked for the first time into an open grave, a strange and terrifying experience for a young boy. Then the old country minister adjusted his glasses and read the words of Jesus: "I am the resurrection and the life." "Let not your heart be troubled." Dr. Newton wrote, "Never shall I forget the power of those words! It was as if a great, gentle Hand, stronger than the hand of man and more tender than the hand of any woman, had been put forth from the Unseen to caress and heal my spirit. From that day to this I have loved Jesus beyond the power of words to tell!" That is what Paul means when he writes about "the power of his resurrection."

To know Christ means to enter into fellowship with him in suffering. As Christ suffered for the sins of others, even so Paul, in his limited and faltering way, would suffer for and suffer in the service of others.

For half a century I have been writing my thoughts in prose and verse; history, philosophy, drama, romance, tradition, satire, ode and song; I have tried it all. But I feel I have not said the thousandth part of what is in me. When I go down to the grave I can say like many others, "I have finished my day's work." But I cannot say, "I have finished my life." My day's work will begin again the next morning. The tomb is not a blind alley; it is a thoroughfare. It closes on the twilight. It opens on the dawn.

—Victor Hugo

Proper Use of the Eyes

They shall not hurt nor destroy in all my holy mountain, saith the Lord (v. 25b).

The far look gave Isaiah hope, and what a dream he had. He saw every life fulfilling its purpose; a child would live to be a hundred years old; houses would be built and the people would live in safety in them; they would plant their vineyards and eat the fruit thereof.

Lord Northcliffe, a British leader of the nineteenth century, was threatened with blindness. The greatest specialists of the day gave his case their closest attention. Six weeks were spent in examining, testing, and diagnosing. At the end they came up with the conclusion that the eyes were not only sound but abnormally quick and keen. In a fast-speeding car they were able to read relatively small print in shop windows, but they concluded that the eyes were the eyes of a hunter and gamekeeper. They were designed for, and had been trained for, use in far-stretching country, wide spaces, distant horizons. When forced to change their focus, compelled to concentrate day after day on columns of newspaper print, the tired optic nerves had finally rebelled.

The remedy was quite simple and yet completely successful. There was added to the hurry and breathless activity of a great city office, with its many things having to be concentrated upon at once, a touch of country life, large gardens, far vistas, and wide-flung acres. When given a chance to extend and stretch themselves, the optic nerves were satisfied and gladly performed their function.

It is so easy for life to be cabined and cribbed. There is the oft-repeated observation that it is easy to be pessimistic by the year, but you have to be optimistic over the years. The near and immediate must not be ignored; the far distances and vast stretches of time must be taken into account.

If God is in the future, why not trust the future?

"A Lamp Unto My Feet"

Thy word is a lamp unto my feet, and a light unto my path (v. 105).

Years ago I lived in the city of Baltimore. Frequently I visited in the hospitals. The operator of the elevator I chose on this particular day was a giant of a man. As I stepped into the elevator, he closed the book he was reading. I saw it was a copy of the Bible. He looked up, smiled, and asked, "What floor, sir?" Fortunately, I wanted the top floor and I was the only passenger. At other times I had seen this man reading his Bible; I wanted his story. I hurried my call and returned to the same elevator and operator. It was an interesting conversation:

For twenty-five years this man had read his Bible through each year. Each day during those years he had memorized a verse of Scripture from his reading. Each year, in addition to the daily verse, he had memorized three chapters, one from the Old Testament and two from the New Testament. He told me that any chapter and verse he had ever memorized he still "knew by heart" and could recall anytime, day or night. The psalmist's words came to mind, "I love thy law." "Thy word have I hid in mine heart, that I might not sin against thee." "Peace have they that love thy law."

Human speech is a wonderful thing. It has been estimated that one speaks on the average of 30,000 words each day; that is a fair-sized book! In a normal lifetime one would fill a library. All of these books are by the same author, and not one can be taken from the shelf or withdrawn from circulation. How good to know that the "daily volume," as well as the accumulation of the years, is generously laced with the words of life!

"Glory on a Windswept Hill"

Her daughter was made whole from that very hour (v. 28*b*).

If you could live again any hour of your life, what hour would you choose? The editor of a metropolitan newspaper asked his readers that question.

One woman wrote, "After months of waiting, planning, longing, two days and nights of awful pain, a sweet little baby girl lay in a crib beside me. Strapped to the bed and unable to hold her to my heart, for one hour I looked at her. . . . In my mind I saw her grow up, my pal, my best friend, one who could understand a woman. The next morning the crib was gone. The memory of her brings tears to my eyes and a great longing to my heart, for there can never be another baby in our home. But that one brief, golden hour was my own. Gladly would I go through all the waiting and pain for just such another hour, no matter what the cost."

A friend used to visit an old lady in her nineties. He went under the guise of bringing her comfort, but he always received more than he gave. For she was a radiant soul, though an invalid, and for more than a score of years she had scarcely known one hour free from pain. One day the friend asked her for the secret. The lovely, pain-wracked ninety-year-old said, "I had an hour of glory upon a windswept hill!"

The biblical writers knew about these giant hours. Isaiah wrote, "In the year that king Uzziah died I saw also the Lord." Paul always remembered, never missed an opportunity to tell, about his great hour; he would say, "I was not disobedient unto the heavenly vision!"

Holy Father, never let us forget that life is made great by these giant hours, never by pygmy years. Amen.

"The Game's Only Half Over"

My Lord and my God (v. 28).

Thomas made a mistake, a serious mistake. He absented himself from the warm fellowship of his fellow disciples. Thomas could not, would not, believe what they told him. But, the game was not over. There was time remaining for him to confess, "My Lord and my God!"

California Institute of Technology was playing in the Rose Bowl football game against Georgia Tech. Early in the game a Georgia Tech man received the ball and was instantly tackled by the California players. He was hit so hard that the ball bounced out of his arms and right into the hands of Roy Riegels, the California center. As Riegels started down the field, three Georgia men headed for him. Riegels reversed his movement, cut the other way, and circled to avoid his would-be attackers. Suddenly he saw an opening and headed for the goal line.

Then an interesting thing happened. His own teammates began to bear down on him, trying in every way possible to tackle him themselves. But Riegels was headed for "pay dirt." No one could overtake him. There was just one thing wrong. Riegels was running in the wrong direction. He raced sixty-three yards before he was finally brought down by one of his own teammates. Roy Riegels was tagged; the tag remained—"Wrong Way" Riegels.

Years later Riegels gave a sequel to that story. He told what happened at halftime. He said he had never been so embarrassed and humiliated in his life. When he and his fellow players went into the clubhouse, he knew that the coach would "skin him alive" for what he had done. The rest of the squad sat together; he sat alone waiting for the storm to break but the storm never broke. The coach spoke quietly to all members of the team; he gave suggestions and encouragement; he pointed out errors and gave approval. As the whistle sounded for the second half, the coach walked over to Riegels, put his hand on the dejected player's shoulder and said, "All right, Roy; the game is only half over; get back into the game." Roy Riegels played the rest of that game as he had never played before.

There is no score until the runner crosses home plate.

On Loving the Unlovable

. . . That he who loveth God love his brother also (v. 21).

A good friend of mine, a teacher, used to say to his classes, "Well, men, I'm mean and common and not much of a teacher, but you've got to love me, for if you don't you can't go to heaven." You cannot love God and hate your neighbor. Love is a whole and complete experience.

It has often been said that the world has become a neighborhood; we now have to make it a brotherhood. No man lives to himself, we are "bound in the bundle of life"; we experience "entangling alliances" as we have never known them before.

Think of how you and I are tied in with the rest of the world. You sleep in pajamas that are East Indian in origin; you get out of a bed the pattern of which originated in Paris; you check a clock which is a European invention. You use a bathroom, the glass of which was invented by the ancient Egyptians, glazed tile by the Syrians, porcelain by the Chinese. You shave and remember this rite was developed by Egyptian priests. Your soap was invented by the Gauls; you dry yourself on a Turkish towel. Your shoes are made from hides prepared by a process invented in Egypt. Your breakfast food is placed before you in vessels stemming from China; the fork is an ancient Italian device; the spoon is a copy of a Roman eating invention. On and on, we are dependent upon others.

There are many tests for religion. In one part of the world one test applies; in another part another test is applied. In one denomination is a certain rule; another communion emphasizes a different code. At one point in church history one requirement was used, while at another time a different standard was applied. But always and everywhere we must love one another. For to love is to fulfill the law.

Those who love deeply never grow old; they may die of old age, but they die young.

—Sir Arthur Wing Pinero

On Boxing with God

The sin of Judah is written with a pen of iron (v. 1a).

Thomas Carlyle, historian, declared that if the French Revolution had not come he would not have been able to believe in God. That revolution was a cruel and bitter business; the innocent suffered with the guilty; the beautiful was destroyed along with the hideous. But Carlyle believed in the divine justice of God. "Be not deceived, God is not mocked for whatsoever a man soweth that shall he also reap," wrote Paul. That verse has been paraphrased to read, "Don't kid yourself; you can't get away with it!" And, James Weldon Johnson said to the prodigal son, "Young man, young man—your arm's too short to box with God!"

Along with the figures of the prophets and apostles on the walls of the Sistine Chapel in Rome, Michelangelo painted the figures of the sibyls. The sibyls were to the pagan world what the prophets of the Old Testament were to the believing world, it was thought that the sibyls could see into the future. One of the sibyls, goes the story, offered her nine books of wisdom for sale to the legendary founder of Rome. The proud Tarquin felt that her price was too great; he declined to buy.

The sibyl burned three books and offered to sell six for the price of the nine. Again, the Tarquin refused to pay. The sibyl burned three more books and offered to sell the remaining three at the same price for which the nine could have been bought. The founder of the city became alarmed; his advisers pleaded with him to pay whatever was asked, lest wisdom perish from the earth. So, he got three books of wisdom where he might have had nine. But, there was no bargain-basement price.

We haggle over prices and insist on cutting corners and driving bargains. The price remains the same. It is, "Do justly, . . . love mercy, and to walk humbly with thy God" (Mic. 5-8).

"Closing Time, Gentlemen"

Search . . . to see if you can find a man, one who does justice (v. 5, RSV).

In 1870 the De Goncourt brothers made reference to a prophecy by the chemist Bertholet to the effect that within a hundred years man would know the secret of the atom. To this the De Goncourts said they had no objection, but they did have the feeling that when such a time came God would come to earth swinging a bunch of keys and say, as shopkeepers say to customers at the close of day, "Closing time, Gentlemen."

That was in 1870. One hundred years have come and gone, and the secret of the atom has been fathomed. There have been times when we feared the jingling of the keys, accompanied with the ominous, "Closing time, Gentlemen." And, it brings such a feeling of helplessness! What can one person do?

For years it has been my privilege to go onto college and university campuses for preaching missions and religious emphasis weeks. I have gone to vast universities, to small colleges; some of these were church-affiliated schools, some private, some state institutions. Do you know what I have found in almost every instance? Wherever there has been a strong Christian current on the campus, there has been one or perhaps a few individuals who were responsible. On the floor of the dormitory, on the athletic field, in the fraternity or sorority, in the social group or in the classroom there was one, or a small number of individuals, who set the pace and gave the Christian tone and color to the whole.

Few have put it better than the poet:

> One man with a dream, at pleasure,
>   Shall go forth and conquer a crown;
> And three with a new song's measure
>   Can trample an empire down.

—William Edgar O'Shaughnessy

"This Business of Living Together"

[He] hath made of one blood all nations of men (v. 26a).

A teacher of mine reported that following the death of F. Scott Fitzgerald there was found among his private papers a list of suggestions and ideas which he intended to work into short stories. One of these read, "Suggestion for a short story—A widely separated family inherits a house in which they all have to live together." What if he had developed that idea!

Of course, the idea was not original with Fitzgerald; God had the idea first. Man inherited from God a house—the world—and God declared in effect, "Here is your inheritance. It is a big house. The requirement is that you live in this house together. I want you to live in peace and harmony, in love and kindness, in helpfulness and in cooperation. I want you to live in this house the way a family should live.

"You may choose to live in a different way. You can partition off the house, put up 'No Trespassing' signs, and get guards and armies to protect boundaries. You can start rumors, call one another names, harbor suspicions, and deal treacherously with one another.

"All this you can do, if you insist. But I remind you that you are a 'widely separated family and that you have inherited a house in which you all have to live together.'" These are the terms, take it together or leave it together. There is no other earthly house available to you.

They helped every one his neighbour; and every one said to his brother, Be of good courage (Isa. 41:6).

"A Man Can Grow"

The zeal of thine house hath eaten me up (v. 17b).

Strenuous effort is essential. John Morley explained Prime Minister Gladstone's freshness and enthusiasm by saying, "He kept himself upon the line of discovery." Ruskin wrote, "The law of nature is that a certain quantity of work is necessary to produce a certain quantity of good, of any kind whatever. If you want knowledge, you must toil for it; if food, you must toil for it; if pleasure, you must toil for it." "Nature," wrote Goethe, the German poet, "knows no pause, and attaches a curse to all inactivity." Emerson said of Napoleon, "Having decided what was to be done, he did that with might and main; he put out all his strength. He risked everything and spared nothing—neither ammunition, nor money, nor troops, nor generals, nor himself."

Our concern is chiefly with the spiritual. And it must be said that some of the best spiritual gifts do not come through strenuous effort but through a patient waiting. The psalmist said that it was those who waited upon the Lord who had their strength renewed. So much of the spiritual life depends upon *reception,* being willing to receive.

However, we should not be misguided. While there is need for waiting and for receiving, there is also need for all-out commitment. The case has not been stated better than by John Bunyan when he wrote of the man with the stout countenance who, after looking carefully and weighing deliberately the cost of the Christian life, went up to the one who had the pen and inkhorn and said to him: "Set down my name, Sir, for I have looked this whole thing in the face. Cost me what it may, I mean to have Christlikeness and will." I like that!

> Though his beginnings be but poor and low, Thank God a man can grow.

Yes, he can!

"Darkness and Dawn"

To open the blind eyes, to bring out the prisoners from the prison (v. 7).

Paul McElroy tells of an attractive girl stopping by a hospital bed to visit with a stone-deaf war victim. The soldier talked and the young girl wrote her answers on a pad of paper. As she was leaving, the deaf boy asked, "Won't you come to see me again? It's awful not knowing what people around you are saying." The girl reached for her pad of paper and wrote, "Oh, I don't know that it is so awful. I'm as deaf as you are. Why don't you learn to read lips as I have been reading yours?"

Van Wick Brooks gives it as his opinion that novelists thrive best on irritations. He says, "Hawthorne throve on the dust and winds of Salem. Flaubert, Stendhal, Sinclair Lewis, Dreiser are other cases in point; and do not Henry James's early novels show that this was also true for him? As long as he dealt with native Americans, who irritated him all the time, everything went well with James. England was too pleasant for him, and hence so much of his later work faulty. Perhaps," he continued, "the less we satisfy our tastes, the more they serve to give us a scale and a measure." The psalmist said, "God setteth the solitary in families: he bringeth out those which are bound with chains, but the rebellious dwell in a dry land" (Ps. 68:6).

There is no virtue in darkness for darkness' sake. Let us rejoice for all light and be grateful for all humanitarian movements that bring it. But forget it not, there is a razor's edge between the hardship that releases and the hardship that cripples. As we legislate against all darkness and all hardship, let us be careful not to legislate against all greatness and excellence. Wright Morris once wrote, "If you are going to take the troubles away from a man—be careful what you take . . . you may take away the man instead of the troubles." Remember James Montgomery's hymn, "In the hour of trial, Jesus plead for me."

"Learning to Forget"

[I] will not remember thy sins (v. 25b).

A wise forgetfulness is essential to spiritual growth. Much is said and more is written about the importance of remembering. Magazine articles are written, books are published, courses are offered to help us remember. Have you seen one of the "memory experts" come into a civic club and after being introduced to a hundred people, one hour later be able to call each of them by name? It is difficult at such a time not to break the Commandment which says, "Thou shalt not covet!"

Still, the truth is this: most of us remember too much rather than too little. Many of us would pay more for a course that would teach us to forget. The old Greek, Themistocles, prayed, "Teach me the art of forgetting; for I often remember what I would forget and forget what I would remember." The philosopher Kant once wrote himself a note when hurt by a man named Lampe. The note said, "Remember to forget Lampe."

It does not take an expert in the field of physical and mental health to tell us that it is often what we remember that is responsible for our undoing. It is frequently those whispering, gnawing, clawing, half-conscious memories of the past that destroy our peace of mind, make us ill, and make us do less than our best.

The apostle Paul testified that he was "forgetting those things which are behind." Of course, he did not mean, and we would not be so foolish as to desire, to forget all the past. He meant, and we desire, to forget those things which would hinder us from running an effective Christian race. The rest of our past should be given voting rights in the present.

> I sit beside my lonely fire
> And pray for wisdom yet:
> For calmness to remember
> Or courage to forget.

—CHARLES HAMILTON AÏDÉ

"A Thousand Years the Same"

Upon this rock will I build my church (v. 18b).

Canon Streeter estimated that St. Paul's Cathedral was moving down Fleet Street at the rate of about one inch every hundred years. Someone remarked that his estimate was probably right, for that was about the speed at which the churches were moving!

Yet, who will deny that the churches are the purest of organizations? What fraternal order, social fraternity, economic group, political party is as clean in body, mind, soul, motive, and conduct?

The church is the tenderest community. It is the mother of institutions of healing and of mercy. It is the sponsor of those who are weak and sinful; it is the champion of women and children. It is rich in memory of brides, mothers, boys, girls, and the aged. It is made precious with loving hands, gentle hearts, and shining tears. It lifts the fallen; it strengthens the weak; it shows mercy, bestows kindness, and offers a friendly hand to the rich on the avenue and the bum on the corner. It brings the freshness of youth. It gives "beauty for ashes, the oil of joy for mourning, the garment of praise for the spirit of heaviness."

We can say that the church is the most persistent army. What other force has endured for two thousand years, has had all the resources of hell thrown against it—armies, dictators, and tyrants? The Herods have tried to kill it in its infancy; the Pilates have tried to crucify it in its days of glory; the Constantines have tried to compromise it by joining it with the military and political forces of the world; the monks have taken it to the deserts; the priests have tried to hush it by dim lights and the smell of incense; social reformers have tried to make it into an arm that cares only for physical need. But—

> Where are kings and empires now,
> of old that went and came?
> But, Lord, thy church is praying yet,
> a thousand years the same!

> —ARTHUR CLEVELAND COX

Church Discipline

Purge out therefore the old leaven (v. 7a).

Corinth had its moral problems. One man in the church was living with his stepmother in open adultery, common-law marriage apparently. Others were being tempted; some were yielding. Even the pagan condemned this sort of living. Paul was shocked! And, what shocked Paul more than the conduct of the man was the attitude of the church. The church was complacent about the matter; they should have been grief-stricken. The surest guard against sin is to know its sinfulness, to be shocked and repulsed by it. To have an easygoing attitude toward sin is to be in peril.

It is well worth noting that Paul's severe attitude was not for the protection of the church, nor was it for the punishment of the man, at least not primarily so; it was in the hope that the man would see the evil of his ways and repent.

It is fearfully easy to become so accustomed to the sin about us that we are no longer disturbed by it. Can it be that we have come to a place where purity is no longer a goal, no longer expected?

Should it be possible for a member of a church to fall into sin without the membership of the church searching its heart to see if the membership has failed? If the members had been more aware, thoughtful, attentive, loving, supportive, would the person have fallen? This is not to say that we, as a church, can assume full and final responsibility for every member in the church. No. God has given freedom of will. But, if a member falls into sin, the membership of the church should search its heart and ways. A loving, caring fellowship is needed.

On Dedication

And for their sakes I sanctify myself (v. 19a).

Archbishop Temple observed that he thought John 17 was the most sacred section of the Bible. Here we see Jesus sanctifying, consecrating, and dedicating himself. Professor Donald MacLeod says that probably, in one sense, it is sacrilegious to apply this prayer of Jesus to ourselves. None can make the surrender he made; none can come close to the devotion, sacrifice, and love. Yet, if we come with thoughts of dedication, where better than this passage can we go? He did say, "As my Father hath sent me, even so send I you." He did promise that as we went at his bidding and in his service, we should have his Spirit with us.

There are several helpful points in this story. Jesus said, "I consecrate [sanctify] myself." Consecration is a personal act; no one can do that for you, in your stead. And this consecration, this dedication, is a complete surrender; not a part of life, it is total life commitment. A historian wrote of Mary, Queen of Scots, that everything became a weapon in her hand to further her cause: her wit, her charm, her beauty, everything—nothing was held back!

Jesus was dedicating himself for our sakes, which suggests that dedication must be associated with a definite task, person, or persons. It is easy to dedicate yourself to helping humanity; it is hard to dedicate yourself to transforming your own personality or family.

An additional truth in the passage for our reading today is this: he sanctified himself for our sakes that we might be sanctified through the truth. That is, to the end that we might fulfill the tasks and dreams God has for us!

> Jesus, I my cross have taken
>   All to leave, and follow Thee;
> Destitute, despised, forsaken
>   Thou, from hence, my all shalt be;
> Perish ev'ry fond ambition,
>   All I've sought or hoped or known;
> Yet how rich is my condition:
>   God and heav'n are still my own!
>
> —HENRY F. LYTE

"Like a Man in Love with God"

God hath made me laugh (v. 6b).

Suppose you had been dead for four days and by some miraculous power brought back to life. What do you think would be your reaction to life, to the people around you, to circumstances and conditions about you? Would you feel pity, anger, frustration, victory, joy, humor?

The dramatist Eugene O'Neill comes to grips with that in his lesser-known, but highly significant play, *Lazarus Laughed*. The first scene is in the home of Lazarus in Bethany. Lazarus has just been raised. The people are gathered. The father of Lazarus is giving a banquet. Lazarus is about fifty years of age; powerful in build; his face is dark and ruddy, forehead broad and noble. There is a slight halo about his head and his body seems to give off a soft illumination.

The guests talk about the change that has come over Lazarus. He does not look or act the same; he does not talk the same. Before, there was deep sorrow in his eyes; now there is a ruddy, life-giving glow on his face. Before the miracle he never seemed quite sure of himself, others, or conditions, now he is sure, now his very presence says, "Yes!" He was sad; now he is glad; before he wept; now he laughs. He laughed when he came out of the tomb. Jesus looked into his eyes and Lazarus suddenly said, "Yes!" as if he were answering the question he read in the eyes of Jesus. Then Jesus smiled and called him, "My brother." The Master turned and walked away; Lazarus watched him go, and began to "laugh softly like a man in love with God."

I am the resurrection, and the life: he that believeth in me, though he were dead, yet shall he live: And whosoever liveth and believeth in me shall never die (John 11:25-26).

117

April 21   Read 1 Corinthians 15:20-26
"The Tragedy Had an Epilogue"

The last enemy that shall be destroyed is death (v. 26).

Dr. Samuel Johnson shrank from death. His biographer, Boswell, once commented that at times he had no fear of death. Johnson replied that he had never known a moment when death had not appeared terrible to him, he felt that no rational man could die without apprehension. To him death was so real and fearful that all life was an effort not to think of it! "The last enemy to be banished," wrote Paul, "is death."

Into the arena where reigned the monster called death, came Christ, our champion, friend, and Redeemer. Through his life, death, and resurrection he brought life and immortality to light! The disciples saw and experienced this victory; they went forth with its glory in their hearts and its song upon their lips. "He is risen!" they cried. It was this conviction which gave rise to the missionary enterprise and the establishment of churches.

Klausner, the Jewish historian, had difficulty in accepting the reports of the resurrection, but there was no question in his mind as to the crucial significance of it in the origin and development of Christianity as a universal religion. He closed his chapter on the crucifixion with the words, "And so the burial ended. Here ends the life of Jesus, and here begins the history of Christianity." His next chapter begins, "The tragedy had an 'epilogue': Christianity would, otherwise, never have been possible." It was not possible for death to hold the Christ.

The true end of life is to know the life that never ends.

—WILLIAM PENN

Get the Total Message

If in this life only we have hope in Christ (v. 19a).

We think of the cross as being the center of Christianity; and it is. And, yet, apart from the resurrection, the cross stands for death, not life. It is possible for us to stand on the wrong side of Easter. The significance of Easter is the resurrection of Jesus. Every worshiping congregation represents that resurrection; every Lord's Day symbolizes that resurrection; every New Testament is an assurance of the resurrection; every redeemed person is a testimony to the resurrection. "If Christ be not raised, your faith is vain; and ye are yet in your sins."

Calvary was stark tragedy for the disciples. The entire band of apostles watched the bloody business from afar, saw his pierced body taken from the cross. One of them had betrayed him; another had cursed and sworn that he had never known him. All had turned and fled for their lives, forsaking him. When he was placed in the tomb and the stone rolled against it, it seemed the end of their hopes. No wonder the sun was dark! Then came Easter!

One of the traditions the English like to pass on to those who visit the old cathedral at Winchester is how the news of the battle of Waterloo was received. They say the news was brought by sailing boat to the south coast of England, and then it was caught up by signal flags and wigwagged across the country to London. When the message reached Winchester, the signal man on top of the cathedral began to spell out the message, "W E L L I N G T O N D E F E A T E D . . . " and then the fogs closed in, hiding the signal from view. The message, sad and incomplete, went on to London, and the entire country was bowed in mourning. "Wellington defeated."

But after a bit the fogs lifted, and the signal man was continuing to give out his message, "W E L L I N G T O N D E F E A T E D T H E E N E M Y." Then, there was great rejoicing. Wait for the full message. There was a third day!

April 23 Read Philippians 4:1-7

Now the God of Peace

The Lord is at hand (v. 5b).

One of the great affirmations of the resurrection is found in the Book of Hebrews. The author says, "Now the God of peace, that brought again from the dead our Lord Jesus, that great shepherd of the sheep, through the blood of the everlasting covenant, Make you perfect in every good work to do his will, working in you that which is well-pleasing in his sight, through Jesus Christ; to whom be glory forever and ever" (13:20-21).

Think of the meaning of those words! The message of the resurrection is that something tremendous has taken place, and it has taken place through the direct intervention of God. "Now, the God of peace, that brought again from the dead our Lord Jesus." That is God's doing. The early Christians preached that; they believed that. They believed that God had vindicated everything that they had lived for and that they had once thought was defeated. They believed that God had brought Jesus from the dead; the resurrection said that the kind of life Jesus had lived was the kind of life that was powerful; that the principles he had enunciated were the principles by which we would live or perish.

They believed the resurrection said that no power on the face of God's great earth could defeat the love of God. They believed that any life anchored in God through Jesus Christ was on the solid rock; that any group that staked its life on Christ, his message, his death, and his resurrection was sure of success; and that any nation and any world that betrayed that message, that did not seek to follow it and live it was doomed. It might be long, it might be short, but doomed it was—a life, a family, a group, a church, a nation, a world. They saw that in the resurrection.

Halford Luccock has reminded us that in each of the four Gospels the story of the resurrection is the story of a succession of footraces. There are eager faces, flashing eyes, bated breath, and rushing footsteps. The disciples couldn't walk; they had to run to tell the news. And what about you and me?

120

"This Whole Business About Easter"

Their words seemed . . . as idle tales and they believed them not (v. 11).

Margaret Sangster told the story of a family she knew. The family lost three children in one week from diphtheria; there was only one child left, a three-year-old daughter. But on the next Sunday the father and mother were in their place at church, the mother teaching her Sunday School class and the father at the superintendent's desk, where he presided as usual and carried on in a wonderful way. Going home, one twelve-year-old boy said to his father, "I guess Mr. and Mrs. Blank believe it, don't they?" The father turned and asked, "Believe what, Son?" "Oh," said the boy, "believe the whole thing, this whole business about Easter."

Let's approach it another way. Following the death of Schumann, the great German composer, it was discovered that no one was able to interpret his music quite so wonderfully as did his widow. Others who, by all rules of the game, should have been able to do with it what she did, and more, were not quite able to match what his widow did. Soon the secret came out. It was found that always before a concert, she would go to her room, get and read some of Shumann's old, faded love letters that he had written to her in days past and gone. In that way she caught his spirit and learned what the motive of his life was, the passion of his spirit; then she went out and interpreted him to the waiting throng. Others did not have that insight into his life and into his love.

It was through Christ—in the volume of their memory of his life and death and resurrection, aided by the Holy Spirit—that the early Christians found victory over every difficulty. All they had to do was to give themselves to him. He did the rest—this resurrected, living, reigning Lord!

It has been noted that if Robert Browning were to come into your life, you could write poetry; if Shakespeare were to come in, glorious dramas would flow from your pen; if Napoleon were to take possession, you would know how to plan and map campaigns. But if the Lord Jesus were given central control of your life, you would know how to live as a child of God; and the necessary resources to so live would be available.

Where Christ Lives

Now ye are the body of Christ (v. 27a).

The suggested passage deserves a second, third, and fourth look. There Paul says, "Ye are the body of Christ." That is a tremendous thought, one that we have not begun to appreciate fully. Christ is no longer in the world in a body; the body of Jesus of Nazareth is no longer available to him.

It was a wonderful body. It did his will, but now he has to use other bodies. If he wants a child taught, someone has to do it; if he wants people clothed, he has to work through bodies to accomplish that; if someone is hungry, he requires another body to help; if he wants a story told, he has to find a storyteller.

Here, then, surely is one of the glories of being the people of God. We can actually serve as the eyes, ears, hands, feet, tongues, and hearts of God.

So, Paul writes, "Ye are the body of Christ." Let your mind and heart play on that bit of mystic realism! We need each other. The body never functions properly unless all the members of the body function together. Let a finger become infected and you feel that everything that you do is done by that finger! We need to be careful that we do not become so deeply engrossed in our own particular tasks that we feel other members of the body are unimportant. One of the marvels of a well-functioning body is its unselfishness; each "member" helps every other member.

"Is your father home?" someone asked the village doctor's son. "No, he's away." "Where do you think I could find him?" "Well," said the boy thoughtfully, "you've got to look for him somewhere people are sick and hurting, someplace like that. I don't know where he is, but he's helping someone."

Read Genesis 32:24-31 April 26

Surprise Party

I will not let thee go, except thou bless me (v. 26).

Jacob was the twin son of Isaac and Rebekah; he cheated his brother Esau and had to flee. He married and became highly successful. After some years he returned home. On the way he got word that his brother whom he had cheated was coming to meet him with four hundred armed men. Jacob sent presents to his brother, hoping to appease him; then, Jacob sent his family and all his possessions across the stream and he was left alone. There follows an intensely dramatic and suggestive experience, an experience that is a surprise from beginning to end.

The time is a surprise. Jacob was a mature man; normally we think of these religious experiences coming to the young. And yet, it is not just the young who have these life-changing, soul-shaking experiences. Elton Trueblood has commented that the great conversion experiences can come only to the mature. Think of Saul, John Newton, and C. S. Lewis.

The circumstances of the experience are a surprise. Jacob was a successful man; often we think that only the broken can meet God. And it is true: only when some people fail will they recognize God; not so here. Jacob had been successful in love, in business, in body, and health. One does not have to fail to meet God!

The order of the experience is a surprise. Jacob did not seek God; God sought Jacob. And for the first time in his life, Jacob was no match for his opponent. Jacob was defeated; then, when he was defeated, he became the aggressor. He said to the angel, "I will not let thee go, except thou bless me." So, Jacob got a new name, a new desire, and a new power; " . . . hast thou power with God and with men, and hast prevailed." Surprise!

The Riddle

For to me to live is Christ (v. 21a).

Mark Guy Pearce, a London evangelist, told a short and quaint story he called, "The Riddle of Ubique." *Ubi* means, in Latin, "everywhere." So, the preacher was writing about everywhere.

A traveler found himself in a strange city called "Ubique" and was impressed by the fact that the people who lived there were barefooted. He saw that it could not be because they were poor; they were well dressed. But in the cold, over the hard, frozen ground they painfully walked without shoes. This was all the more surprising, for in the city were massive shoe factories; owners of the factories were among the leading citizens. Impelled by curiosity, the traveler went to one of their factories and attended a noon meeting, where after reading from some popular book, the leader addressed the group on, "Is There Such a Thing as a Foot?"

He later discovered that the factories where he had thought shoes were made were only places where the people discussed shoes and their advantages. At last the visitor did locate a humble cobbler who made shoes, good ones, no nonsense about it, solid, comfortable shoes. The stranger rushed out into the streets and avenues proclaiming the good news; now the people could have shoes! But, instead of flocking to buy shoes the people began to criticize the stranger; newspapers ridiculed him; the ladies commented it was vulgar to take people's measurements for shoes.

It was Henry Van Dyke who said, "May I never tack a moral on my tale, nor tell a tale without a moral." Pearce, the quaint, old London preacher, did not tack a moral onto his tale; he left us to draw our own conclusions. Probably you and I should do the same.

"God, Now, What Can I Do for You?"

It is more blessed to give than to receive (v. 35b).

When Charles M. Schwab was in his seventies, he became the victim of a nuisance suit. The sum for which he was sued was extremely large. The case could have been settled out of court for a fraction of the amount named. Mr. Schwab refused to settle, fought the case through to a finish, and won the case. Before leaving the court, he asked permission to say a few words relative to the matter. The judge gave permission. The old man said:

> I'd like to say here, in a court of law, and speaking as an old man, that nine tenths of my troubles are traceable to my being kind to others. Look, you young people; if you want to steer away from trouble, be hardboiled. Be quick with a good loud "No" to anyone and everyone. If you follow this rule, you'll seldom be molested as you tread life's pathway. Except [and the old man paused, as a big smile lightened his features] except—you'll have no friends, you'll be lonely—and you won't have any fun!

And, one might add, "You will be missing the spirit and teaching of Jesus." Linking our lives with others offers a great opportunity for wider usefulness. We achieve our greatest good when our lives become linked with the lives of others, when we can receive and give strength. So many of life's needs cannot be met by working in isolation.

In his poem, "Rugby Chapel," Matthew Arnold pays tribute to his father, Thomas Arnold, legendary headmaster of Rugby:

> But thou wouldst not alone
> Be saved, my father! alone
> Conquer and come to thy goal,
> Leaving the rest in the wild.
> We were weary, and we
> Fearful, and we in our march
> Fain to drop down and to die.
> Still thou turnedst, and still
> Gavest the weary thy hand.

In the Eye of the Beholder

I was in the Spirit on the Lord's day (v. 10a).

John of Revelation was on an island fortress; he was there as a prisoner for his witness to and of Jesus Christ the living Lord. And John writes: "I John, who also am your brother, and companion in tribulation . . . was in the isle that is called Patmos, for the Word of God, and for the testimony of Jesus Christ. I was in the Spirit on the Lord's day." There, in that place, under those conditions, John was "in the Spirit on the Lord's day." And, in that place, under those conditions, he heard the voice of God!

The following quotation appeared in the *San Francisco Chronicle* on March 24, 1963; I clipped it:

> We hate to leave our place. The climate is wonderful—very little fog—and beautiful plants and flowers grow very nearly everywhere. There are lots of little night-singing birds, seagulls, cormorants and a few pelicans. But the best thing is our million-dollar view. From our window we can see from the Golden Gate Bridge to the Bay Bridge, and the sunsets are spectacular. And at night, with all the lights aglow, San Francisco is indeed a glamorous city! We shall miss our lovely home very much.

Do you not envy Mrs. Freeman Pepper, the writer of those words? She had lived for twenty-one years in that enchanted, enchanting, place. Many of us have never even visited such a place on vacation! Lucky Mrs. Pepper! But wait, let me tell you where Mrs. Pepper's home was for those twenty-one years: Alcatraz Island, the most feared, dreaded, total-security prison in the United States. I could see that tiny island fortress from my office window in the Golden Gate Baptist Seminary where I taught for ten years. I know that view from my window, but Mrs. Pepper's home? Mrs. Pepper's husband was a guard at Alcatraz; their home was on that rock fortress. From "The Rock" she saw and experienced all the beauty and loveliness of which she wrote.

"The Holiest or the Brainiest"

Sanctify yourselves therefore, and be ye holy: for I am the Lord your God (v. 7).

It is not enough to strive only for knowledge; we must also strive for holiness. Paul wrote, "Knowledge puffeth up." It may and it will if void of holiness and love. In Marc Connelly's drama, *Green Pastures,* God holds a conference with Abraham, Isaac, and Jacob. God discusses with them his plan for bringing the children of Israel out of Egypt into the Promised Land. He wants to know if they have any suggestion as to who should lead in this important undertaking. Isaac asked God if he wanted the "brainiest" or the "holiest" man. And God answers that he wanted the "holiest," for if the man has holiness, then God can make him brainy. If one wishes to persist about that scene, he might add that probably *only God* can make some "holy men" brainy!

Connelly is right; he is scriptural. Holiness does come first; the heart does precede the head. Either without the other is incomplete. In one case you get a blown-up world; in the second case you get an ineffective irrelevance. Holiness is a prerequisite for Christian thinking.

Today there is a strange suspicion of holiness. Modern man is afraid of the entire concept of holiness; he would rather be accused of being evil than of being holy. Perhaps modern man equates holiness with the "holier-than-thou" attitude. Still across the ages comes God's command, "Ye shall be holy for I am holy."

Holiness is the symmetry of the soul.

—Philip Henry

To Transform the Face

It was needful for me to write unto you (v. 3).

This word is about the value of personal letters, the letters which do not have to be written, yet, if they are not written, something beautiful may not become a reality. Such letters work within the realm of the heart, the spirit, and personality, lifting and transforming as surely as the skill of the plastic surgeon transforms the face. Let me explain.

Christmas was approaching. Stanley Slotkin asked his secretary: "Betty, what would you like for Christmas this year?" Betty was ready with her answer. Hands clenched and eyes tightly closed to hold back tears, she said, "Mr. Slotkin, I'd like a new face." She was taken to a plastic surgeon who straightened her nose and modified her mouth and chin. Mr. Slotkin and his wife took Betty into their home and cared for her during her convalescence. After that they took her to a hairdresser, then to the city's most elite shop for a new outfit. Betty was beautiful!

The experience started Mr. Slotkin, a successful businessman, on his hobby; he became a sort of year-round surgical Santa Claus who gave new faces. He has been the good saint to more than twelve hundred people. They have been transformed by the touch and the money, and the love of Stanley Slotkin: a prisoner "who was a thief because he looked like a thief"; a girl who had no chin but through "Santa's" magic became a professional singer; a small boy who was tormented by his classmates for his "sugar-bowl" ears. Psychological changes have been as dramatic as physical. For example, Mr. Slotkin's secretary, Betty, learned to smile, gained a new personality, fell in love and married, and became a mother. Oh, yes, Mr. Slotkin had to get a new secretary.

Now, wouldn't you like to do for others what Stanley Slotkin has been able to do for all those people? You can do it through warm, encouraging, sympathetic personal letters.

What Will You Do with the Horn?

Sing, O ye heavens; for the Lord hath done it (v. 23a).

A prominent physician said to his minister that the most deadly disease was one that his medicine could not reach nor the surgeon's knife remove. "Cancer?" asked the minister. "No," replied the doctor, "we shall one day be able to deal effectively with cancer. This disease of which I speak is boredom. It is our worst enemy. It is not only deadly in itself, it is also the cause of other serious problems such as gambling, drinking, dope, immorality, and death itself. The reason many people die," continued the physician, "is not that they have a reason for dying but that they have no cause for living."

Many of the followers of the Master caught something of his joyous spirit. They sang in prisons and amid earthquakes; they rejoiced as the caskets of their loved ones were lowered into the ground; they lifted their voices in thanksgiving as the wild beasts rushed upon them in the arenas and, as the fires snuffed out their breath, they sang their doxologies. No wonder the people stormed the church doors, trying to bribe and buy the secret of this joy and triumph!

The little Salvation Army lass had been rescued from the lower depths of crime and the gutters. She loved music and was placed in the band. But her loud blasts on the trumpet made it impossible for any other instrument to be heard. The conductor spoke to her; she promised to ease up on the volume, but soon she was back at it again; the sound of her instrument drowning out everyone else. Again the conductor spoke to her. "I am sorry; it is not that I do not want to be a member of the band and cooperate in all that you ask me to do. It is just that when I think of what the Lord has done for me I could blow this . . . horn straight!" One need not approve the deleted adjective to hail the spirit of enthusiasm and joy!

"Too Glad to Be Good"

The Son of man is come eating and drinking (v. 34a).

If the Gospels could be read with no preconceived notions and prejudices, probably one of the dominant impressions received would be that Jesus was a well-adjusted, harmonious, happy, and triumphant spirit. We would see that he delighted in feasts, relished banquets, and rejoiced in social conversation. A recent cartoon shows a tired business tycoon at his big mahogany desk. He presses a call button and says to his secretary, "I'm lonely; get me a gifted conversationalist." So much of life is like that, except we cannot demand a "gifted conversationalist."

Again and again the Gospels tell us that Jesus went into a house to eat, that it came to pass as he sat at meat, that they made for him a banquet, that there was a feast and Jesus and his disciples were invited. It has been said that for much of his public ministry, Jesus was "society's most sought after dinner guest." Leslie Weatherhead said the straightlaced thought he was too glad to be good and too happy to be holy! It was this side of his life that caused some the severest criticism to fall upon him.

His popularity was amazing. The crowds pressed him so there was no time for him to eat. They "thronged him" in the streets; they crowded him on the shore; the multitudes followed him great distances, unmindful of hunger and inconveniences. Women ministered unto him; children were given into his arms. His teachings were no less exciting than his life. When he told a story, there was color, movement, and drama; banquets, harvests, treasure hunts, kings setting out to battle, hypocrites on parade, demons on the warpath, weddings, and celebrations. He called himself the "bridegroom"; he said the kingdom he came to establish was like a wedding. John said he began his work with a wedding and ended it on a fishing trip! They said, and no wonder, "The world has gone after him!"

"Have Faith in God"

And Jesus answering saith unto them, Have faith in God (v. 22).

Were the Master among us today, and he is; but, were he among us today so that with physical eyes we could see him, and with physical ears we could hear him, and if each were to go to him, as each would go to him, and ask, "Master, what lack I yet?" would he not say, "Have faith in God"?

Might he not say, "You think your great problem is a pagan culture; you think it is strife and lawlessness in your streets. You think your problem is a break in the dam of morality, the break-up of homes, promiscuity, illegitimacy, alcohol, and dope. You think your problems are inequality between races, a lack of deep caring on the part of the privileged for the underprivileged, that your present home, the earth, is being polluted"?

"All this," I think he might say, "may be quite true enough, and tragic enough, but there is something more basic and fundamentally wrong, *you do not have faith in God*. And until you have faith in God, you begin at no beginning and you work toward no desirable end. If you had faith in God, all things would be possible for you; if you had faith in God, you would be pleasing to him."

I am not saying that faith is a sort of magic, a wand to wave over serious problems with the assurance that the problems will disappear, as in childhood fairy stories. But this is what a great faith will do: it will give adequate motivation, assist in choosing appropriate goals, reveal proper evaluations and priorities, and guarantee unfailing endurance and adequate resources.

Without faith we are stained-glass windows in the dark.

—Anonymous

This I Do Believe

I have not found so great faith, no, not in Israel (v. 10b).

If only in the light of the Lord's face each person could make his own private confession of faith! Allow me to state mine, believing, as I do so, that I shall be stating the faith held by many readers. To the best of my knowledge and experience these things I do believe, on these I stand, after these I do not place question marks, I place exclamation marks! I seek new light upon the implication of these affirmations, as to their reality and their reliability, my heart is fixed. In affirming this faith I am not boastful, but I am bold, not in myself, but in the truth that is affirmed.

I affirm the reality and the goodness of God, that for me is a closed issue;

I affirm the faithfulness and trustworthiness of Jesus Christ, here I raise my voice and with the psalmist cry, "My heart is fixed, O God!"

I affirm the relevancy and the value of the Holy Scriptures for the instruction and the nurture of the Christian life. Here my "yes" is yes and my "no" is no.

I affirm the efficacy of prayer; like the man born blind, there may be, and there are, many things I do not know but of a few things I am sure, one of these is the difference to my spiritual welfare that prayer makes.

I affirm the divine origin, the creative place, and continuing purpose of the church in the plan and purpose of God for the good of mankind.

I affirm the moral quality of this universe; the scales are weighted on the side of righteousness and the stars in their courses fight against evil.

I acknowledge my personal responsibility for making this faith known; I admit that I am a debtor.

When Henry David Thoreau was a boy, someone asked what he was going to be when he grew up. The man in the boy answered, "I shall be unanimous." If only we could be unanimous as a people on some such affirmation of faith today!

If life is a comedy to him who thinks and a tragedy to him who feels, it is a victory to him who believes.

—ANONYMOUS

Profit in Prayer?

The effectual fervent prayer of a righteous man availeth much (v. 16b).

The biblical character Job asked a piercing question: "What profit should we have, if we pray unto him?" (Job 21:15). The Christian would answer, "much in every way." Tennyson wrote, "More things are wrought by prayer/Than this world dreams of."

Prayer will change the person who prays. And that is no small achievement. It is reported that Andrew Carnegie said of prayer: "Why should I pray? I have everything I need." The friend answered, "Perhaps you could pray for humility." Prayer would help us to adore God, put great affirmations at the center of our lives, help us to commit our lives to God, help us keep in communion with God.

Prayer not only will change the person who prays, it will change our attitude toward others. William Law once said that he had proven beyond a shadow of doubt that it is utterly impossible to maintain a spirit of ill will toward one for whom you pray.

Prayer will do this for the person who prays. It will open the floodgates that hold back power for triumphant living. As a child I watched the miracle of water power. Here was giant machinery for grinding corn, making flour, ginning cotton, sawing lumber—corn and wheat and cotton and lumber needing to be changed into usable forms. Here was a great dam, and behind the dam, millions of gallons of water. The need? A power to lift the gate that would let the water come pouring through to reach the mighty turbines that would, in turn, cause the intricate machinery to do its appointed task. Prayer will lift the floodgates of God's grace and power.

> Teach me to pray, Lord, teach me to pray;
> This is my heart-cry day unto day;
> I long to know thy will and thy way;
> Teach me to pray Lord, teach me to pray.[5]
>
> —ALBERT S. REITZ

Spirit with Spirit Can Meet

And Elijah said unto Ahab . . . there is a sound of abundance of rain (v. 41).

Ask Job's question again, "What profit should we have, if we pray unto him?" Much profit. Prayer will change the person who prays, including his attitude toward others. Prayer will also influence the person prayed for. Obviously that is the case if the person being prayed for is aware of the prayer. Examples.

A friend wrote about fishermen off the coast of New England; they were overtaken by a fierce storm late in the afternoon. The skipper saw the clouds, felt the gale, looked at the waves, and said, "Men, about this time the little woman will be sending up a prayer for us to the God who rules the wind and waves." He was silent for a moment, then a shout, "All hands on deck! We've got to get that prayer answered."

When J. Wilbur Chapman came to Bethany Presbyterian Church in Philadelphia, there followed one of the most marvelous ministries this land has ever known. The first Sunday after Chapman preached, one of the laymen came to him and said, "You seem like a very ordinary individual; I am not sure you can make it here. But six or eight men have promised to meet me here next Sunday morning to pray for you, and we are going to spend an hour in prayer that your ministry may be successful." That group grew to five hundred men praying for Wilbur Chapman. They prayed him into success, undergirding his ministry until he could not fail!

> Prayer is the most powerful form of energy one can generate. The influence of prayer on the human mind and body are as demonstrable as that of the secreting glands. It supplies us with a flow of sustaining power in our daily lives.
>
> —ALEXIS CARREL

Privilege and Responsibility

We made our prayer unto our God, and set a watch (v. 9).

We think of prayer as a great privilege, and it is that, but it is more—it is a responsibility. Samuel felt that it was his obligation to pray for the people. It would be a sin if he did not pray for them (1 Sam. 12:23).

Seemingly God rests the welfare of mankind on the prayer life of believing people. God certainly rests the welfare of your family and neighbors on your work, whether or not you do work; the kind of work you do and how diligent you are in doing it makes a difference. If you are hardworking, intelligent, and competent, your influence upon your family and community will be good. If you are lazy, unreliable, untrustworthy, and selfish, your influence will be of a different kind.

Think of a surgeon. Tomorrow he will go into the operating room. There he will perform a delicate operation. The outcome? It may well depend upon the kind of student that doctor was in medical school, how he has continued his education since. Would a loving God allow the work and skill of the doctor to determine the outcome of an operation, but not allow prayer to enter into the situation?

God's *desire* to help persons does not depend upon our prayers, only his *help*. For we are the body of Christ. And, as the body of Christ we are used; there are things Christ cannot and will not do without hands; there are places he will not go without feet; words he will not speak without voices; help he will not give without prayers. He needs our eyes, ears, hands, feet, voices, and prayers.

Prayer is not overcoming God's reluctance; it is laying hold of his highest willingness.

—ARCHBISHOP TRENCH

"We Are Not Amused"

He findeth it swept and garnished (v. 25).

How is evil to be dealt with in the individual life? It does no good to deny its reality and its presence. One cannot escape by hiding; the monastic approach is not for the average person. Besides, according to documented evidence, the walls of a monastery or nunnery are no assurance against the devil; he is good at climbing walls!

There is the way of outright disapproval, the unapologetic frowning upon that which represents or tends toward evil. There is the classic story of young Queen Victoria. A young man was telling an off-color story at the table. The queen asked him to tell the story to her; he said it was not fitting that she should hear it. She commanded him to tell her the story. In embarrassment he repeated it. Then, with a serious face, the young queen replied, "We are not amused."

There is another, more desirable way of effectively dealing with evil in its many faces. It is to make use of "the expulsive power of a new affection." Those words are the title of a famous sermon preached by Thomas Chalmers of Scotland. He said there were two ways of weaning the heart from the ways of the world. The first was to show the evil of the world so the heart would withdraw its affection. The other way was by so attaching the heart to God that one would exchange an old affection for a new one. It is, of course, a central truth in the suggested passage of Scripture for today, a house filled with desirable tenants has no space for vagrants!

> Had I but served my God with half the zeal
> I served my king, he would not in mine age
> Have left me naked to mine enemies.

> —SHAKESPEARE

More Than a King

None is good, save one, that is God (v. 19b).

In his novel, *The Robe,* Lloyd C. Douglas told how the slave, Demetrius, pushed his way through the crowd in order to get a good look at Jesus. Another slave asked if Jesus were crazy; Demetrius was sure that he was not. Then the other wanted to know if Jesus were a king; Demetrius did not think so. The man then demanded to know just who Jesus was. To this perhaps Demetrius replied that he did not know who Jesus was but that Jesus was something more important than a king.

Demetrius was right; Jesus is more important than earthly kings. He rules and reigns as no earthly king ever has or ever will. William Temple said it for us:

> While we deliberate, he reigns; when we decide wisely he reigns; when we decide foolishly, he reigns; when we serve him in humility, he reigns; when we serve him self-assertedly, he reigns; when we rebel and seek to withold our services, he reigns—the Alpha and Omega, which is and which was and which is to come, the Almighty.

Jesus alone is good enough to rule over the hearts of men. This assertion in no way detracts from good rulers, as men and women are accounted good. In ancient times there were good kings and there were bad kings. Queen Elizabeth II of Britain expressed her vows to her people in a high and noble way when she came to the throne.

> I declare before you that my whole life, whether it be long or short, shall be devoted to your service and the service of our great imperial family to which we all belong. But I shall not have the strength to carry out this resolution alone unless you join in it with me, as I now invite you to do. I know that your support will be unfailingly given. God help me to make good my vow, and God bless all of you who are willing to share in it.

On Bell Ringing

I call to remembrance the unfeigned faith that is in thee (v. 5a).

The college of William and Mary in Williamsburg, Virginia, had a difficult time during and following the Civil War. That conflict was waged up and down the peninsula, and the college was left in ruins, along with the rest of the countryside. The school put up a gallant fight, but in 1881 it closed its doors. For nearly seven years there was no school. Yet every morning during those seven years President Ewell rang the chapel bell. Through summer sun and winter snow, the pealing of the chapel bell could be heard. There was no faculty to teach; there were no students to learn, and the rains dripped through the decaying roofs of the deserted buildings; but President Ewell rang the chapel bell. In the tones of that bell the inhabitants of the little town and countryside detected the notes of faith, hope, and love. They detected the notes of courage and defiance. The bell became a symbol of the determination that intellectual, cultural, moral, and spiritual values should not perish from the earth.

Years ago there was a Christian home in England, a humble home that had few of the comforts and luxuries of life, but one that stayed close to the church and welcomed the influence and faith of the church into its relationships. Three daughters were born to the parents of that home. One of those girls became the mother of Burne-Jones, the celebrated artist whose pictures the world has enjoyed. Another daughter became the mother of Rudyard Kipling, the famous author whose writings thrill us. The third daughter became the mother of Stanley Baldwin, former prime minister of England. The family kept the home and the church together; God gave beauty to inspire, books to thrill, and freedom that liberates.

Legend has it that Satan, on being asked what he missed most on being driven out of heaven, said, "The sound of the trumpets in the morning."

Show and Tell

Show what great things God has done unto thee (v. 39b).

When Jesus healed the man of Gadara who had lived in the graveyard naked, the man was so grateful that he wanted to join Jesus and the disciples on their evangelistic tour. He asked "that he might be with him." But Jesus sent him to his own home and family, instructing the man to show his own family what great things God had done for him.

Now that is interesting—I think significant. It probably does not say that home evangelism is always more important than city, associational, state, national, or world evangelism. It does seem to say that the home is the place to begin our evangelizing and our missionary work. "Go home and show what great things God has done for you." That is the place to start.

And it is not an easy place to start. It may be the hardest place to start. Incidentally, there may be a suggestion of that difficulty in the story. We read that the man "went his way, and published throughout the whole city how great things Jesus had done unto him." Do the words tell us that he found it so hard to witness at home that he took on the whole city? Or, is the passage saying that in taking on the "whole city" his own home was included? Not sure about that, we are sure where he was to begin.

Again, it is a hard spot. For one thing the people know us so well! Another thing, everything is so constant at home, no "time off for good behavior." The lady said to the bride, "Now, honey, this housework won't get you down if you'll just remember you are never going to get through!" So constant. Again, we are seldom at our best in the home—in looks and dress, in words and attitude, in courtesy or cooperation. It's hard to show what God has done for us. But, there is where it starts.

"How She Got Her Soft Face"

Then said the Jews, Behold how he loved him! (v. 36).

In *Margaret Ogilvy,* the story of his mother's life, Sir James M. Barrie told a tender and touching experience; he said it was how his mother got her soft face. It came through suffering. She had a young son away in school—a bright, merry-faced lad. When news came that the boy was seriously ill, the mother's face was terrible in its calmness as she set about "to get between death and her boy." The family trooped down to the little station. The ticket was purchased. As the mother said good-bye to the children, she was wearing her "fighting face." Then the father came out of the telegraph station and said huskily, "He's gone." The family turned quietly about and went back up the hill to the home.

At first the mother was crushed to the point of death because of the sorrow. Gradually she gained victory. Sir James says, "That is how she got her soft face . . . and her large charity," and why other mothers in the community instinctively turned to her in their trouble. He said, "When you looked into my mother's eyes you knew, as if He had told you, why God sent her into the world—it was to open the minds of all who looked to beautiful thoughts."

In such a way—though with a thousand times more reality and depth—tired, weary, and tempted souls have turned to Jesus, the "Captain of their salvation." They have known that he was a high priest who could be reached with the feeling of their infirmities, since he has been tempted in all points as they are tempted and will be tempted. So, no one has, no one ever will, be able to say to him, "You do not understand."

God had one Son on earth without sin, but never one without suffering.

—AUGUSTINE

What to Do for the Child

The child grew, and waxed strong (v. 80a).

A great need in child training is to guide them into independence. Wise are the parents who are able to give the child a sense of independence and, at the same time, love and proper guidance. If the child can feel that he is being allowed, and expected, to make his own decisions, to make these decisions within the love and concern of his parents; and, that the parents are available when help is needed, the feeling of healthy independence can be experienced by the child.

In writing about his mother, Ramsay MacDonald said that she thought of her children as treasures given to her to guard and protect, but not to mold in her image. He said that she knew the child was an individual and not an appendage; she felt it was her duty to enrich the life of the child by teaching him to use his own talents. He felt she was saying to the child, "I am at hand to hold and help you if necessary, but I want you to develop your own little selves so that when you are men and women you will be persons of a free will and not creatures of circumstance."

A delightful incident in the life of the great Chief Justice Oliver Wendell Holmes speaks to this truth. One day while walking, he was joined by a little girl. They walked and talked together for a bit, and then the little girl announced that she had to go home. Justice Holmes suggested that if her mother asked her where she had been, the child might say she had been walking with Oliver Wendell Holmes. To this the child replied, "And when your folk ask you where you have been, tell them that you have been walking with Mary Susan Brown." Magnificent!

The little child is the only true democrat.

—HARRIET BEECHER STOWE

"As the Twig Is Bent"

Seek ye out of the book of the Lord, and read (v. 16a).

There are few things, apart from the Christian faith, that a family might more earnestly pass along to its children than a love of reading. And while parents cannot bequeath to their children a love for reading as they might pass along a piece of real estate, still there is much that can be done toward helping children acquire a love of reading on their own.

W. Taliaferro Thompson in *An Adventure in Love* says there are certain basic principles which apply to the home:

First, the principle of suggestion—there is a tendency for the child to accept and make a part of his own thinking what he hears his parents say.

Second, the principle of sympathy—there is a tendency for the child to feel as the parents feel.

Third, the principle of approval—there is a tendency for the child to do and to say what will win the approval of parents.

Fourth, the principle of imitation—the child is inclined to do what those he most admires do.

Fifth, the principle of belief, there is a tendency on the part of the child to interpret beliefs in terms of what he sees his parents do rather than on the basis of what he hears them say.

These principles apply on a broad field of life. Consider how they apply to raising a thirst for reading. If there are books and magazines in the home; if these books and magazines are handled carefully; if they are spoken of in tones of appreciation; if reading is turned to eagerly and joyfully; if biblical, historical, literary, poetic characters are easy and comfortable companions, of course the child will be influenced.

Then I thought of reading—the nice and subtle happiness of reading—this joy not dulled by age . . . this lifelong intoxication.

—LOGAN PEARSALL SMITH

A Time of Celebration

In the day of your gladness . . . they may be to you for a memorial (v. 10).

Family worship in our own home has been enriched by making use of special days and seasons. All members of the family participated in these celebrations. The events were carefully planned. One of the traditions of our home has been a time of deep and reverent worship about the open fire, before the Christmas tree, before the opening of presents on Christmas Eve or Christmas morning. At such times our worship was touched with joy and our Christmas spirit with reverence. The Easter season was another time of special significance in our family worship. I feel that my own denomination has not always made the most of the Advent season, the season of Lent, and other emphases that our liturgical friends have. But with freedom of form, content, and understanding, the seasons can enrich our worship.

It is so very easy to complain about these special times and seasons being "commercialized." The truth of the matter is that in our churches and Christian homes we have not done a lot to give these times and seasons a Christian interpretation. Our heritage would teach us to "go and sin no more." Simply to name special days and times in our church and national history suggests opportunities for Christian interpretation and teaching that should not be overlooked in family worship: Thanksgiving, New Year's Day, Father's Day, Mother's Day, Children's Day, Labor Day, Washington and Lincoln's birthdays, the Fourth of July, Veteran's Day, and there are others. For example, birthdays, wedding anniversaries, or the anniversary of the death of a loved one.

> Monday's child is fair of face,
> Tuesday's child is full of grace,
> Wednesday's child is loving and giving,
> Thursday's child worked hard for a living.
> Friday's child is full of woe,
> Saturday's child has far to go,
> But the child that is born on the Sabbath-day
> Is brave and bonny, and good and gay.

What Mean Ye by This Service?

What she has done will be told in memory of her (v. 13*b*, RSV).

Special days and seasons are a rich source of help for family worship. This approach is scriptural, too. It was one of the binding forces of the Hebrew home—binding from the standpoint of family ties and from the standpoint of religious heritage.

The ancient festival of the Passover was a family celebration presided over by the father but participated in by all members of the family—the selection of the lamb from the flock, securing the wood for the fire, lighting the flame, gathering the herbs, baking the bread. Even the youngest child, or the oldest, could ask the pivotal question: "What mean ye by this service?" Then the father would answer, "It is the sacrifice of the Lord's passover, who passed over the houses of the children of Israel in Egypt, when he smote the Egyptians, and delivered our houses" (Ex. 12:26-27).

The Feast of Weeks was another annual festival that all members of the family shared. The mother and daughters would grind the meal, knead the dough, and bake it in the oven. Specific instructions were given in Leviticus 23.

The Feast of Tabernacles was a celebration with a festive atmosphere that lasted for a full week. The family lived in tents. It was a time of special thanks to God for the bounty of the harvest, close to our Thanksgiving. The religious truths for the family were never lost sight of. "That your generations may know that I made the children of Israel to dwell in booths, when I brought them out of the land of Egypt: I am the Lord your God" (Lev. 23:43).

> With joy we hail the sacred day
>   Which God has called His own;
> With joy the summons we obey
>   To worship at His throne.
>
> —Harriet Auber

All Together Now

Keep the commandments of the Lord your God which I command you (v. 2).

Many families have been surprised to learn how easy it is to begin family worship, how cooperative the different members of the family are in the project. G. Ernest Thomas reports the experience of a family in Philadelphia. The father in the home, a businessman, determined to lead his family in daily worship. The man admitted that he was embarrassed and self-conscious as he prepared to carry out his plan. On a certain Monday morning he decided to "dive in." He waited until his two high school sons were at the table. The boys took their seats and were reaching for their food when the father barked, "Wait a minute, before you drink your orange juice; we are going to have family devotions every day from now on." Then he looked about the table as if daring anyone to argue about his decree!

All were silent as he read a passage from the Bible and comments from the devotional guide. He led the group in prayer and then said, "All right, now you may go on with your breakfast; we've had our devotions." The procedure continued for the next three mornings. On Wednesday evening, while waiting for dinner, he began reading the evening paper. His youngest son, a sophomore in high school, came and stood by his chair. The father looked up and said, "Out with it; what's on your mind?"

"Well," began the boy, "there's something I thought I ought to tell you. Last summer when I went to youth camp, I made an agreement that I would try to persuade our family to have family worship each day. But, when I got home and looked at you and mother, I lost my courage. I just wanted to tell you how glad I am that we are having family worship."

> The Crown of the home is Godliness;
> The Beauty of the home is Order;
> The Glory of the home is Hospitality;
> The blessing of the home is Contentment.
>
> —Author Unknown

Careful with the "Escape Clause"

Men ought always to pray, and not to faint (1b).

There is a Methodist church in the heart of Chicago that claims to be "the tallest Methodist church in the world." Above the church is a great skyscraper office building; above the office building is a tall slender steeple. Years ago the church decided to install a system of bells in the top of the steeple so that around the clock, and on the hour, the crowds that milled about the streets below might be reminded of the things for which a church and its steeple stand. The bells were installed and then a discovery was made. The busy, anxious, hurrying people in the canyon streets below were not able to hear the bells. The distance was too great, the canyons were too deep; the people were too busy!

It is close to a parable on the family and its worship. High sounds, deep streets, hurrying people, are all present. Yet, let us be honest; let us admit that it is not the pattern for all families. Many families are together at set times during the day, or could be together. It may be about the breakfast table, around the dinner table, or late in the evening before the family retires. These families should not excuse themselves from family worship.

The homes which seek this "escape clause" should be reminded of the words of William Temple when he said that when we fail in our discipleship (family worship) it is always for one of two reasons—either we are not trying to be loyal to Christ or we are trying to be loyal in our own unaided strength and find that it is not enough.

> God, give us Christian homes!
> Homes where the Bible is loved and taught,
> Homes where the Master's will is sought,
> Homes crowned with beauty thy love hath wrought;
> God give us Christian homes.[6]

—B. B. McKinney

Paul, Priscilla, and Aquila

Whom when Aquila and Priscilla had heard, they took him unto them (v. 26)

Aquila and Priscilla were an interesting couple. They formed an intimate friendship with the apostle Paul that lasted many years. The name Priscilla appears first in four of the six times their names are mentioned. That could mean that she was from a noble family; it may mean that she was simply the stronger of the two personalities. It may mean that her work and courage were more outstanding than her husband's. There are several ways in which this couple aided Paul and the cause of Christ.

They created a Christian marriage. They stayed together through "thick and thin," through persecution and being dispelled from Rome. They so lived and worked and loved that their names are forever linked. No one can think of Aquila without thinking of Priscilla, or of Priscilla without thinking of Aquila.

The second thing this couple did was to create a hospitable home out of that Christian marriage. They did not selfishly guard that loving relationship of theirs, they shared it. Their home was open to Paul, it was open to Apollos, and, we may be sure, it was open to others.

Third, this couple gave themselves to helping and guiding the young. Apollos was eloquent, mighty in the Scriptures, fervent in the Spirit, he taught diligently. But, according to the Scriptures, he knew "only the baptism of John." I guess that means that he knew Jesus only in an ethical and moral way. Aquila and Priscilla helped him to know the way of the Lord more perfectly. They loved the church of Christ; they were willing to risk their lives for its progress. Great couple!

"Consider Yourself Dead"

. . . But alive unto God through Jesus Christ our Lord (v. 11).

Paul wrote about dying to sin. He stated repeatedly that this dying was the way to freedom from sin, that since the Christian had died to sin, it no longer had control over him. To be in a state of death is to be in a state of nonresponse. The dead person does not respond in the area of the five senses. Even so, said Paul, sin gets no response from the person who has died to sin; therefore, death to sin is the way to freedom in Christ.

The reason people will not leave the discussion of everlasting life alone is because death will not leave people alone. So, age after age the question comes back, "If a man die, shall he live again?" (Job 14:14). Strange that the question would be stated that way. "If a man die?" Man does die; man always dies; so far as we know man will always die. As some wag put it, "You are never going to get out of this life alive." What a noble statement! The only way to get out of this life is to die. That is true in more ways than one.

At the beginning of World War II, I had a wonderful friend who was minister of education in the church I served as pastor. Like millions of others, this young friend of mine was drafted. He came to talk with me about it. He did not mind going into service; he was patriotic, glad to serve his country. But, in order to get his affairs at the church in order he needed sixty days, not thirty, which was the regular time allowed. So, he and I went to the draft board with our request for an extension. The members of the board heard my friend's statement. Then the chairman, said: "Mr. Morgan, what would the First Baptist Church do if you were to die?" "Why, Sir, it would get along without me." "Then," said the chairman of the draft board, "consider yourself dead, Sir. That will be all." The First Baptist Church had no control over him; he was "dead" so far as that institution was concerned.

God, the Just Judge

I the Lord, search the heart (v. 10*a*).

The fact that God is personal in no way weakens the doctrine of his holiness. He accommodates himself to our finiteness, but he is great and holy and majestic and infinite.

Henry Gray, in *A Theology for Youth,* tells about the ancient sculptor, Phidias. He built one of the most beautiful and significant buildings of all times. It was perfectly proportioned; it was graceful in design; it was imposing in appearance. No other building ever enclosed so much matchless art. Phidias carved the statue of Athena himself. To the casual observer it was a disappointment and a distortion. The statue was out of proportion to the size of the Parthenon, the building that housed it. There Athena sat, high, almost reaching the ceiling, dwarfing everything about her. From her height the goddess looked down with imperial majesty.

What Phidias was trying to say through his statue is what we believe about God. He is high and lifted up, He is great, we cannot attain unto him. He is majestic; we dare not be careless in our worship. He is holy; he cannot and will not abide sin. God is creator, God is personal, God is holy, and God is judge. This is not to indicate that God is one who spies on us and is vindictive in his pronouncements. Wherever that note creeps in, let the life and teachings of Christ correct it. He seeks constantly to save the sinner; he always condemns the sin. Few notes are more needed than that!

Nathaniel Hawthorne, in *The Scarlet Letter,* makes Dimmesdale try to hide from his sinful past. But the day came when conscience was too strong; he could no longer run and hide. To the marketplace he came; there he stood beside the girl he had wronged. To his fellow townsmen he cried: "Stand any here that question God's judgment on a sinner? . . . Behold a dreadful witness of it!"

Judge not that ye be not judged (Matt. 7:1).

Beams of Light from the Past

The Lord answered me, and said, Write the vision, and make it plain (v. 2).

Frederic Myers, in an essay on Virgil, notes how many lines in Virgil's writings have a long and cumulative history; how certain lines have moved individuals. He writes:

> On this line the poet's own voice faltered as he read;
> At this one Augustus and Octavia melted into passionate weeping;
> Here is the verse which Augustus quoted as typical in its majestic rhythm of all the pathos and glory of pagan art, from which the Christian was bound to flee.
> Look, this is the couplet which Fenelon could never read without tears;
> This line Filippo Strozzi scrawled on his prison wall, when he slew himself to avoid a worse ill.
> These are the words which like a trumpet call aroused Savonarola to seek the things that are above.
> And, look, here are the lines that Dante heard on the lips of the church Triumphant, at the opening of the paradise of God.[7]

If the poet Virgil had such influence, think of what a story might be told about a thousand lines in God's holy Word! The Australian preacher, F. W. Boreham, has a book of sermon-essays on favorite texts of great men; he gives background and experiences of times and places when a particular verse spoke in a special way to the life of these persons. And, Arthur John Gossip, the master preacher of Scotland, wrote on how good it would be if the minister had some way of replacing certain sections, leaves, of his Bible for after a few years these were so worn and soiled that one could only with great difficulty read the precious words. He said that of course the first section to be replaced would always be John 14, that: "In my Father's house are many mansions" (v. 2).

Remember, the highway patrol wants you to have a good rear-view window, as well as a clean windshield. In life we need to know from whence we come in order to navigate the future successfully.

Three Crucial Questions

If ye will inquire, inquire ye: return, come (v. 12b).

In Thornton Wilder's spiritually perceptive play, *Our Town,* Emily, the young girl, asks three pertinent questions after being allowed to view life from the perspective of the "cemetery." Her first question, "Do any human beings ever realize life while they are living it?" Question two, "Are we always at the mercy of one self-centered passion or another?" And, third, "Don't we ever come close to one another?"

She is told that probably a few of the saints have been able to realize life as they lived it, doubtful that others have. Probably we should add that a few of the poets have. "O world," one cried, "I cannot hold thee close enough . . . My soul is all but out of me . . . Let fall no borning leaf!" It does seem that we are driven by the "Furies" of passion, first one and then another and, worst of all, frequently all the passions at once. Do we ever come close to one another? It was what disturbed Emily the most. Her mother could not, would not, look at her.

One of the most effective and dynamic lecturers at Harvard University was George Santayana. He held his classes spellbound as he walked about the room, pausing now and then to punctuate his speaking. Joseph Auslander, then at Harvard, told about one beautiful spring morning when Santayana seemed at his best; members of the large class were eager to capture every beautiful phrase.

Again and again the teacher went over to the window and looked out upon the disturbing yellow of a hedge of forsythia. Finally he paused for a long time, longer than usual, while members of the class sat with pencils poised to take down his next words. At last he turned to the class and said, "Gentlemen, I very much fear that last sentence will never be completed. You see, I have an appointment with April." He walked out of the room; he never lectured regularly again.

I am come that they might have life, and that they might have it more abundantly (John 10:10).

"Reading Maketh the Man"

How knoweth this man letters, having never learned? (v. 15b).

For many years one of the great industrial organizations had as its slogan, "Send Us a Man Who Can Read." It is a good slogan. The person who reads is the growing person, the person with ideas, the person who dreams dreams and sees visions. When a friend says to Mr. Mifflin—in *The Haunted Bookshop* by Christopher Morley—that he always thought a book shop was a very dull place, Mr. Mifflin responds:

> Far from it. Living in a book shop is like living in a warehouse of explosives. Those shelves are ranked with the most furious combustibles in the world—the brains of men. I can spend a rainy afternoon reading, and my mind works itself up to such a passion and anxiety over mortal problems as almost astounds me. It is terribly nerve-racking. Surround a man with Carlyle, Emerson, Thoreau, Chesterton, Shaw, Nietzsche, and George Ade—would you wonder at his getting excited? What would happen to a cat if she had to live in a room tapestried with catnip? She would go crazy!"

The prophet of old spoke of "eating" the book. "Thy words were found," he wrote, "and I did eat them; and thy word was unto me the joy and rejoicing of mine heart" (Jer. 15:16). This indicates how by reading a person grows and matures. There is a saying that clothes make the man; another that we are what we eat. Neither is entirely true; both are pertinent enough to make us consider. Francis Bacon observed that "reading maketh the man." It is more true to say a man is what he reads.

As a person assimilates what he reads, it becomes a very part of his being and results in "joy and rejoicing." Joseph Fort Newton once described Emily Dickinson as "stardust, lightning, and fragrance all mixed up with a smile."

> *Therefore whosoever heareth these sayings of mine, and doeth them, I will liken him unto a wise man, which built his house upon a rock (Matt. 7:24).*

Too Good to Be True

Christ Jesus came into the world to save sinners (v. 15c).

The good news of the gospel swept the tired and bruised Roman world like a prairie fire! The worth of all persons, God's love for all persons, available salvation for all persons, God's plan and purpose for all persons. But it seemed too good to be true. Within a few hundred years of the New Testament those great truths were being deemphasized.

Society was broken down into groups and classes. God "called" only those at the top. The soul of *every* man was precious but, according to the Roman Catholic Church, God dealt with the common man only through the uncommon man. During the Middle Ages, that period of intellectual darkness between the fifth and fifteenth centuries, there were four classes in society.

At the top was the *clergy*. They were the most favored; through them, by the administration of the sacraments, the masses received salvation.

After the clergy came the *nobility*. They did the fighting, maintained law and order under the authority of the clergy, not along beside the clergy, but in the service of the clergy.

After the nobility came the *peasants,* the working people. The peasant was probably a serf or freeman in the service of the nobility. It was the belief of the day that God did not deal directly with him; when he attended church he had no intelligent part in the service; he did not understand the language used.

Merchants, traders, and businessmen made up the fourth group. They were often thought of as parasites; they did not create; they lived off what others created. Certainly, God had no direct dealing with these people! Wow, what a change!

Too Good Not to Be True!

Have the workers of iniquity no knowledge? (v. 4a).

Following the Middle Ages, with its narrow and restricted classifications of groups, came the Reformation of the sixteenth century, when a serious effort was made to bring back the true teachings of the gospel. In the Protestant lands there was the "sound of a going in the tops of the mulberry trees," as 2 Samuel 5:24 says.

Four solid biblical facts were proclaimed by Luther, Calvin, Zwingli, and others. First, *the sinfulness of man*, all men, all persons, every person. Since all are sinners, all stand on equal ground before God.

Second, *Christ died for all*! He died for all, not for any particular group or class but for all. If the sinfulness of all brought the upper classes down, the love of God for all, revealed in Christ, lifted the lower classes up. No one could earn or merit salvation; salvation was a free gift.

Third, *salvation is by grace through faith.* Salvation does not come, said the Reformers, through a sacramental system administered by a privileged class, the clergy. It is a free gift of God and it is by grace through faith.

Fourth, *all are called.* All persons have dealings with God. All are called to know, to accept, to obey, to love, to serve Christ. God is interested in; he cares for; he supplies resources for all who work and glorify God; God aids his children. Heady stuff, that! Too good not to be true!

> I hear the Savior say,
> "Thy strength indeed is small,
> Child of weakness, watch and pray,
> Find in me thine all in all."
>
> Jesus paid it all,
> All to him I owe;
> Sin had left a crimson stain,
> He wash'd it white as snow.
>
> —ELVINA M. HALL

"Be Useful Where Thou Livest"

And the common people heard him gladly (v. 37b).

Mark says that "The common people heard him [Jesus] gladly." Of course they did. They felt a particular bond with him; he was of, by, and for them.

On December 23, 1863, John Hay, one of President Abraham Lincoln's private secretaries, recorded in his journal that the President had a dream the night before. He was in a large group of plain people. When it became known who the President was they began to comment on his appearance. One said, "He is a common-looking man." Lincoln responded, "Common-looking people are the best in the world; that is the reason God made so many of them."

Think of how "the common people" must have felt when they heard Martin Luther preach the following:

I can just imagine the people of Nazareth at the judgment day. They will come up to the Master and say, "Lord, didn't you build my house? How did you come to this honor?" Luther said that after the Virgin Mary received the astonishing news that she was to be the mother of the Redeemer she did not vaunt herself or go off into isolation, no, she went back to milking cows, scouring kettles, and sweeping the house like any other housemaid. And the shepherds worked. They had a tough job to do but after they had seen the baby, they went back to tending their sheep. And with irony Luther said, "Surely that must be wrong. We should correct the passage to read, 'They went and shaved their heads, fasted, told their rosaries, and put on cowls.' Instead we read, "The shepherds returned." Where to? To their sheep. The sheep would have been in a sorry way if they had not.[8]

And, think, how the world has been humbled and made glad by the song Mary, the mother of Jesus sang before the birth of the Savior:

He has shown strength with his arm,
he has scattered the proud in the imagination of their hearts,
he has put down the mighty from their thrones,
and called those of low degree;
he has filled the hungry with good things,
and the rich he has sent empty away (Luke 1:51-53, RSV).

"Let Something Good Be Said"

He that receiveth a prophet in the name of a prophet (v. 41a).

For the first nine years of his life Bryan Sharp lived with the Babemba tribe in Southern Africa. In the book, *Contact: The First Four Minutes,* by Leonard and Natalie Zunin, his story is told. He said this was the way the tribe dealt with delinquents and criminals. The person was brought to the center of the village. He was left alone, unbound. All work ceased and the entire population gathered in a large circle about the accused. Then each person in the tribe, young and old, began to speak about the accused. Every good thing the person in the center of the ring had ever done that could be recalled, all the good deeds, his kindness, his helpfulness, his strength, were recounted. Not a word of criticism was allowed. No exaggeration was permitted, but every factual good deed in his life was recalled and spoken. Sharp said that the tribal ceremony frequently lasted for days. At the end, when no one was able to think of anything else good that the person had done, the tribal circle was broken, a joyous celebration took place, and the offending member was received back into the tribe with warmth and love. A backward tribe?

But the growth and development is not only to the receiver, it is to the giver as well. The bestowing of thanks and praise requires skill no less than painting a picture or singing a lovely song requires art. We learn by doing and the artistry can be learned. The eye can be trained to see the worthy deed; the heart can be educated to respond to the noble act; the mind can be enlightened to react appropriately. "Practice makes perfect." And as we become aware of the good that is being done in the world, life becomes more meaningful.

In his fine play on Abraham Lincoln, John Drinkwater says that when we admire the "high heart," celebrate the clear vision, and worship greatness passing by, we ourselves are great.

Choose Your Memories

Remember his marvellous works that he hath done (v. 5a).

What a memory the man had! As you read Psalm 105 you are led to believe the psalmist had the history of his nation at his mind's fingertips.

The ability to recall is a wonderful gift. We have played the game when we would be allowed a certain number of minutes in a room and then we were tested on our ability to recall what we had seen. In his book, *The Art of Thinking,* Ernest Dimnet tells of two Frenchmen who broke the monotony of prison life by recalling all they could remember of history, literature, and philosophy. They had neither pen nor paper, books nor magazines, yet, through the sheer process of memory the hours in the prison were shortened and made profitable. It is a stimulating exercise to recall all that you can of the places visited, the works of art seen, the biographies read, the famous people you have met.

The range and extent of memory is one gauge of a person's education. An uneducated person has few long-range memories about nations, people, and events. An educated person extends his memory to include vast stretches of time. In his great novel, *The Brothers Karamazov,* Dostoevski has one of his characters say:

> You must know that there is nothing higher or stronger and more wholesome and good for life in the future than some good memory, preserved from childhood, or home. People talk to you a great deal about your education, but some good, sacred memory, preserved from childhood, is perhaps the best education. If a man carries many such memories with him into life, he is safe to the end of his days, and if one has only one good memory left in one's heart, even that may sometimes be the means of saving him.

"If a Child Comes"

And a little child shall lead them (v. 6b).

Shortly after Jean Kerr published her delightful book, *Please Don't Eat the Daisies,* one of her sons had to write a book report as his school assignment. It was a natural thing for him to choose his own mother's book to review. He sought to give a fair and objective review. But when he came to give his own evaluation of the book, he gave his mother a poke under the fifth rib! He wrote: "Mrs. Kerr has written a very funny book although the parts about her children are grossly exaggerated and in some instances downright lies!"

It is difficult for parents looking back upon the childhood of their own sons and daughters, now grown, with established homes, to be objective. Yet, even allowing for the enchantment that distance lends, we know that some of earth's most rewarding experiences came when we were on vacation, alone in isolated settings, with the family. Somehow small things became large; large things seemed less important. Laughing heartily at a family joke that would mean nothing to one not a part of the family: sharing the "happiest moment" of the day with each other; recalling the most beautiful object seen during the day; the item of food most enjoyed; the favorite passage read during the day; the choice verse from the Bible memorized that day; the item, object, person for whom each is most thankful—family togetherness.

Rewarding discussion came over vocational choices. We knew, and probably the children knew, that those vocational choices would change over the years. I remember one of our daughters announced, when she was five, that when she grew up she was going to be "a return missionary." When our son was seven, his ambition was to be a "church janitor just like my friend Luke." The fact that he became a lawyer does not change the fact that he was impressed by a good man doing an honest job as a janitor.

Children are a great comfort in your old age—
and they help you reach it faster, too!

—LIONEL KAUFFMAN

"It Was in Cana of Galilee"

Thou hast kept the good wine until now (v. 10b).

It was in Cana of Galilee that Christ attended a wedding and blessed it. I am glad when they were making out the invitation list that the name of Jesus was included.

In the early part of the eighteenth century Francis Herries, a character in Hugh Walpole's book, *Rogue Herries,* met an old clergyman. Herries complained that the place was isolated from the world. The old minister replied that the place was the world, all the world. Anger, vanity, covetousness, lust, charity, goodness, and sweetness of soul were all there within those hills and on that piece of ground. He said that God and the devil both knew those fields and often walked thereon.

Now, Cana is the world; there universal truths are stated. Cana is the world of creative living, of happy marriage, of joyous obedience. Cana contains the secret of how to live "happily ever after."

This incident shows what life is like without Jesus—the wine runs out, joy and enthusiasm ebb, weariness of spirit takes over. It shows what life can become through the presence and blessing of Christ—beauty and enthusiasm return, the music of life is heard, the purpose of life is clear. It shows what the future holds for those who invite Christ to their wedding and do what he tells them to do—then the best wine, life, will come last. Life will get better and better; it may get harder and harder, but Christ will see to it that the last of life is what the first was made for.

> By a Carpenter mankind was made, and only by a Carpenter can mankind be remade.
>
> —ERASMUS

"Look, Ma, No Hands!"

They let down the bed wherein the sick of the palsy lay (v. 4b).

We are God's children; we are also God's instruments. God uses persons. I am amazed at what amputees can do, in sports, business, professions, labor, and entertainment.

One of the most beautiful weddings I ever had the privilege of conducting dealt with great handicaps. The bride was armless, had never had arms, was born without arms. She was beautiful, highly intelligent, a graduate of a fine university, but armless. Yet, we had a double-ring ceremony. That service moved so smoothly, the bride was so accomplished in the use of her feet and legs, that people in the audience did not know that she was armless. The groom placed the ring upon her toe; she took, with her toes, the groom's ring from my fingers, and placed it upon his finger. She did this while standing so erect that, with her long train stretched behind her, no one knew of the handicap that was being overcome.

Yet, when all has been said and recognized and admired, there are things that people who have arms and hands can do that those who do not have arms and hands cannot do. In a very real way, we are God's arms and hands and feet and eyes and ears. He can do things in and through his people that he cannot do, will not do, without his people.

Many years ago Harry Emerson Fosdick wrote a fine little book on prayer. He affirmed that there were three things that God could not do and would not do, without his people. There are things that God will not do until his people *think*; there are disease and death, but God waits for his children to go into laboratories. There are things God will not do until his people *work*; he builds no churches and hospitals. There are things God will not do until his people *pray*; it is written into the fabric of the universe.

"Walking Along with You"

Can two walk together, except they be agreed? (v. 3).

Only the relationship between the individual and holy God is more significant and precious than the marriage relationship. For as a man stands at the marriage altar by the side of a lovely woman and hears her say, "I do," he knows that unworthy though he be, this person is paying him the highest tribute that it is possible for one human being to pay another. Her words affirm, "I choose this one to share my life, my dreams, my happiness, my laughter, and tears. I choose him to be the father of my children; I wish to face the sunrise and the sunset with him by my side. And, he in turn, says:

> I just want to walk along with you, where the trail is not too wide, where there's only room for you and me walking side by side, where the ferns lean over the pathway, and the jack-in-the-pulpit grow, where adder's tongues with drooping heads nod shyly too and fro.
>
> I want to walk where the sun is bright and the trail is all aglow, where the rippling brook is aglint with gold, where butterflies come and go; and our eyes will be filled with the golden rain, while every vagrant breeze is a kiss from a nymph or a pixy bold, who lives, we are told, in the trees.
>
> And I want to walk where the shadows lie—there are shadows on every trail—that my presence may be a comfort to you through the darkness of the vale; and if across the path some chasm yawns, where you might pause in fear, then I'll be a friend of the trail indeed with a helping hand so near.
>
> But, let the trail be rough or smooth, in shadow or in the sun, there'll be joy of life in every mile and joy of the course we've run. So, let me walk along with you, where the trail is not too wide, where there's only room for you and me walking side by side.
>
> —Arthur Haper

The Bible is a family book, its language is family language. Only God and the marriage relationship were allowed to come between a son and his father, but a man was to leave father and mother and cleave to his wife. A man is to love his wife, even as "Christ loved the church." So, the two cease to be two and merge into one.

On the Opening of Eyes

And Jesus increased in wisdom and in stature, and in favour . . . (v. 52).

Jesus grew as a normal boy, as borne out by this text. He set a pattern for children of every generation to develop and mature in understanding.

As a pastor I often wrote to the deacons in our church at Christmastime. By starting the first of December and writing one, two, or more letters each day, predating, the letters were sealed and ready for mailing by Christmas Eve. By marking the letters, "Special Delivery," I was assured of delivery before midnight. There was frequently gratifying response. Example:

The deacon was a fine man, a trusted official of a great university. He had an only son, an executive in a national young men's political party. The relationship between father and son was no more distant and strained than is frequently the case. Still, the brilliant son was sure the father had been born thirty years too soon to have any real understanding of life and the present world.

My letter was delivered on Christmas Eve. The letter sought in warm, sincere, honest terms to convey my appreciation. The letter named times and occasions during the past year when this man's voice and vote turned the tide for God and good. It brought as much of a grateful heart as I could pack between the folds of one envelope.

The father read the letter and left it on the arm of his chair. At breakfast on Christmas morning he casually mentioned the letter and told the family that they might feel free to read it if they desired to do so. (The father reported to me what happened.) The son on returning to the living room, picked up the letter, read it, reread it. Then, visibly moved, he walked over to his father and said, "Dad, I am embarrassed to admit that your minister knows you better than your son does. But now that his letter has opened my eyes, I want to make a confession: I think you are a great man, Dad, and I am proud to be your son."

"The Church Is a Living Thing"

And he is the head of the body, the church (v. 18a).

In *The Servant in the House* Charles Rann Kennedy wrote of the church:

> This [church] is no dead pile of stones and unmeaning timber. *It is a living thing.* When you enter it you hear a sound—a sound as of some mighty poem chanted. Listen long enough, and you will learn that it is made up of the beatings of human hearts, of the nameless music of men's souls—that is, if you have ears. If you have eyes, you will presently see the church itself—a looming mystery of many shapes and shadows, leaping sheer from floor to dome. The work of no ordinary builder!
>
> The pillars of it go up like the brawny trunks of heroes: the sweet human flesh of men and women is moulded about its bulwarks, strong, impregnable: the faces of little children laugh out from every cornerstone; the terrible spans and arches of it are the joined hands of comrades; and up in the heights and spaces there are inscribed the numberless musings of the dreamers of the world.
>
> It is yet building—building and built upon. Sometimes the work goes forward in deep darkness: sometimes in blinding light: now beneath the burden of unutterable anguish: now to the tune of a great laughter and heroic shouting like the cry of thunder. Sometimes, in the silence of the night-time, one may hear the tiny hammerings of the comrades at work in the dome—the comrades who have climbed ahead.

Only a great artist with a fine Christian spirit could write so beautifully and meaningfully. But, in our own way and words, we, too, could give our testimony of what the church is and does. Donald F. Ackland writes in *Joy in Church Membership*:

> For the strengthening of our own experience, for our continuing instruction in the Christian way, for the contribution that we can make to the faith of other believers, for the privilege of fellowship in worship and witness, for the more effective influence of a united testimony, for obedience to the revealed will of Christ our Lord, it is required of Christians that they be church members.

He Was a Good Fisherman

And he gave some, apostles; and some prophets, and some evangelists (v. 11).

Swanson Yarbrough's health was bad. He had heart trouble and a collapsed lung; he had asthma and allied complications. Three hours each afternoon he spent in bed. He followed an extreme and rigid diet; he knew painful relapses.

Yet from 1947 to 1956, the year he died, he was responsible for bringing almost a thousand people into the membership of his church, the First Presbyterian Church of Tyler, Texas.

How? By knowing and loving the Lord, by prayerful, consistent and friendly visiting. During these years, Mr. Yarbrough spent four to five evenings each week ringing door bells to talk with people about Christ and his church. He got the names of the people from friends, local newspapers, banks for new accounts, utility people for new accounts. One man said of him, "He was at my home before I got my suitcase unpacked."

How did Swanson Yarbrough tap the springs of power? He firmly believed that God had called him to the task; his wife supported him in the work; they started each day with a time of worship; he maintained a time of Bible study each day, no interruptions allowed. Dr. J. Sherrard Rice, his pastor, wrote in a letter to me, "I have never known as devoted and effective and consistent a winner of men." I have before me as I write, an expression of appreciation for this wonderful "fisher of men" from his church.

In the musical *Camelot*, the legendary King Arthur instructs his knights to ask every person they meet if they have heard the story of Camelot; if they have not heard, the knights are to tell the story loudly and clearly. They are to remind themselves every night, "from December to December," of the "flaming wisp of glory called Camelot." Jesus said, "You are my witnesses."

Just Six Hours!

What God hath cleansed, that call not thou common (v. 15b).

God fulfills himself in many ways," wrote an unknown poet. One of the ways God fulfills himself is through using the faithful unknown to call out the faithful known. He used a faithful deacon, do you know his name? to bring the great preacher, George W. Truett, into the ministry.

The Truett family moved from the mountains of western North Carolina to Whitewright, Texas. There young George worked, attended junior college, and at night read law that he might fulfill his lifelong ambition to be a lawyer. Then . . . but let Dr. Truett describe what took place:

> One Saturday night I went to church where all our family were members. . . . After the sermon a revered old deacon got up to speak. He began with generalities, some talk about the duty of individuals and the duty that belong to the group. But presently he got painfully specific and personal. Then everyone in the house knew he was talking about me. He was urging that I decide at once for the ministry. I protested. I had done so before when the deacon mentioned it to me privately. I had joined the church at nineteen; I was willing to be a faithful lay member, but I had other plans for a career. But there was the deacon talking to the church. The members prayed. Exhortations were heard. Finally they agreed unanimously that God was calling George Truett to the ministry.

Young George asked that he be given six months for an answer. They gave him six hours. Throughout the night George Truett roamed the Texas fields of his father's farm, roamed and prayed. The next day he was ready with his answer; he, too, agreed that God was calling him into the gospel ministry. He was ordained.

> Brethren, we have met to worship
> And adore the Lord our God;
> Will you pray with all your power,
> While we try to preach the Word?
> All is vain unless the Spirit
> Of the Holy One comes down;
> Brethren, pray, and holy manna
> Will be showered all around.
>
> —GEORGE ATKINS

Careful! You Might Get It

When they had opened the door, and saw him, they were astonished (v. 16).

H. G. Wells had a humorous and disturbing story about an arch-bishop. The archbishop had a problem. He decided to pray. Now the archbishop had "said his prayers," ah yes, he had done that. But he had not prayed directly, trustingly. He decided to try this. He would state his case simply and faithfully, just as he saw it and remain on his knees for an answer.

Slowly he sank to his knees, put his hands together. He was touched by childlike trustfulness. "Oh, God," he began and paused. As he waited a sense of imminence, a monstrous awe, gripped him, and then he heard a voice. The voice was clear and distinct. It said, "Yes, what is it?"

They found his grace, the archbishop, the next morning. He had slipped off the steps where he was kneeling and lay sprawled on the crimson carpet. Plainly his death had been instantaneous. But instead of the serenity which was his habitual expression, his countenance, by some strange freak of nature, displayed an extremity of terror and dismay. That is Wells's story.

Smile over the story, then become serious. Then, ask yourself some questions. Are we surprised that our prayers are not answered? Would we be more surprised if they were answered? It disturbs us that God is silent while evil rages; would we be more surprised if he did anything about it?

L. P. Jacks, a British minister, wrote, "I began to see that this hearsay, second-hand stuff about God and Christ, in which I was so prolific, was not religion, but at best only a ghost or reminiscence of religion—in short, though that might *go,* it would not *do.* Not for life's journey."

Read Psalm 20:4   June 9
"Tunes Heard in the Streets"

Grant thee according to thine own heart (v. 4a).

Martin Luther always kept his eye on the peasant when he was
writing. He said that if he could write so that the peasant would
understand, then all classes would be instructed and helped. Deep
water is usually clear; if the child cannot understand something of a
book, it may be that the book is muddy rather than deep.

The poems of Homer were appreciated by Pericles, but the sausage
sellers in the markets of Athens loved them, too. The poems of Virgil
were valued by the vineyard dressers and the shepherds no less than
by the Emperor Augustus. Shakespeare was loved by the sophisticated
minds in the court of Elizabeth I, but he was popular, too, among the
people of the poorer sections of London. When one of Thackeray's
books attained a degree of success among the brilliant minds of the
day, the novelist was not impressed. He said, "My tunes must be heard
in the streets."

A case in point. A fine Christian scholar in one of our worthy schools
of higher learning. The teacher was a friend of mine; the student, now
a fine pastor, is a friend of mine. The student was concerned about the
course; his grades for the course were low; he feared he would fail the
subject. He went to see the Christian professor, that friend of mine,
with the request that he be allowed to drop the course. The professor
was silent for what seemed a long time; the student thought the
request had not been understood.

Then the professor said: "Two points. First, permission to drop the
course is denied. Second, you are a good student, a conscientious
student, if you are having difficulty with this course I am to blame, not
you. I promise to take care of that problem." And he did. Before
graduating, the student was asked to be that professor's assistant. It
was said of the teaching and preaching of Jesus that "the common
people heard him gladly" (Mark 12:37).

Corn Bread and Molasses

And the streets of the city shall be full of boys and girls playing (v. 5a).

I am told that feeding a young guest calls for resources and ingenuity different from anything else a hostess ever faces. I do not know, except views from the observation deck and the paying line. The sight is one to amaze the stoutest heart and the paying can make any pocketbook appreciate the virtue of humility!

It was the only time I can remember when we had a real, live governor of the state as a dinner guest. Governor J. M. Broughton and Mrs. Broughton, were longtime friends. Such excitement! It was a small dinner party, just the governor with Mrs. Broughton and a few other choice friends. Patricia, our young daughter, had been duly instructed. Of course, she was a member of the party, she was a member of the family.

All went well. Good food, good conversation—a light, urbane, and somewhat sophisticated atmosphere prevailed, but Patricia was not eating her food, unusual for her I might add. Finally, her mother said, "Well, dear, what is wrong? May I get you anything else?" That did it. Patricia came forth immediately, in a high-pitched, child's voice with, "Yes, Mummy, may I have some hot corn bread and molasses?" For a moment there was stillness, a stillness akin to that which prevails at the heart of a hurricane, then the storm broke. The group roared with laughter, led by the governor! He said, "Bless you, Patricia! Just what I would like, too, if your mother has enough for two servings." No wonder he was elected governor of the state and later U.S. senator! The dinner was, we thought, a total success, and no one made a larger contribution than Patricia.

Dear Father God, keep us mindful of the words of your Son, our Lord and Savior, who taught that we must become like little children to enter the kingdom. Give us the freshness, the honesty, and the trust of the child. Amen.

Only Get the Work Done

I will glory of the things which concern my infirmities (v. 30).

One of the great encouragements of life is to see how others overcame handicaps. Paul is a case in point within the text for today. For example, Augustus Caesar, the adopted son of Julius Caesar, was known as the "increasing god." He was on the throne of Rome when Jesus was born in Bethlehem. Augustus is considered by the historians to have been one of the very greatest of the Caesars. He completed the conquest of Spain; set up and made effective the administration of Gaul; with his great army and navy he extended Rome's frontiers until the Empire covered a hundred times more than it did during the Punic wars. Yet, Will Durant says he was a frail and nervous invalid, had a sort of ringworm, had rheumatism that weakened his left leg and made him limp, his right hand was stiff, he suffered from something akin to a plague in 23 BC. He suffered from stones in the bladder and he had insomnia.

Or, look at a more noble character. The world has loved the writings of Robert Louis Stevenson. For years the eyes of the literary world were focused on the little island in the Pacific from which came his "faultless writings," as they were called. It seemed that everyone wanted to write like "RLS." Yet we know that he fought a lifelong battle with illness. His doctors said that he would have to live as if walking on eggs. They said he had to live the life of an invalid; he could endure no shocks, no surprises; he could not eat too much, walk too much, drink too much, or even laugh too much. His life was one long battle with colds, congestion, hemorrhages, and sinking spells, in which he lost the power of speech. In 1893 he wrote a friend that for fourteen years he had not known one day of real health. He had awakened sick and gone to bed weary, that he had written his books in bed and out of bed, written them when worn out with coughing. But he said that sick or well was only a trifle as long as the work got done!

We thank thee, dear Lord, that he who is within is greater than anyone or anything without and that "through Christ we can do all things." Amen.

"The Skin of Our Teeth"

The exchange of it shall not be for jewels of fine gold (v. 17).

What a family spends its money for is revealing, whether the amount of money is much or little. Thoreau noted that we spend more on almost every bodily ailment than on the mind's ailment. Thoreau's neighbor and friend, Ralph Waldo Emerson, wrote that it is pitiable to observe the things by which a person is considered rich or poor. He said that just a few more coins, a little more carpet, an additional amount of stone, wood, or paint, and the educated and the cultured often became no better than a naked savage, who marked his riches by a string of glass beads or a colorful feather. What is of real value to us? What are our priorities?

In *The Skin of Our Teeth,* Thornton Wilder knew what his values were. The play merges time and sequence; mixes wars and floods, deluge and bombing. But whether it is Noah building an ark or a dictator building a tank, the spirit of man is about the same. Mr. Antrobus comes home from the war. All is in ruins; he is discouraged. He observed that in some ways war is better than peace, for in war you think about a better life, while in peace you think only about a more comfortable life. He remembers that during the war, when he could see the clearest, there were three factors that always went together: the voice of the people in their need, the thoughts of his home and family, and his books.

Mr. Antrobus knows that life means struggle; all that is good stands every minute upon the razor edge of danger and has to be fought for constantly. Still all he has ever asked for was a chance to build new worlds; God has always given that. As he opens a book and fingers it lovingly, he muses that God has "given us voices to guide us . . . and the steps of our journey are marked for us here."

And he said unto them, take heed, and beware of covetousness: for a man's life consisteth not in the abundance of the things which he possesseth (Luke 12:15).

Five Handshakes Away

The Sun of righteousness [shall] arise with healing in his wings (v. 2b).

Richard L. Aldington wrote in his autobiography that he was sure he was a real poet because he was only five handshakes away from Shelley. Then he set out to prove his case. He said he once shook hands with Swinburne; Swinburne once shook hands with Southey; Southey once shook hands with Landor; and Landor was the intimate friend of Shelley. There it is. QED! Only five handshakes away!

In a significant way, Aldington's contention has merit. We are only so many physical, mental, and spiritual "handshakes" away from the great, regardless of what their day and generation may have been. We are caught in a network of influences that are tied with Gordian knots that no Alexander can cut.

We are influenced by our parents; each of our parents had two parents, making four; they each had four, making eight. Run that back for ten generations and you are in a human network of one thousand and twenty-four. Trace it back twenty generations and you are caught in a web of one million, forty-eight thousand, five hundred, and seventy-six. Each of these was "shaking hands" with his contemporaries and passing that handshake along to you.

Abigail told David that his soul was bound in "the bundle of life." That is so very true. No person lives to himself; no person dies to himself. Each person's loss diminishes me; I am blessed by whatever blesses you. The good that I do is not to my merit alone; others have made it easier for me. And—by the same token, in some way—others have contributed to the stain that colors me.

Local Addresses Are Important

Hearken unto me, ye that follow after righteousness (v. 1b).

One of the basic assumptions of all civilized life is that you do not have to do everything over from the beginning. It is possible for mankind to see, experience, think, write, and form laws and constitutions. This accumulated wisdom becomes capital for future generations; they do not have to begin all over again; the accumulated capital can be drawn and used. A new generation does not have to begin "from scratch." It needs to be remembered that if you have no change, you know no progress, but if you have no traditions you experience no civilization.

A friend of mine was surprised and humbled when his mother's will was read. There was a large family; it was a closely knit family. But, when the will was read, this is what it said: "I leave everything I own to my son Blank, to do with as he pleases, because he always pleases to do right." Liberty: "To do with as he pleases." Discipline: "Because he always pleases to do right." The freedom of rivers, the discipline and staying power of oaks. It takes both to make a worthy life.

This principle applies locally as well as on wider horizons for it applies to all of life. Banking hours were over for the day. The janitor was cleaning. The telephone rang and he answered it: "This is the First National Bank." The calling party said, "I want to know what the Federal Reserve discount is, what the prime paper rate is, and if you think this foreign travel is going to upset the currency?" A few seconds of silence. Then, the voice of the janitor again: "Mr., when I said, 'Hello,' and 'this is the First National Bank,' I told you all I know about banking." Local addresses and identifications are important. Streams of liberty, oaks of discipline are needed locally and abroad.

"The Dice of God Are Loaded"

Behold, thou art there (v. 8b).

There is a dual purpose that prompts prodigal sons (or daughters) to leave home: first, to seek what they think cannot be found at home; second, to escape what they have at home. The prodigal wants to escape the Father's house, will, and love. He wants to live his own life without his Father's discipline.

But that is impossible; it has always been impossible. The psalmist could have told him. If he ascends "up into heaven" God will be there; if he makes his bed in hell, God will be there; if he takes the "wings of the morning" and flies to the uttermost limits, even there he will find God's hand ready to guide him.

A truth that ancient and modern prodigals are slow to learn is this: One does not avoid the Father's presence by fleeing the Father's house and the Father's people. The prodigal may choose the form that the Father's presence and discipline will take, but escape these? Never! One does not escape the laws of health by ignoring them: see the crowded hospitals, sanitoriums, clinics, and doctor's couches! It would be as easy to avoid the law of gravity, logic, and health by denying their existence as to avoid the presence and will of the Father by the same means. The prophet Amos said that the ever-present God might be likened unto the experience of a man fleeing from a lion and meeting a bear, rushing to his home for safety and a serpent bites him! The "form" of God's presence we may choose, but not his presence itself.

> The dice of God are always loaded;
> Every secret is told,
> Every crime is punished,
> Every wrong is redressed in silence
> And in certainty,
> The thief steals from himself;
> The swindler swindles himself.
>
> —RALPH WALDO EMERSON

On Finding Yourself

He said . . . I will arise and go to my father (vv. 17-18a).

Random Harvest by James Hilton was popular decades ago. It is the story of Charles Rainier, a man who was shell-shocked in the war and suffered amnesia. When he regained awareness, he was back in his native England but the past was blotted out, no memory of it at all. He became very successful in business and in politics. He married; her name was Helen; there was harmony but no closeness between them. He was lonely; his past haunted him.

Then gradually his memory began to return in bits and pieces. He remembered that he had been married before, married to a girl by the name of Paula. That first marriage, he knew, had been completely happy and fulfilling. He wondered about that first wife, Paula. Was she alive; had she remarried; was she, somewhere, waiting for him? He had to find Paula.

And, find her he did. There came clarity of mind, partially. He drove to a small town; parked his car and climbed a hill. There he found two small windswept hills and, lying between, a small lake. He knew it was here that he and Paula had first declared their love. He dropped to the ground and gave himself to remembering. And, then, she came to him, his long-lost Paula. They went into each other's arms, never to be separated again.

But what about Helen, his present wife. No problem; Helen and Paula were one and the same person. Helen had found him, knew him, and still loved him. Caused him to love her; married him. She longed to tell him who she was, who he was, who they were together. But she knew he would have to "come to himself" for that. She waited. Now that he had "come to himself," they were reunited.

Parable? Almost. "And when he came to himself he said . . . I will arise and go to my father."

"I Leave My Love"

Who shall separate us from the love of Christ? (v. 35).

Think of the boldness of Paul! In the suggested passage for today he says that "nothing" shall separate us from Christ. Does he mean our love for Christ or Christ's love for us? Both, I suspect, but primarily God's love for us.

Once in a great while you find a human love which seems to approach, in a small way, something of that enduring quality. And, when we do, it is cause for gratitude as few things we are permitted to witness are.

For example, there is the lovely and tender little book by James Davidson Ross called *Margaret.* It is the true story of a girl, fifteen years of age, dying of cancer. The book was written by her brother-in-law. He writes so beautifully, so tenderly, and so understandingly that you lay the book down with a sob and a shout! The girl dictates her last will and testament; she dictates from the depths of pain. On the surface her bequests seem small and trivial: a small piece of rope to her father, a locket to her sister, a prayer book to her brother, several toys to her nieces.

Then, along with these material items comes a more precious bequest: "To everyone who has been so wonderful to me these past months, I leave my love, my trust, and my faith in Christ." For her brother-in-law she gives her most precious bequest. She wrote: "To Jim: my savings certificates and myself: 'Lo, I am with you alway, even unto the end of the world.'"

It is a beautiful message. Nothing short of the triumphant realization of what Paul meant could produce it.

> The man is happy, Lord, who love like
>   this doth owe;
> Loves thee, his friend in thee,
>   and for thy sake, his foe.
>
> —RICHARD C. TRENCH

A Letter of Recommendation

Jesus began to say unto the multitudes concerning John . . . (v. 7a).

If you were asked to write a character reference for this man, John the Baptist, what would you write? How would you react to the following:

"Dear Sir: This word is written in response to your letter requesting a character reference for John the Baptist. This man is honest and truthful. He will swear to his own hurt and never change. He is loyal to the highest and best that he knows, cost what it may. He is wise, having the strange ability to recognize true greatness when it appears in a person no matter how carefully it may be concealed. He is courageous in person and in speech. He fears not the face of man; he calls the shots as he sees them, cost what they may.

"He has perseverance, once he puts his hand to the task you can count on him to see it through to completion, no matter how hard the going gets, no matter how he may be criticized or persecuted. He is humble. He never tries to usurp the place of a superior. He recognizes his place and stays in it. He can, and will, place others above himself.

"I should warn you that he is not the most diplomatic person in the world. He has a way of speaking the truth, the whole truth and nothing but the truth, as he sees it.

"I should warn you, too, that this has been known to get him into trouble with the boys, and the girls, of power and influence who feel that nothing derogatory about them, their personal lives, and administration, should be released to the public. But if you want an honest, truthful, courageous, and humble man, you can get no better than Dr. John Baptist. He will work no miracles but you will find that many people will believe on Jesus because of this man's testimony."

Would you sign it?

The Real Rewards of Prayer

O come, let us worship and bow down (v. 6a).

About one hundred and fifty years ago Ralph Waldo Emerson was a young theological student at Cambridge, Massachusetts. Ill health caused him to spend some time at his uncle's farm nearby. While recuperating he got to thinking about a subject for his first sermon. One day when talking with some of his uncle's hired hands, one of the men said to young Emerson that men were always praying and that their prayers were always answered. The young Emerson latched on to the idea for his sermon. Choosing as his text the words of Paul, "Pray without ceasing" (1 Thess. 5:17), he developed a sermon with three points: "First, Men are always praying; Second, All their prayers are granted; Third, Beware then what you ask." Soon, thereafter, Emerson put the sentiment into verse:

> And though thy knees were never bent,
> To heaven thy daily prayers are sent;
> And whether formed for good or ill,
> Are registered and answered still.

Jesus taught his disciples that men ought always to pray and not to faint; that is, do not become weak and cowardly. That would seem to say that Jesus believed if men would pray they would not faint, that through prayer men would find strength and courage. This suggests one of the fundamental areas of prayer relationships. True prayer is setting up and maintaining a relationship with God, the fountainhead of strength and courage.

Prayer is, in one sense, a sort of "mutual aid society." Our giving is in the form of "offering." We offer unto God our adoration, praise, thanksgiving, penitence, commitment, faith, our very selves. In return, through prayer, God gives to us his very self. That is the major transaction. There are by-products, but these are incidental to the giving of self.

"Take with You Words"

Take with you words, and turn to the Lord (v. 2a).

In *The Screwtape Letters,* C. S. Lewis has Screwtape, a senior devil, say to Wormwood, a junior devil, "Do not be deceived, Wormwood. Our cause is never more in danger than when a human, no longer desiring, but still intending, to do our Enemy's (God's) will, looks around upon a universe from which every trace of Him seems to have vanished, and asks why he has been forsaken, and still obeys."⁹ And, that is to say, let us leave moods, circumstances, feelings, observable results in the hands of God and get on with our praying!

When the disciples made their request to Jesus that he teach them to pray, he said, "When ye pray say . . . " Words are important in prayer. The prophet advised his people to take words and turn to God; words are important.

The poet Coleridge said he had ceased to pray with "moving lips and bended knees." He merely "composed his spirit to love." To that one might say, "Poet, stick to your poetry!" Prayer is more than the composing of the spirit, the creation of a mood induced by soft lights and easy music, plus the sweet smell of incense.

Man is an animal. Yet he is more than an animal. He is made in God's image. But he is an animal with animal habits and appetites. So, what we do with our vocal cords and knees affects our total selves. The psalmist was wise when he called for us to "kneel." That is not to say, of course, that we cannot pray except on our knees, nor is it affirmed that all prayers have to be vocal. The Bible gives examples of kneeling, standing, and reclining as prayers are made. But voice and posture are important in praying. Jesus instructed, "When you pray, say . . . "

Now when Daniel knew that the writing was signed, he went into his house; . . . and kneeled upon his knees three times a day, and prayed, and gave thanks before his God, as he did aforetime (Dan. 6:10).

How to Pray

The Spirit itself maketh intercession for us (v. 26b).

For what and for whom do you pray? Do we not very quickly run out of subject matter in our praying, so that it is a matter of repetition or very short prayers? In his book, *Teach Yourself to Pray,* Stephen F. Winward makes valuable suggestions. He says that we should take the Bible reading into our prayers. In conversation your words have some relationship to what the other party says to you. So, when God has spoken to us through his word let us respond with some reference to what he has said to us. If the passage has included, "I am the light of the world," would we not naturally respond to that? Wherein do I need light, my family, my church, my friend, my nation, and the world?

The content of our prayers would also have reference to the circumstances of the day in which we live. As we meet God in the morning, before we meet persons, let us anticipate the day: we shall meet these people, go to these places, have these responsibilities, read these books. We shall want to pray about these.

When evening comes, let us ask questions on the threshold of our prayer time: What have I done today that could have been done better? What thoughts or acts call for God's forgiveness? What calls for special thanks and gratitude? Whom have I seen today who needs my prayers tonight?

And, our heart's desires need to be taken into our prayers. It may be that our heart's real desires do not get into our praying. Are we ashamed, do we feel they are too small, unworthy of God's concern? But, if he notes the sparrow's fall . . . And, he KNOWS; so, better face the matter in prayer.

In the morning, prayer is the key that opens to us the treasures of God's mercies and blessings; in the evening, it is the key that shuts us up under his protection and safeguard.

—ANONYMOUS

179

Come, Let Us Worship

Wherefore God also hath highly exalted him (v. 9a).

Ritual, forms of worship, "God's table manners," must be sincere and honest. However, sincerity of heart does not relieve one from observing correct and appropriate "table manners." Once the heart is right, and that is a first requirement, appropriate forms become more, not less, important. The motive must not be taken for the deed, even though the motive preceded the deed.

Another caution about these "table manners" is that the form must be an aid to help us come into the presence of God, not a substitute for his presence. At this point there are dangers inherent in all forms. The handshake is good, a symbol of friendship, but it must not become a substitute for friendship. Salute the flag? Yes, the flag is a symbol of the nation, but let not the flag nor the salute we give it become a substitute for faithful citizenship and worthy Christian patriotism. God cannot be worshiped appropriately without some form but the form must not be substituted for the life.

In his book, *The Glory of Christian Worship,* G. Edwin Osborne wrote of the early building that housed the Seventh Street Christian Church in Richmond, Virginia. In doing research on the old building in preparation for the celebration of the church's centennial, Dr. Osborne discovered that when first erected the building had a large stained-glass window in the wall behind the pulpit and choir, a picture of Holman Hunt's *The Light of the World.* Further investigation revealed that the picture was still in its original place. The outside had been bricked over by an adjoining building, the inside by massive organ pipes. The author wondered if something akin to that has not happened to public worship with artificial devices covering up the disturbing call of God! Disturbing preacher, Dr. Osborne!

"A Lot of Catching Up to Do"

If a man love me, he will keep my words (v. 23a).

One of the strong arguments for eternal life is the cry and desire for love and human relationships. When friendship means so much here, the heart responds that it must be continued there. Jesus felt this. Read very carefully of his actions and words in the "upper room" on the night before he was crucified. He had great difficulty in leaving the disciples and going to the garden. He finally asked God that he and the disciples might be together forever.

Someone asked Grandma Moses once how it felt to have millions of Christmas cards made from her pictures. She answered, "Oh, I don't think about fame much. I keep my mind on what I am going to paint next. I have got a lot of catching up to do."

One day a group of us were talking with a wealthy man, converted late in life, who was being wonderfully generous with his money. We tried to express our admiration and appreciation. He said, "Well, when the Lord saved me, I decided that I would try to make up for time and service and generosity lost during a lifetime, but for the life of me I cannot do it. Every day the Lord lets me live I get deeper and deeper in debt to him."

You are immortal; you know it by and through the grace of Jesus Christ. How does it affect your praying and your living? P. T. Forsyth wrote in *This Life and the Next,* "There are those who quietly say . . . I know that land. Some of my people live there. Some have gone abroad on secret foreign service, which does not admit of communication. But I meet from time to time the Commanding Officer. And when I mention them to him He assures me all is well."

"Go and Tell"

Jesus saith unto her, Mary (v. 16a).

Everlasting life seems impersonal. You come to the grave to leave the body of a loved one. Great truths are spoken, but in the midst of your sorrow and tears these truths seem vague and distant. What you need is the sense of personal identification, participation, that comes when you hear your own name spoken. That is just what Mary did hear; that is just what the "Marys" always hear. We are assured that he calls his own sheep by name. Easter has your own name and address on it, even zip code!

When Mary did recognize her Lord, she wanted to rejoice in her newfound happiness and "let the rest of the world go by." Jesus had to restrain her from clinging to him. Mary was content to remain in the presence of Christ and not share her new discovery with others. The bent knee and the swift foot must go together. There is need for adoration and worship; there is need for evangelism and missions. A place for the glad heart and a place for the joyous tongue.

Every pastor knows the tragedy of the person who experiences the death of a loved one and becomes a recluse because of it. That person is as much in a tomb as his/her departed spouse. The very balm that would heal, one often refuses to use. One may cease to be grateful for the years he had because of the loss of years he is denied. We must share; we must tell.

Albert Schweitzer once said to a group of students, "I don't know what your destiny will be, but one thing I do know: the only ones among you who will be really happy are those who will have sought and found how to serve." The word to Mary, and to us, is: "Go and tell."

The "Bandanna" Makes a Difference

His righteousness remaineth forever (v. 9c).

I knew a successful businessman, a member of the church of which I was a pastor. There was no depth of understanding or devotion, apparently, to his religious life. Illness struck without warning. The doctors broke the news gently, but to me they were more frank. When I asked how long they thought the man had to live, they said it would probably not be more than sixty days. Then came a transformation. For the first time God became real, personal, and loving. The man said to me, on one of my numerous visits to his hospital room, "Pastor, I do not know what I would do now if it were not for God. I simply hand the burdens over to him, and that is the end of it."

Suffering reveals a man to himself, a self, it may be, that he never knew before. True, what is revealed will depend in no small degree on what was in the man before the suffering came.

The citizens of a Western city gave a dinner for their leading businessman. After the tributes were all in, the man was asked for an expression. He said, "I am deeply moved. This town has been good to me; you have been wonderful friends. When I came here fifty years ago, I had one suit, it was on my back. The rest of my possessions were tied up in an old red bandanna. Now I own the bank, the newspaper, two hotels, five oil wells, and a radio station. Yes, sir, this town has been good to me and I am grateful." A person sitting close by said, "Tell us, Bill, what was in that old red bandanna." "Well, Son," said Bill, "to the best of my recollection I had $450,000 in cash and $750,000 in negotiable securities tied up in that rag." What you have in the bandanna is important; but sometimes nothing short of tragedy will reveal it.

When Columba, the missionary, settled on the island of Iona, conditions were crude and cruel. Often refugees came to him. For these the missionary appointed counselors. He called these "Soul Friends." And, remember, "There is a friend that sticketh closer than a brother."

"In the High Street"

Glory to God in the highest, and on earth peace, good will toward men (v. 14).

It is easy for religion that does not find its source in the heart to go off on a tangent. The externalist chooses his own area of concern. In contrast, the person who has God within his heart gets his concerns from the heart of God. He will have "blind spots," all persons do. But he will ask forgiveness for that.

One of the requirements for sainthood in the Roman Catholic Church is that the person must have been "radiant." In fair and in foul weather, in hard times and in good times, in victory and in defeat, there must have been that quality of "radiance." The chances are slim that you or I will ever be "canonized." We do not desire it from men, and our understanding of the Scriptures forbids us to expect it from God. But don't you like the emphasis upon "radiance"? Do you not feel that it is an authentic Christian note?

External conditions have little to do with whether a person is radiant or not. Comfortable people, physically, are often very drab. Some of the most radiant persons we have known were those in dire circumstances.

E. P. Dickey got two good sermons during one hour of worship. That, I would say, is better than the average! One of the sermons came from the pulpit, where a man of God had made faithful preparation. The second came from a stained-glass window. A slight defect in the glass obscured one letter in the Scripture quotation, making it read: "Glory to God in the high st." That is what religion of the heart does. It puts glory to God in the high streets—and in the low streets of life.

> He is a portion of the loveliness
> Which once he made more lovely.
>
> —Percy Bysshe Shelley

"Whenever I Doubt of Life"

He is before all things, and by him all things consist [hold together] (v. 17).

Lloyd C. Douglas has an interesting passage about a little boy in his novel, *The Robe*. The boy's name was Jonathan and he had been given a beautiful donkey that he cherished. Yet, the next day he gave the donkey to another. Marcellus, the Roman, thought about that and mused: *This Jesus must have been a man of gigantic moral power. He has been dead and in his grave for a year now, but he had stamped himself so indelibly onto the house of Justus that even this child has been marked! . . . It was as if this Jesus had taken die and hammer— and had poured the image of his spirit into this Galilean gold, converting it into the coin of his kingdom! The man should have lived! He should have been given a chance to impress more people! A spirit like that—if it contrived to get itself going—could make the world over into a fit habitation for men of good will!*[10]

Follow that with another picture. From history there emerges a glamorous character who caught the world's imagination during the First World War. He was known as Lawrence of Arabia, an Englishman who sought to influence the desert tribes of Arabia to cast their lot with the Allies. The tribesmen said to him: "If you lead us, you must eat the same food that we eat, find shelter in the same tents in which we dwell, accept the same risks that we accept, meet the same difficulties that we meet, live the same life that we live, and live it better than we do." And, "The Word was made flesh, and dwelt among us, . . . full of grace and truth" (John 1:14).

And now a Scotsman's tribute. George Matheson, the blind preacher-poet, wrote:

O Son of Man, whenever I doubt of life, I think of thee. Nothing is so impossible as that thou shouldest be dead. I can imagine the hills to dissolve in vapor and the rivers to empty themselves in sheer exhaustion, but I feel no limit in thee. Thou never growest old to me. Last century is old, last year is an obsolete fashion, but thou art not obsolete. Thou art abreast of all the centuries. I have never come up to thee, modern as I am.

What a Doctrine!

Of a truth I perceive that God is no respecter of persons (v. 34b).

One of our dearly bought truths, greatly loved, long cherished but weakly proclaimed and poorly demonstrated, is the *priesthood of all believers.* Who is a priest?

The Roman Catholic says that a priest is one who has, through ordination, been given the right to receive the authority to administer the sacraments of the church and to grant absolution to individuals. By the granting of absolution, they mean "a judicious act," an act that is performed by the spoken word and is effective even if the word is spoken in jest. According to Roman Catholics one is absolved of one's sin in no other way than by and through the priests—priests as a class. These, and these alone, have this power and therefore can retain or remit sins. So, they have in their hands the keeping of the keys of the kingdom. For unquestioned obedience, salvation is guaranteed.

Who is a priest? Baptists, and a large portion of the Protestant world, answer: A priest is one, anyone, everyone who has voluntarily believed on and accepted the Lord Jesus Christ as personal Savior; that person has thereby become a representative of God through Christ for the Christian group. He is one, anyone, everyone, who goes to God for the people and comes from God to the people. He has been given this privilege and required to assume this responsibility, not because of some ordination at the hands of men, but by reason of the fact that he has willingly and voluntarily accepted the redemption revealed and made available by the sacrificial death of Christ. He has just as much authority as his brother in Christ, every brother in Christ, that much, and no more.

Between those two positions "a great gulf is fixed." It is difficult to see how there can be compromise on that.

"A Deed of Gift"

Ye turned to God from idols to serve the living and true God (v. 9b).

Christians often suffer as non-Christians never do. The Christian assumes burdens, undertakes tasks, endures persecution, experiences separation, pledges life and fortune as a non-Christian never does.

One area in which a Christian suffers as a non-Christian does not is in self-surrender. We are sinners; we love self. We suffer in the surrender of self. The surrender of self is the hardest thing that a Christian is called upon to do for Christ. Stanley Jones once said that he had known missionaries who had given up everything for Christ, everything but self.

It is said that a lawyer once came to Dwight L. Moody, the evangelist, held out an important-looking legal envelope, saying, "I want you to take this." Mr. Moody looked at the sealed and waxed envelope and said, "Take it away; this has nothing to do with me; I know nothing about legal matters." "But," said the man, "it does have to do with you, it grows out of your preachng." Mr. Moody said, "Then what is it?" Here is the story:

"It is a deed of gift," said the lawyer. "I have been attending your meetings. You kept saying, 'Give yourself to God.' I felt like it; I wanted to do it; but I did not know how to do it. All of a sudden it came to me. I said to myself, *Why again and again, in your profession as a lawyer, you have executed a deed of gift for a client. A certain sum has been transferred to a child or to a friend or to an institution.* So, I said to myself, *I'll do that for God.* So, this morning when I went to my office I got a deed of gift drawn up. I gave my life to my Savior. Then, sir, I called my office staff in and got them to witness to my signature. So, here is my deed. I give myself to God."

"Great Expectations"

According to my earnest expectation and my hope (v. 20).

Years ago I lived in a part of the country where a giant dam was to be built. Thousands of acres of land was bought from farmers. A date was set for flooding the entire area. All families would have to be relocated, with a period of four years time. During those four years the people lived in a mood of "so what." There was no future for the old homes, everything would have to go, no use making improvement to the homes, farms, barns, fields, and orchards. The people were robbed of all "expectations."

For twelve months I pastored a church where the building was to be sold. We were rebuilding on a different location. There was no incentive to "keep up" the property. We were robbed of all "expectations" for the present location.

By way of contrast, let a life be lived in the firm expectation of everlasting life—in the full belief that the life we live in the here and now will affect our eternal welfare in the there and then, that "there shall never be one lost good"—then all that we do takes on a divine aspect.

It is only the uninformed who say that a belief in the afterlife robs the present life of incentive. The Christian says, "This is my Father's world." He says, "The earth is the Lord's and the fulness thereof; the world, and they that dwell therein" (Ps. 24:1). When he says this, he knows that *every* living soul, *every* foot of earth, *every* hour of time, *every* opportunity for service to man, *every* privilege for giving glory to God has eternal significance.

The love of heaven makes one heavenly.

—SHAKESPEARE

Keys, Chests, and Breasts

Thou art beautiful, O my love (v. 4a).

James Howell wrote, "As keys do open chests, so letters open breasts." That is as true in the home between members of the family as anywhere. The Bible is a family book. If you doubt it, read through it and be alert for all such references. For causing the fires of love to burn more brightly, for deepening the spirit of gratitude for each other, for sheer joy and beauty of life, the written word is of great value.

Recently my wife was returning home after an engagement. I was unable to be there to meet her. The next best thing? The written word, a very personal note. Laying hold of a valued quotation, making it my own, I wrote: "Welcome home! I love you: more than yesterday, not as much as tomorrow." The friend who brought my wife home, saw the note and said, "You lucky dog!"

Leave the notes in frequented places: by the telephone, under the breakfast plate, on her, his, pillow, stuck to the vacuum cleaner handle, taped to the steering wheel of the car, tucked in his suitcase when he is leaving on a trip. If you cannot come forth with an original that does justice to your ardor, lay "violent hands" upon the oft used; your spouse will give you credit for research! "Sweetheart, you are not a woman; you are a memorable occasion!" "Honey, you are pure joy and the only way you could create unhappiness for me is being absent." "Wow! but you're great!" "When God made you, I think he just sat around the rest of the day feeling real good!"

Henry Luce, of *Life* and *Time* fame, received a letter from one of his subscribers. It informed Luce that the man's wife was going to leave him until she read the article in *Life* about divorce suits. "Now she says she's going to stay. Please cancel my subscription."

Husbands, love your wives, even as Christ also loved the church (Eph. 5:25).

"I Think You're Wonderful!"

And the Lord turned the captivity of Job when he prayed for his friends (v. 10*a*).

In his beautiful book, *A Touch of Wonder*, Arthur Gordon tells of making an enriching discovery. His mother was leaving the old place that had been home for the family for nearly one hundred and fifty years. Over those years a tremendous amount of family possessions, mostly junk, had accumulated from basement to attic. Obviously, most of this could not be moved; he and his sisters were asked to check through the accumulation and to discard everything except what the family could not afford to part with.

He found a trunkful of old letters, grimy with dust, faded by time. The letters were not of great historical significance, nor were they passionate love letters. They were simply a chronicle of the lives, actions, and reactions of ordinary people. The surprising thing was the freedom of the letters in expressing sentiment and gratitude. The reserve and restraint that is so familiar today was not present in those old, faded letters.

When someone did something that was good, there were those to commend. When a person was cherished, there were those who said so. Mr. Gordon said that again and again he found such words as: "When you left, I felt as if the sun had stopped shining." "Have I told you lately what a wonderful person you are?" "Never forget how we admire and love you."

There were faith, affection, approval, encouragement, congratulations, sympathy, humor. The trials, the victories of life were shared. A person did not walk alone. A written note spoke from and for the heart.

> Your words have caused men to stand on their feet.
>
> —JOB

Assignment—Vacation

Six days thou shalt do thy work, and on the seventh day thou shalt rest (v. 12a).

"You see," wrote Henry Van Dyke, "we are all scholars, boarding scholars, in the School of Life, from the moment when birth matriculates us to the moment when death graduates us. We never really leave the big school, no matter what we do. But my point is this: the lessons that we learn when we do not know that we are studying are often pleasantest, and not always the least important. There is a benefit as well as a joy in finding out that you can lay down your task for a little while without being disloyal to your duty. Play-time is a part of school-time, not a break in it."

No matter how much you love your work—and I have loved mine—there is an unequaled exhilaration when the last bag is placed in the trunk of the car; the casual clothes and walking shoes have been hung and stuffed; the last box filled with cherished books; the paper boy, milkman, and postman informed; the pets have been taken to the kennels; the last call has been made to the office; the family stuffed into the bulging car . . . and you are safely out on "the road again," leading to your vacation spot.

You are out of reach of the telephone; only the most urgent mail will reach you. You are on "Assignment Vacation!" It may be the mountains, "I am homesick for my mountains, my heroic mother hills," you sing. Or, with Masefield you shout, "I must go down to the seas again, to the lonely sea and sky."

Charles Lamb once wrote of old Simeon Stylites, the first professional pole-sitter, that he had a great talent for "doing nothing." That does call for a special talent; and, we need to learn how to do a little "doing nothing." But, in my own case, a little of "nothing" goes a long way. But a few hours of work, along with careful planning for the year ahead, the rest of the day spent with family and books and on nature's trails! And time flies!

"One Solemn Watchword"

A word spoken in due season, how good is it! (v. 23*b*).

Words to be effective must have a timeliness about them, they have to be spoken "in time" or "on time." It is this that the proverb indicates, "A word spoken in due season, how good is it!"

If spoken in time, words can be more encouraging than actions. For example, why is Nathan Hale so firmly anchored in American history and lore? He was a brilliant young man who volunteered for a dangerous mission. So? Thousands of young men volunteered. They, too, gave their lives for their country. Why the special honor to Hale? One of the reasons is that he said on that September morning in 1776, just before the British hanged him, "I only regret that I have but one life to give for my country." That did it! Those words were what the Revolution needed; they are what we still need. One sentence and Nathan Hale's place was secure in American history.

There are other examples. Patrick Henry was a patriot. His actions were not always as noble as some other patriots. But Patrick Henry made a speech, "I know not what course others may take, but as for me, give me liberty or give me death." With those words he would never be forgotten!

It would be difficult to estimate what the outcome of the Second World War would have been but for the words of Winston Churchill. He wanted his people to so live that if the British Empire were to endure for a thousand years men would always say that "This was our finest hour." When Churchill died, England's eighty-seven-year-old poet laureate, John Masefield, wrote:

> When, in a mess of nations overthrown,
> This England stood at bay, and stood alone,
> His figure, then commanding, stood as stone,
> Or, *speaking* uttered like the very breed
> Of Francis Drake, disaster being near,
> One solemn watchword, to have done with fear.
> Thence, with no other drumbeat, all took cheer,
> Content with such a captain, such a creed.[11]

A Lover's Quarrel

Receive us (v. 2).

Did you ever look in on a lover's quarrel? Or better, still, did you ever participate in one! Did you not almost feel that the "make-up" that followed was worth the quarrel? Do Paul's words make you think of a situation like that?

Have you ever read Tennyson's "Guinevere"? Read about Arthur's leave-taking? He says,

> . . . think not that I come to urge thy crimes;
> I, did not come to curse thee, Guinevere,
> I, whose vast pity almost makes me die
> To see thee, laying there thy golden head,
> My pride in happier summers, at my feet.
> . . . .
> All is past, the sin is sinn'd, and I,
> Lo, I forgive thee, as Eternal God
> Forgives! do thou for thine own soul the rest.
> . . . .
> . . . I love thee still.
> Let no man dream but that I love thee still.

Arthur did not forgive as the "eternal God forgives." There was in Arthur's forgiveness something akin to God's forgiveness. However, as you read the words of Paul on forgiveness, you feel that he was even closer to the forgiveness of God.

Paul was not like the husband and wife who had quarreled, "Come, now," he said, "you agreed to forgive and forget." "Yes, I did," she shot back, "but I don't want you to forget that I have forgiven and forgotten!"

The books of a beloved doctor were examined after his death. A number of accounts had been crossed out with the words, "Forgive—too poor to pay." The physician's wife decided that the accounts would have to be paid; she proceeded to sue for the money. The judge asked, "Is this your husband's handwriting?" "Yes." "Then there is no tribunal in the land that can obtain this money when your husband has written the word 'Forgiven.'"

"Preparing for His Exile"

But lay up for yourselves treasures in heaven (v. 20).

Freud once told a beautiful story about a shipwrecked sailor. The sailor was saved by the natives on a tiny island. The man was surprised at the treatment he received from the natives. They placed him upon a throne and obeyed his every wish. He soon learned that it was the custom of these strange people to make a person their king for one year; during that year the people did everything he commanded. The sailor was delighted with this arrangement until he asked what had become of the former kings. He then learned that at the end of the year the kings were exiled to a tiny, uninhabited island where they starved and died of thirst. But for one year he was their king and they would do his bidding.

So the sailor put the natives to work making boats, transporting fruit trees, flowers, and shrubs, as well as building houses and digging wells on the barren island. Consequently, when the time came for his exile, he was sent not to a barren island to die of hunger and thirst, but to a paradise of beauty and plenty.

The Bible is clear in its teachings about how a person lives, but what he does with his possessions will relate to his future status. A person is judged according to the deeds done in the body. We are admonished to make friends of "the mammon of unrighteousness" (Luke 16:9). We are warned to "lay up treasures in heaven." If a person does not properly handle the gifts of mammon here, what right has he to think that he will be entrusted with the gifts of the kingdom? This certainly does not indicate that a person gets into the kingdom by his works and gifts. Only the love and death of Christ can get us in, but what we do, how we live, will have something to do with the treasures in the life to come.

The War Is Over

Neither shall they learn war any more (v. 3).

One bitter cold morning in February, 1958, a hunter stumbled into the police station in northern Japan and mumbled, "I've seen it; I've seen it!" The man looked as if he had seen a ghost. The police commissioner was unable to get anything out that made sense, but he was convinced that the man had seen something. A search party was organized, and they started looking. Accompanied by the frightened hunter, they waded through the snow; they combed every inch of the territory, it seemed, where the hunter said he had seen "it," and found nothing. The search party was at the point of giving up when one of the detectives poked what looked like a pile of leaves under an overhanging bank. The mass of leaves "exploded"; an apparition arose; a pair of dark eyes stared out from a dirt-encrusted face. "It" tried to speak but could scarcely make itself understood. "It" put its fingertips together in an attitude of prayer and bowed thrice; the searchers decided that whatever "it" was, "it" was human and more frightened than they.

Finally the story came out. He, "it," was Liu Liang-i. He was forty-six years old. He had been captured by the Japanese fifteen years earlier and brought from Shantung Province. He had made his escape from his captors and for fifteen years had been hiding out. He had experienced no communication with any human being in all that time. He knew nothing of what was going on; he did not know that the war had been over for thirteen years; he thought the Japanese were still his enemies and that if he showed himself he surely would be killed.

With all the power and ability at his disposal, Paul sought to let people, all peoples, know that "the war is over." That Christ came to reconcile us to God, not God to us. For God was not mad at his children—he was in Christ reconciling the world unto himself.

A Delayed Answer

Many waters cannot quench love, neither can the floods drown it (v. 7a).

Joseph Fort Newton, eminent clergyman and journalist, once wrote a letter to a child on her first birthday, telling her the kind of woman he hoped she would become. The child's mother kept the letter and on the daughter's seventeenth birthday gave it to her. The girl answered the letter, sending Dr. Newton her picture, and telling him the kind of young woman she considered herself to be. She had not "sprouted wings," but she did consider herself a normal, wholesome, happy American girl, and she was deeply grateful for the letter. The letter reached Dr. Newton in England where he was living at the time. Later, when he was on a speaking tour in Dallas, Texas, the young woman came and introduced herself and the young man to whom she was engaged to marry.

I have in my library a copy of the letter that Robert Browning wrote to his friend, Alfred, Lord Tennyson, on the eve of Tennyson's eightieth birthday. The letter reads:

> My dear Tennyson: Tomorrow is your birthday—indeed, a memorable one. Let me say that I associate myself with the universal pride of our country in your glory, and in its hope that for many and many a year to come we may have your very self among us—secure that your poetry will be a delight to all those appointed to come after. And for my own part, let me say further, I have loved you dearly, may God bless you and yours.

> At no moment from first to last of my acquaintance with your works, or friendship with yourself, have I had any other feeling, expressed or kept silent, than this which an opportunity allows me to utter—I am and ever shall be, my dear Tennyson, admiringly and affectionately yours,

> —ROBERT BROWNING

The writer of Proverbs says, "A man is judged by his praise." And Seneca, the Roman philosopher wrote, "There is as much greatness of mind in acknowledging a good turn as in doing it." When did you acknowledge in a letter the good that someone did?

"Murder Most Foul"

And the Lord said unto Cain, Where is Abel thy brother (v. 9a).

In the suggested Bible passage for today there are two "firsts"—the first recorded human death and the first question addressed to God by man. We are not sure how Cain killed his brother Abel; we do not know what kind of instrument was used. There are many ways to kill. Some murders are committed quickly; some occur over a long period of time.

On December 4, 1961, the *San Francisco Chronicle* carried a report of an address by Dr. Fred T. Kolouch, surgeon, of Twin Falls, Idaho. He was speaking to the delegates of the Western Surgical Association meeting in San Francisco. Dr. Kolouch stated that conversation could be as dangerous as bacterial infection. He further declared that patients in deep anesthetic sleep might be susceptible to suggestions, inadvertent remarks made by operating surgeons, or even silence, to the point that they might be literally scared to death. Dr. Kolouch affirmed that there were cases on record where the patient had been so deeply influenced by a remark that before the patient could recover it was necessary to put the patient in a hypnotic state and remove the negative suggestion. Frightful!

Suggestions that are discouraging, demeaning, fear-inspiring, have probably taken a larger toll of life than we realize. In contrast, recall that wonderful compliment paid to Job, "Your words have caused men to stand on their feet." If the words could be true, there are few words of approval that we would rather have spoken of us.

> He who is good is free, though he be slave;
> he that is evil, a slave, though he be a king.
>
> —AUGUSTINE

"Ol' Man Adam and His Chillun"

And the Lord God called unto Adam, and said unto him, Where art thou? (v. 9).

In Adam's fall, we sinned all." We have quoted it, sung it, and practiced it! On the recognition of inherited sin, great systems of theology have been anchored.

Roark Bradford's book, *Ol' Man Adam an' His Chillun*, has a good title; for Adam is old, and we are certainly his "chillun," and there is the suggestion of an ancestor problem. Roy L. Laurin has a book of biographical sermons called *Meet Yourself in the Bible* in which he affirms that in the characters of the Bible you can find yourself and your relatives, that all problems and difficulties have been set forth in characters of the Bible.

One of the loveliest scenes in the Bible is the picture we have in the early chapters of Genesis of the confidence, communion, and fellowship that existed between God and Adam and Eve.

In entrusting to Adam the keeping and dressing and naming and enjoying all the garden, save the "tree which is in the midst of the garden," God gave man a great responsibility. This responsibility would not have been bestowed had there not been faith in man on the part of God.

From the beginning of time God has invited man to be a "fellow laborer" with God, not as a servant but as a son. Even here in the early pages of the Bible are suggested the words Jesus had the father speak to his elder son, "Thou art ever with me, and all that I have is thine" (Luke 15:31).

> Thou madest us for thyself, and our hearts are
> restless, until they rest in thee.
>
> —AUGUSTINE

"Too Close to My Price!"

Arise, O God, judge the earth: for thou shalt inherit all nations (v. 8).

It is difficult to be just in the home and family relationships. It is easier to be just to the neighbor's child than it is to your own. It is easier to be courteous to your neighbor's wife than it is to be courteous to your own wife! We make allowances for the neighbor; we seek additional facts before we blame; frequently, it is not so with those who are closest to us.

An outstanding example of this insensitivity to those nearest to us, is John Wesley's letter to his wife:

> Suspect me no more, asperse me no more, provoke me no more; do not any longer contend for mastery, for power, for money, for praise; be content to be a private, insignificant person, known and loved by God and me. Of what importance is your character to mankind? If you were buried just now, or if you had never lived, what loss would it be to the cause of God?

We do not like to admit it but we judge, and are judged, by less than adequate standards. We are judged by race, by culture, or lack of it, by our economic status, by the clothes we wear, or do not wear, by politics and religious affiliation. We are judged, and judge, by association. Someone has said that before we judge another by his associates it should be remembered that Judas Iscariot traveled in the best of company.

A famous story tells of the captain who was maintaining a blockade of one of the Southern ports during the War Between the States. Blockade runners approached him with a big bribe if he would turn his back while they piloted their ship past his blockade. He said no. They came back with the suggestion of a larger bribe. His answer was no. They came back a third time, with an even bigger bribe. This time the old captain leaped to his feet and shouted, "Out, out, get out; you are getting too close to my price!"

"You Might Have Been"

Our light affliction, which is but for a moment (v. 17a).

Recall the story of Joseph. About the best thing that ever happened to him was his "pit experience." He was a spoiled, egotistical, selfish youngster. He became competent, big, generous, and an unselfish provider. And, it looks as if it was hardship, the "pit," that had much to do with it.

Some years ago there appeared a delightful book, *Mr. Smedley's Guest.* Mr. Smedley was rich; Mr. Smedley was influential; Mr. Smedley was concerned with "things"—stocks and bonds, houses and lands, and holdings. One evening the family went out and left Mr. Smedley alone in the house. He began to nod and doze.

He was awakened by the entrance of a guest, an uninvited guest. At first Mr. Smedley was angry that anyone would enter his home unbidden. However the visitor was so charming that Mr. Smedley was soon delighted that he had come.

The guest talked charmingly and learnedly of many things in which Mr. Smedley, himself, had at one time been interested. The guest talked about the book that Mr. Smedley had written, which had made such an impression on the world. At first he could not recall having written the book, but the guest described it with such clarity that Mr. Smedley finally remembered it in detail. The guest went over to the piano and played one of Mr. Smedley's own compositions. At first he could not remember having written the composition, but as the guest played it all came back to him. Finally, when the guest arose to go, Mr. Smedley expressed his delight with the visit, but said that he did not get the guest's name. The guest replied, *"I am the man you might have been."*

Perhaps if Mr. Smedley had been thrown into a pit?

On Serving an Apprenticeship

Is not this the carpenter? (v. 3a).

Walter Smith has a little poem in which he talks about the dearness of the cross and the tomb in which the Savior lay. Then the poet goes on to say that, while all this is true, still Jesus walked the same road and bore the same load when he made common things for God in the shop at Nazareth. It was at the baptism that the voice of God came, "This is my beloved Son, in whom I am well pleased." Yet, Jesus had not preached a sermon, healed a lame limb, or raised anyone from the dead. He had been in training, that was well pleasing to God. Preparation for service is within the will and purpose of God no less than service itself; indeed, can you be sure where one begins and the other ends?

Where are you serving your apprenticeship? Is the place plain, hard, and unromantic? Do you wonder if any good can come out of your Nazareth?

There is a story about a plain old Scot and his four sons working in a field noted for its barren soil. A tourist watched the five digging in a cabbage patch where the plants could scarcely be seen for the rocks. Addressing the father, the tourist asked, "Tell me, what *can* you raise on this rocky hillside?" The old Scot gave him a withering look, raked a dirty fist across his sweating face, and all but spat out his answer, "Men!" he said.

When God called Moses to lead the children of Israel out of Egypt, Moses was keeping sheep on the backside of the desert. There God said to him, "Put off thy shoes . . . for the place whereon thou standest is holy ground" (Ex. 3:5). I lived near Stanford University. There beneath a window in the chapel with a picture of Jesus in the carpenter shop are these words:

The highest service may be prepared for and done in the humblest surroundings. In silence, in waiting, in obscure, unnoticed offices, in years of uneventful, unrecorded duties, the Son of God grew and waxed strong.

"God's Family at Home"

Behold, how good and pleasant it is for brethren to dwell together in unity (v. 1a).

In his commentary on the Gospel of Mark, William Barclay tells the story of a great artist who was commissioned to paint a fine window for a great church. His subject was the lines in the hymn, "Around the throne of God in heaven, thousands of children stand." The artist worked hard; he fell in love with his task. Finally the window was finished; he went to bed and fell asleep.

During the night he seemed to hear a noise in his studio. He went to investigate. There he saw a stranger with a brush and palette working at the artist's picture. "Stop," cried the artist, "you will ruin my picture." "It seems you have already done that," said the stranger. "You have many colors on your palette, but you have used only one for the faces of the children. Who told you there are only children with white faces in heaven?" The artist said he had just thought that way. Then the stranger began to paint the faces of the children: red, yellow, brown, black, white.

"Who are you?" demanded the artist of the stranger. "Once in the long ago," said the stranger, "I said, 'Let the children come unto me and forbid them not, for of such is the kingdom of heaven.' I am still saying that."

The dream ended and the artist rushed to the studio. The faces of all the children were white. He seized his brush and began to use his colors. When the committee came for the picture, they were pleased. They said, "Why, it's God's family at home!"

> We build an altar here, and pray
> That Thou wilt show Thy face,
> Dear Lord, if Thou wilt come to stay,
> This home we consecrate today
> Will be a holy place.
>
> —LOUIS F. BENSON

"On Painting Seven Bishops"

Give to him that asketh thee (v. 42a).

When the English artist, Sir William Orpen, set himself to the task of painting the portrait of the Archbishop of Canterbury, Cosmo Gordon Lang, he soon learned that he had a difficult task. He finally said, "I see seven archbishops. Which shall I paint? There is the proud and ambitious prelate; there is the busy executive; here I see a genuine, sincere, passionate preacher of the gospel . . . Which one shall I paint?" Conflict.

That strife is within and without. There is strife between man and his better self, between groups, classes, political parties, economic philosophies, sections of the country, nations of the world. A tourist stopped at a service station and was surprised to see a sign, "I am a 200-percent American!" Being curious, the tourist asked what the sign meant. The attendant said, "Well, you know about 100-percent Americans; they are the ones who hate this group or that group; well, the boss, now, he hates everybody; so, I say he is a '200-percent American.' "

At times we seem to dislike people just for the conflict itself; we would be hard pressed to explain just why we dislike this person or that group.

> I do not love thee, Doctor Fell,
> The reason why I cannot tell;
> But this alone I know full well,
> I do not love thee, Doctor Fell
>
> —THOMAS BROWN

The cost of these conflicts is enormous. The cost of wars, the cost of strikes, the cost of domestic strife is bankrupt nations, thousands out of work, divorce courts crowded. And, there is strife within the churches and denominations. God alone can estimate the cost in terms of weak evangelism and lukewarm kingdom building. "Blessed are the peacemakers: for they shall be called children of God" (Matt. 5:9).

The Widest Gate

And I shall dwell in the house of the Lord for ever (v. 6b).

F. W. Boreham, the Australian preacher-storyteller, paints a beautiful picture of a dream. He saw a marvelously beautiful city. On asking its name, he was told that it was known as the "City of Blessedness." The city had eight gates. Each gate was pure gold and over each was a carved motto.

All the gates seemed to be the same size, except one. This gate was several times as large as all the others and the traffic was much greater at that gate; the traffic was so great that he was unable to read the motto above it. The other mottoes could be easily read; one read, "Blessed are the poor in spirit." Other gates were marked for those who mourn, the meek, the merciful, the pure in heart, the peacemakers, the persecuted. He wondered about the gate that was so much larger, where the crowds were so much greater. Many people were turning from the other gates and coming to the large one.

He joined one of the groups and asked what was the meaning of their going from one gate to another. They told him they had come hoping to enter the city of the blessed, but there seemed to be no gate that would admit them. They were not poor in spirit, though they would like to be. They did not mourn for their sins and the sins of the world as they knew they should. They were not meek, though they wished they were. So, they had gone from gate to gate, to everyone but the big gate; it was so crowded they had not tried it.

On making inquiry, however, they learned of a truth about the city of blessedness. Just as there is sin in the desire for sin, so, there is grace in the desire for grace. In the desire for meekness, purity of heart, there was merit. So, the large gate was for these. It's motto was, "Blessed are they which do hunger and thirst after righteousness: for they shall be filled." While David was not allowed to build the Temple, the Lord told him it was good that he desired to do so.

"I Had to Preach"

His commandments are not grievous (v. 3*b*).

One evening years ago, I spoke at a youth banquet down on the Florida Keys. The pastor was Dr. John L. White, well into his nineties. Yet, he was vigorous, the young people loved him, crowded about him, loved to talk with him. On the return trip to Miami, I said, "Dr. White, what is the meaning of this? More than fifty years ago you were pastor of the church that I now serve; a dozen years ago you retired; you are close to a hundred years in age. Yet, tonight you were alive, vital, and effective with young people; explanation, please?"

He was quiet for just a moment and then spoke, "Well, Son, I'll tell you about that. My wife died a few years ago, and a few days before she died, we had a long talk together. We talked about our children, the churches we had served; we talked about you, as you now are pastor of one of those churches." His voice dropped almost to a whisper, " 'Lover,' that is what she called me, 'Lover, I have asked God to let me live longer than you in order that I might continue to love and care for you. But God has denied my request. I am going first, and that is all right. I shall be waiting for you. But, I want you to promise me that when I am gone, you will preach Christ; preach him as only you can preach him!' You know," he said, "she was prejudiced about that."

Dr. White became silent; I waited for I was sure he had not given me all the story. Then he said, "Son, I had to preach! And, Son, I tell you, I have a freedom and a joy in preaching today that I have never had before!"

And now the words of the Savior:

Go ye into all the world and preach!

"I Got a Glory"

Righteousness shall look down from heaven (v. 11b).

O ne of my favorite writers, Archibald Rutledge, relates a lovely story about "Sam," the engineer on a tugboat on a lazy South Carolina river. The writer says that of all the abodes known to men the engine room of a small tugboat on a lazy river is the worst! The odors from the kitchen, smokestack, and engine combine to make reaching the farther shore a greatly desired goal!

Dr. Rutledge had often crossed the river on the old tugboat, *The Foam*. But on one memorable day he climbed aboard and saw a new engineer! Sam sat in the doorway of the engine room reading his Bible. He was immaculate in person and in dress. There was a strange splendor of ancient wisdom in his eyes. In his countenance there was evidence of a deep peace—peace with himself, God, and the world.

And the engine! A thing of beauty. Its brasses shone. Gone was the bilge water beneath the seat. Gone were the filth, stench, and grime. Instead, there was order: clothes, brooms, mops, and tools were all in place, and there sat the master of the transformation, quietly reading his Bible.

The change was worth investigating. How on earth and water did such a transformation come about? "Cap'n," said Sam, "it's just dis way: 'I got a glory!' "

The eloquent words were strangely reminiscent of words that could be found in the Book that Sam was reading. "The Lord will give grace and glory" (Ps. 84:11). "Let the whole earth be filled with his glory" (Ps. 92:18). Remember the words of the old spiritual, "I know the Lord has laid his hand on me." Sam had his glory!

"Just Dumb About Different Things"

Then Pilate entered into the judgment hall again, and called Jesus (v. 33a).

Every person is judged by God in Christ. This is the judgment that Pilate faced. Certainly Pilate judged himself. Pilate was judged by his superiors in Rome, by his fellow Romans in Palestine, and by the Jews in Palestine. But, most important, Pilate was judged by Jesus.

In the spring of 1941 William McChesney Martin, Jr., was inducted into the U.S. Army as a private. Early in his training he had real difficulty in properly executing some maneuvers in close-order drill. The sergeant in charge barked: "I've seen some stupid people, but you are by far the worst. It's a lucky thing you got in the army, for you would never be able to make a living anywhere else." Interesting! For, you see, before Martin was inducted into the army he was president of the New York Stock Exchange. Human judgment is subject to correction!

Every person must face the judgment of self; we must stand before the bar of conscience and receive sentence. We are limited in our ability to rightly judge ourselves; the sentence may be too severe, it may not be severe enough. Every person must stand before the bar of others. A person may say, even boast, that he does not care what others think of him; it is usually not the truth.

Macauley, writing about Gibbon's reasons for the rapid spread of Christianity as opposed to the relative stagnation of the Jewish faith, commented: "It was before Deity embodied in a human form, walking among men, partaking of their infirmities, weeping over their graves, slumbering in the manger, bleeding on the cross, that the prejudices of the Synagogue . . . and the swords of thirty legions, were humbled in the dust."

> When the saints and the sinners
> Shall be parted right and left,
> Are you ready for that day to come?
> Are you ready, are you ready?
> Are you ready for the judgment day?
>
> —W. L. THOMPSON

The Attractiveness of Goodness

He turned to the woman, and said unto Simon (v. 44a).

There are few scenes in the Scriptures which show the irresistible attractiveness of Jesus as this story does. Let not familiarity with the incident close your eyes to the bold act of the woman. Every law and social custom of the land, every sentiment and courteous reserve, was against her appearing at this public and social gathering as she did. Yet, she was there, drawn by the irresistible attraction of perfect goodness joined with perfect love. Goodness, in and of itself, is not always attractive. The little girl's prayer is understandable: "Dear God, make all the bad people good and all the good people nice." Simon was a perfect example of the appropriateness of that prayer.

Along with attractive goodness, this story reveals Jesus' unlimited ability and warm eagerness to forgive. Let us never end, or grow tired of, reminding ourselves that there is no limit to the forgiving love of Christ.

In *The Secret Woman,* Eden Phillpotts has Ann and Salome meet in the churchyard. Salome had stolen Ann's husband, who has since died. Ann offers her own forgiveness to Salome and urges that Salome receive the forgiveness which God offers. Salome feels that she is too small and insignificant for God to notice—that he will not forgive. Ann cries out: "Naught's too small for Him and naught's too great. I've learned that, and I've learned what God's forgiveness means. Ours be but the shadow of his. He comes three parts of the way . . . The haste o' God. Quicker'n lightning. A sigh of sorrow brings Him or one humble thought."

> Dear Lord and Father of mankind,
>   Forgive our foolish ways;
> Reclothe us in our rightful mind;
>   In purer lives thy service find,
> In deeper rev'rence, praise.

> —JOHN GREENLEAF WHITTIER

Christ, the Master of All Things

Except a man be born again (v. 3*b*).

Christ never can become one's master until one has been born again, born from above, and born of the Spirit.

John Ruskin was a brilliant and gifted individual. No thoughtful person assesses nineteenth-century England without considering the man. This brilliant man had a redeeming experience a few days before Good Friday in 1852. He was seriously ill at the time. He wrote about his experience and the record has been preserved.

Ruskin started thinking about his past life, the fruit of it, the joy of it, the hard work of it; all these had passed away and he found no comfort in any of it. He thought of his studies of the Bible. He found no comfort there either—yet he decided that he had no comfort in the past; he had no faith and hope for the future.

Ruskin was a very sick man. As he thought of his condition, he decided that, despite his feelings, he would trust and act as the Bible directed. If the instruction were not true, he would be no worse off. So, he determined to believe in and take Christ as his Master in all things. He testified that having reached this decision, he fell asleep. When he arose in the morning, he felt a deep sense of peace.

Medical science is not too confident about repairing old tissue; psychological science has questions about changing the foundations of character after a person reaches thirty. Educational persons are strong for working with the young. Even many branches and communions of religion rely almost solely upon the children for their recruits. "How can a man be born when he is old?" Good question. And, the answer? Well, now, flesh can take us far; it cannot take us into the kingdom. The earthly cannot produce the heavenly. But while the new birth cannot come from the flesh, it can come from the Spirit.

> Lord, as of old at Pentecost
> Thou didst thy pow'r display,
> With cleansing, purifying flame,
> Descend on us today.
>
> —CHARLES H. GABRIEL

209

"Someone to Die for Them"

While we were yet sinners, Christ died for us (v. 8b).

It is a "mad" story, and it comes to us from Taiwan of two hundred years ago. The story goes that the inhabitants of the island at that time were murderous headhunters. The Chinese, who had control of the island, sent a man by the name of Gaw Hong to be the magistrate of the island. He won the trust and affection of the people by his fair and honest dealings. Little by little the barbarous custom of headhunting was being eliminated. The deadly conflicts between the tribes were being moderated; an era of goodwill and cooperation seemed to be dawning.

But a religious feast was approaching, and the leaders of the tribes were troubled. How could they appease their gods if they did not have the heads of their enemies to offer as sacrifices? They went to Gaw Hong about the matter. He reasoned and postponed, pointing out that the old feuds between the tribes would break out again. They acknowledged that this was probably true, but they knew no other way to worship. Finally Gaw Hong gave his consent, with the understanding that they would take only one head where and when Gaw Hong directed; to this the tribesmen agreed.

When the feast day arrived, they were ready for the hunt, hunting where and when Gaw Hong had directed. The hunters waited in the dawn light; they saw the enemy approaching; the arrows found the mark. The head was severed from the body almost before the body had fallen to the ground. When the head was removed from the bag where it had been placed by the hunter, it was the head of their beloved Gaw Hong.

We are told that vows were made against headhunting that day, vows that were kept. And, it is reported, that even today, when life is hard and the going is tough, the islanders remember and long for a Gaw Hong to come and die for them. Mad? Of course, it is mad, but there is a cross on a lonely hillside.

"The Field Is the World"

The field is the world (v. 38a).

In *The Light of Asia,* Sir Edwin Arnold tells the story of Gautama Buddha's great cry of anguish and commitment. Arnold takes poetic license in telling the story, of course. Gautama was born into a home of wealth and influence. Because his father had suffered greatly he resolved that his son should not suffer; he should have all that his heart desired; he should be shielded and protected.

But one day Gautama discovered there was another world outside his sheltered palace, a world of pain and tragedy. When this discovery came, he ran outside his protected place crying, "Now I go to help the world." He gave his life for that sorrowing, suffering world. Beautiful! But we know something more wonderful and true.

God loves this world and has invested heavily in it. The writers of the New Testament ran and raced and shouted. They wanted to "wake the town and tell the people" of God's love for the whole wide *world.* "The field is the *world,*" they cried. "God so loved the *world.*" "For God sent not his son into the *world* to condemn the *world*; but that the *world* through him might be saved." They heard God say, "Go ye into all the *world.*" Unto the uttermost parts of the *earth.*" "I am debtor," Paul affirmed, "both to the Greeks, and to the Barbarians; . . . the wise, and to the unwise" (Rom. 1:14).

Once Archbishop Lang of Canterbury was preaching before King George V. The Archbishop knew that the king did not like the theme of foreign missions, but Lang was a follower of One who loved the *world,* so he had to be true to the Bible. The king was cross and said, "Am I to understand that, because I do not believe in foreign missions, I am not a Christian?" Lang answered, "Sire, I am presenting facts, not drawing conclusions."

"Were You Out There?"

They parted his raiment, and cast lots (v. 34*b*).

In *The Robe,* Lloyd C. Douglas wrote that Marcellus, the Roman soldier who was in charge of the crucifixion, was drunk when the order was carried out. However, he was not so drunk that he did not know an innocent man was being crucified. Back in his barracks he said to his gallant slave, Demetrius, "I'm dirty—outside and inside. I'm dirty and ashamed. . . . Were you there when he called on his god to forgive us? . . . He looked directly at me after he had said it. I'm afraid I'm going to have a hard time forgetting that look."

And he did. In the days, months, and years that followed he found it impossible to dismiss the crucifixion from his mind. The memory of it all but drove him mad, causing him to contemplate suicide. He would suddenly stop talking in the middle of a sentence. A strange and faraway look would come into his eyes, and he would ask a question, always the same question, "Were you out there?" If the person to whom he was speaking was poised and steady and answered, "No," then Marcellus would brighten and say, "Of course not; that is good. You should be glad." But soon the drama would be reenacted, as that strange, faraway look came into his eyes, and the question would be asked, "Were you out there?"

The event was so tremendous that he felt everyone must know about it, and it was such an awful tragedy that he felt everyone must have had some part in it; so, the question, "Were you out there?"[12]

And were you? Was I? Were we all and each "out there"? Scripture, doctrine, conscience, poetry, and song—all say that we were.

> We gibed him, as he went, with houndish glee,
>   Till his dim eyes for us did overflow;
> We cursed his vengeless hands thrice wretchedly—
>   And this was nineteen hundred years ago.

—EDWARD ARLINGTON ROBINSON

"Dark Road"

He made darkness his secret place (v. 11a).

Darkness disturbs us. We neither like it nor understand it. So much of life we do not understand; so many experiences have the quality of the unknown about them.

The problem has challenged the best minds. Philosophers and poets have tried to explain, but when all have done their best they feel like "unprofitable servants."

Three intimations may be helpful pointers to an understanding of "why" darkness. First, we live on the earth; the earth is a part of the universe; the universe is regulated by a system of laws. These laws keep the universe in tune, "universe," "one-verse," but the laws are impartial. This means that if through ignorance, disobedience, imperfection, or rebellion we oppose these laws we get hurt, there is darkness.

Second, we are bound in the "bundle of life"; we are not isolated units; we neither live nor die to ourselves. Even Robinson Crusoe had his man Friday. What others do casts light or shadows upon our paths.

Third, God has granted to us freedom of choice, freedom of will. We do not always choose wisely; sometimes we do. Wise choices tend to bring light; evil choices tend to bring darkness.

Most of the rough, steep, dark conditions of life could be placed under one or more of these facts. Whatever the explanations, it is a matter of knowing in part and prophesying in part. What we know is in the experience of the darkness itself.

> Immortal, invisible, God only wise,
> In light inaccessible hid from our eyes,
> Most blessed, most glorious, the Ancient of days,
> Almighty, victorious, thy great name we praise.

> —WALTER CHALMERS SMITH

"What Will You Do About It?"

And the Lord said unto Cain, Where is Abel thy brother? (v. 9a).

The world criticizes the churches. Some of that criticism is just, much of it, unjust. When the world criticizes us for not being sensitive to the needs of others, the world is on target.

This was once brought home to me in a disturbing way. I was minister of a downtown church. The sanctuary was a thing of quiet beauty, Gothic structure, deep wall-to-wall red carpet covered the floor, great organ, windows that told of ancient events in the Christian faith. The order of service conducted there was in keeping with the setting. On this particular morning the deacons had come forward, the offertory sentence had been spoken, the offering of the people was being received, with a background of lovely music. Then I *sensed* that something unusual had projected itself into that lovely service. Lifting my eyes and thoughts from the mood of prayer, I saw him.

He was standing by the communion table. His appearance was entirely out of keeping with everything that I have described. He was dirty, ragged, disheveled; his eyes were far back in deep sockets whose rims were red; his gaze was focused on me. How he got down one of the long, beautifully carpeted aisles without being detected and assisted, quietly of course, to an inconspicuous seat by one of our carefully groomed and well-trained ushers, I do not know, but there he stood by the communion table.

Rising from my plush chair, I bent over and asked, "Yes, what may I do for you?" He replied, "I'm hungry, what are you going to do about it?" Disturbing question, placing the "monkey" on my back.

Not to be misunderstood, it needs to be said that there is a place for quiet beauty and reverent worship. Jesus accepted, and defended, an extravagant gift of anointing. And that gift has been making its contribution for two thousand years. Still there is that "I'm hungry, what are you going to do about it!"

They Were Away from Home

Let thy servant, I pray thee, turn back again, that I may die in my own city (v. 37a).

It would be difficult to find a word picture that more adequately suggests what Christmas really is than this phrase, "Home for Christmas." Home is where the heart is, home is where peace and goodwill are, home is where warm sentiment and tender love reside, home is where God is recognized. No wonder the lovely song, "I'll Be Home for Christmas," is revived each year with its haunting suggestions of snow and mistletoe, presents "on the tree," the place where "love-light gleams."

It is not just a sense of nostalgia and lost innocence; it is more than that. It is a great theological fact: mankind is away from home, and evil is responsible. We are told that at 11:30 on the morning of November 20, 1967, America's population reached, for the first time, two hundred million persons. Yet, the figure had to be an estimate, for at least six million people were not counted. They were away from home! The census taker couldn't find them.

In a deeper sense than that millions are away from home. The Scriptures are very sure of this. It began with Adam and Eve; they were away from home when God came to visit; disobedience was the villain. Cain, their son, was driven from home; evil was responsible. Jacob fled from his home and his brother's face; greed was accountable. Joseph was sold as a slave into Egypt, away from his father's house; wickedness was responsible. The prodigal son left his father's house and wandered in a far country; sin was the culprit. While the ancient prophet says that we have all, and each, turned into his own way.

> Softly and tenderly Jesus is calling,
>   Calling for you and for me;
> See, on the portals he's waiting and watching,
>   Watching for you and for me.
> Come home, come home,
>   Ye who are weary, come home.

> —WILL L. THOMPSON

215

"... and Kissed Her"

The maid is not dead, but sleepeth (v. 24b).

A book I have in mind, long out of print, is *Beside the Bonnie Brier Bush* by Ian Maclaren. Lachlan Campbell was a hard man, a shepherd by trade but theology was his business; he was an elder in the little Scottish kirk. He had an only daughter, Flora. His wife, Flora's mother, died at the birth of the child. There came the day when Lachlan stood before the church and asked that his daughter's name be removed from the roll, for she had left home and gone into the way of sinners. He was crushed, but he did "his duty," as he saw it.

All were helpless until a sainted woman in the community, Margaret Howe, took a hand. She was an avenging angel with Lachlan. Finally she was allowed to write Flora a letter, inviting her to come home that her father was "a wearing his heart out for the sight of her." The father signed the letter, addressed the envelope. That evening he put a light in the window to burn until Flora came home.

It was night when she got off the train at the little station, a mile from her father's house. She saw the light in the window, and was afraid her father was ill. She ran, and exhausted, fell against the door. The dogs recognized her; Lachlan finally got the door open. Later she told Margaret Howe about it, in the presence of her father, saying that there were fifty words in the Gaelic for *darling* and her father used them all! "But," said Lachlan, "there is something I must say and it is not easy." He showed her the Bible where her name had been erased, saying pleadingly, "Will you ever be able to forgive me?" "Margaret," said Flora, "let me have the Book." Flora wrote and then handed it to her father. He read:

> "Flora Campbell
> Missed April 1873
> Found September 1873."

Her father fell on her neck and kissed her.

Dear Father God, never let us forget that there is joy in heaven over one sinner that repenteth. Amen.

"Lantern in My Hand"

Thy word is a lamp unto my feet, and a light unto my path (v. 105).

The above line of poetry has been engraved upon the imagination of the believing world. It is not so much that we remember it as that we cannot forget it! "Thy word is a lamp unto my feet, and a light unto my path."

"Thy word" refers to the Bible. But to the psalmist it meant more than just written words. Again and again, the psalmist's contemporaries, the prophets of God, affirmed, "The word of God came to me saying." They meant they had experienced a direct encounter with God himself. Strickland Gillilan has it, "God kept on talking when his book had gone to press." God did and God does. Of course, the true and living Word of God is Jesus Christ. John wrote, "In the beginning was the Word."

The word *lamp* in the text and the word *light* infer darkness. Were there no darkness there would be no need for a light. The text emphasizes the immediacy of the need. The lamp for the feet means that the need is very personal. Every person needs some assurance about where he will put his feet as he walks the roads of life. There is the suggestion, too, of a rough road; if the road were broad and straight and smooth, there would be no great need for a lamp, even in darkness.

Notice, in addition to the parallelism of the verse there may well be the suggestion that God's Word is a source of help in the light of day no less than in the dark of night. A lamp for the feet by night; a light, the sun, upon the path by day. The psalmist would suggest the need for God's word in the day of success as well as in the night of failure.

The truth of the text is caught up in the haunting lines by Joyce Kilmer in the poem, "Love's Lantern,"

> Because the way was steep and long
>   And through a strange and lonely land,
> God placed upon my lips a song,
>   And put a lantern in my hand.

217

July 30   **Read Revelation 22:1-5**
Between Tears and Laughter

And there shall be no more curse (v. 3a).

In *Between Tears and Laughter,* Lin Yutang reminded us that things neither make for greatness, nor do they satisfy a craving to create it. The Barretts of Wimpole Street did not have the luxury of enameled bathtubs; Charles Dickens never turned the knob of a radio or flicked the switch on a television set; Goethe never clicked the shutter of a camera; Dryden's room was neither steam-heated nor cooled by refrigeration; Bill Shakespeare never read a newspaper, nor did he ever attend the movies.

Man is a spiritual being as well as a physical animal. He cannot live long without bread, but neither can he live by bread alone. This life is temporary; man was meant to prepare for another life. "All this life," Heard said, "man must be learning to diet himself for another way of living."

Within the womb before his birth man develops eyes, but there are no colors for him to see; he develops ears, but there are no harmonies to enjoy; develops feet, though there were no paths of service to walk, and hands, though there were no deeds of usefulness to perform. Just so, man was meant to grow "spiritual organs" while he is here on earth. Through the experience of birth we emerge into a world where every normal growth and development in the womb may be employed and enjoyed. So, through Christian faith, we are convinced that there is a life and an experience beyond this life; there the hopes and the dreams and the sensitivities that cannot find adequate expression here in this life will know complete fulfillment there.

Robert Browning, the poet, was very sure that "There shall never be one lost good," that what had been good would be better, that while here "On earth the broken arcs; in heaven a perfect round."

"Too Late to Change"

Whosoever will save his life shall lose it (v. 25a).

It is difficult for a church to change its course, mend its ways. Old habits are strong; old ways of doing things are comfortable—comfortable like old bedroom shoes. Not only is it difficult to change; it may be too late to change—not too late from God's point of view but from the church's point of view. In *The Ugly American,* Major Monet says, "That's enough gentlemen. Even if you are right we don't have time to change our tactics. We're losing too fast."

In *The Shoes of the Fisherman,* the Pope is speaking to Semmering about Jean Télémond. The Pope wonders if Télémond is justified in taking the risks he does. Semmering answers: "If a man is centered upon himself, the smallest risk is too great for him, because both success and failure can destroy him. If he is centered on God, then no risk is too great, because success is already guaranteed—the successful union of creature and Creator." That is, we believe, a true observation; we know it is a thrilling thought! It reminds us of the words of the Hebrew youths when they were threatened by the king. They answered: "We would not make any defense in this matter; for the God whom we serve is able to save us from the fire of the furnace. . . . But, whether He does or not, be it known to you, O King, we will not serve your gods, or worship the image which you have set up" (Dan. 3:16-18, MLB). A trumpet blast from the "hid battlements of Eternity!"[13]

To the young Hebrews, it was a small thing whether or not God saved them from the furnace. They knew that he could save them; that was all they asked. They were willing to leave the wisdom of such a deliverance to him. Whatever happened to them in the furnace would not change God's character or his care of them.

"The Most Religious Thing You Can Do"

Come ye yourselves apart into a desert place, and rest a while (v. 31a).

Ionce heard a college president criticize one of his professors for not taking time off from his teaching. The president reported that the teacher had not missed a class in twenty-five years and was proud of the fact; instead, the teacher should have been apologetic. Had he taken time off for vacation, for attending learned society meetings, for study and renewal, he would be a better teacher.

It was the Master of life who said to his own students, "Come . . . and rest a while." Jesus knew "what was in man." He knew our abilities, the limits of our endurance, the resources at our disposal, and how best to tap these resources. Certain branches of the Christian faith have given much attention to asceticism and self-denial. It is possible to recognize contributions made by this way of life, yet see dangers in it.

To keep the body—the instrument through which our work in the world is to be done—in good repair is a Christian concern. Christianity at its best has always been concerned with the whole person. It is interested in the bodies of persons, so hospitals have been built. Christianity is interested in the minds of persons, so schools have been built next to churches. It has been interested in the emotions of persons, so, mental clinics have been given a large place in the development of church-related schools of medicine. Sometimes the most religious act a person can do is to take a vacation.

> For the beauty of the earth,
> For the glory of the skies;
> For the love which from our birth
> Over and around us lies;
> Christ our God, to thee we raise,
> This our hymn of grateful praise.

> —FOLLIOTT S. PIERPOINT

"From the Viewpoint of the Dog"

The earth is the Lord's, and the fulness thereof (v. 1*a*).

Carl Jung, the psychiatrist, quotes a patient as saying, "If only I knew that my life had meaning and purpose, there would be no silly story about my nerves." This, one suspects, is more often true for more persons than we would like to admit.

There was the little girl who had always had a crooked spine. Through many operations performed by a famous surgeon the child stood straight and walked without any deformity. The first time she looked in a full-length mirror she cried out to her mother, "Oh, Mummy, I'm crooked!" If life were to take on meaning and purpose, would we know how to interpret it?

When life has meaning, everything is seen from a different point of view. People and things are seen differently. Price tags show the real values.

In *The Higher Happiness* Ralph Sockman told about a room in the New York Museum of Natural History that was arranged as it would appear to a dog. How did they know?! In this particular room the legs of the table were made to resemble large pillars; chairs were lofty thrones; the mantel over the fireplace appeared as an unscalable precipice.

Jesus once dealt with an individual who saw men as trees walking. He dealt with people who considered people of less value than pigs. He knew persons who thought that the sabbath was more important than the persons who observed it. The point of view makes the difference. The goal and purpose of life are all important.

The man without a purpose is like a ship without a rudder— a waif, a nothing, a no man. Have a purpose in life, and, having it, throw such strength of mind and muscle into your work as God has given you.

—Thomas Carlyle

"No More Fancy Tastes"

Go, and do thou likewise (v. 37b).

When life has meaning, a person can make a useful contribution. That is no small matter. Ben Roberts in *Red Hills and Cotton* tells about seeing the following epitaph on a tombstone, "Born 1840. Died 1890. He lived 50 years." Fifty years, that is a long time. What did the man do with those years? Look at what the Master did with fifty days! His public ministry may have extended close to eighteen months, but scholars say that the events of only fifty days are recorded. Fifty days, fifty years, how were they used? George Bernard Shaw said the most fitting epitaph for many men would be, "Died at thirty, buried at sixty."

President Hutchins of Berea College told of a man visiting a mountain store. There he saw a bunch of bananas for the first time. The storekeeper invited the man to eat one. "No," said the man, "I ain't gonna." "Why not?" "Well," said the man, "I got so many tastes now I can't satisfy, I ain't gonna add no more fancy ones to it." If life has purpose and meaning new experiences and tastes can be added without fear.

As a young schoolteacher Wendell Willkie was eager that his students understand the American way of life. He gave each student three buttons: one stood for life, one for liberty, and the third for the pursuit of happiness. The next day the students were to tell the class about each button. The next day one youngster said, "Mr. Willkie, I have life and liberty, but Mama sewed 'pursuit of happiness' on brother's britches." Joy and happiness are easily lost when there is no goal and purpose in life.

Life may be long or short. If it is happy it will seem short. If it is unhappy it will seem long; time is relative.

> Firmness of purpose is one of the most necessary sinews of character, and one of the best instruments of success. Without it genius wastes its efforts in a maze of inconsistencies.
>
> —LORD CHESTERFIELD

This Is Far Better

Seek ye the Lord while he may be found (v. 6a).

The author of Ecclesiastes was certainly right when he advised that one should remember God in the days of his youth. Psalm 90 says the same, "O satisfy us early with thy mercy; that we may rejoice and be glad all our days" (v. 14). The psalmist did not want to be cheated out of a single day of joy and gladness. He seems to have known that to have joy and gladness in the evening of life, one needs to have experienced it in the morning of life as well.

An old Greek was approached by a visitor who asked, "Sir, tell me to what do you attribute your good old age?" The philosopher replied, "You see the trees and orchards I possess. I have them because I planted them as a young man. So, in youth I laid the foundation of my life. I did not wait until I was old to begin to prepare for today."

Marie Stopes wrote, "When I was sixteen, I was vain because someone praised me. My father said, 'You can take no credit for beauty at sixteen. But if you are beautiful at sixty, it will be your own doing. Then you may be proud of it and be loved for it.' "

The author of Ecclesiastes felt that only youth could know joy and beauty; he had a gloomy picture of the grave; he believed that "all is vanity." For him the best "has been." For the apostle Paul, "The best is yet to be." Christ made, and makes, the difference.

I once knew a retired educator who had been the president of a great American university. He spoke to our Rotary club on the joys of retirement and of old age. And he made me envious. I was striding along with reserves of physical strength, living off the overflow of animal energy. Here was one sitting under his own "fig tree with none to make him afraid!" Let us remember, our God is adequate for every age.

August 5 Read Psalm 40:1-5
"My Grandpa!"

Blessed is that man that maketh the Lord his trust (v. 4a).

Today's personality is a man who has given his life to young people in religious education through a great denomination. He retired a half dozen years ago. Less than a month ago I stood by his desk and heard his words: "I am happier than I have ever been. I enjoy my home and family more; my friends mean more to me, and I have more time with them; I am reading more books, and the ones I read mean more to me. My Bible speaks to my mind and heart as it has never spoken before. My church has never meant so much to me, and I am spending more time in it. Jesus is more precious to me than he has ever been before, and I face the future with more hope."

This man's friends know that his words are no idle boast but honest and experienced truth. I remember Oscar Blackwelder's story of the woman who was receiving congratulations on her birthday. One exclaimed, "Why, you are beautiful!" With a twinkle in her eye, the recipient replied, "I ought to be, I'm seventy-four!"

And there is Bennett Cerf's delicious story. It was a Christmas gathering, children, parents, and grandparents. Six-year-old Steven was a member of the group. After dinner the group watched a football game on television, that led to a discussion of sports. One said he liked prize fights the best; another golf; a third baseball. Someone finally asked young Steve which sport he liked best. He looked in turn at everybody in the room; then came over to his grandfather, throwing his arms about his neck, Steve said, "My Grandpa!"

> Leave the flurry
>   To the masses;
> Take your time
>   And shine your glasses.
>
> —OLD SHAKER VERSE

224

A Magnificent Introduction

By whom also we have access [an introduction] (v. 2a).

Look closely at the word *access* (introduction). It is a beautiful word Paul uses for introduction. It carries two pictures. It is the word used for ushering someone, introducing someone, to royalty. It is also the word employed for the approach of a worshiper to God. Paul is saying that it is Jesus who takes us into the presence and introduces us to God. Jesus opens the door and ushers us in; what we find is grace, not condemnation; salvation, not fear.

This word Paul uses for introduction has another meaning. It is the word for the place of ships; it is a harbor; it is a haven. So, Paul lets us see and know that as long as we try to sail the ship of life alone we are tempest-tossed and lost; but, when we turn these lives over to God in Christ, we are safe in the haven of life. Again, a harbor is a place from which ships go out to "do business in great waters" for their owner and master.

The salvation that Christ offers gives shelter and protection from the storms of sin and waves of death. It is salvation that saves us to usefulness and service; it sends us forth to do business and to fight battles for the King of kings and the Lord of lords. We sail forth, flying his colors, stocking his supplies, relying upon his knowledge of waters that are unknown to us; we lift anchor!

> He breaks the pow'r of canceled sin,
>   He sets the pris'ner free.
> His blood can make the foulest clean,
>   His blood availed for me.

> —CHARLES WESLEY

Work and Worship

Be ye transformed (v. 2b).

Few things show the sharp contrast between Paul's thinking and that of the Greek philosophers more clearly than the words, " . . . present your bodies a living sacrifice, holy, acceptable unto God." To the Greek the body was weak, evil, and a nuisance. The Christian believes that the body is not evil; it belongs to God; it can honor God; it can be the "temple of the Holy Spirit." Christ did not hesitate to wear flesh. Paul believes that we should take the work and service the body can perform and offer it all to God as an act of worship.

That word in Romans 12:1, translated by the King James Version as "service," translated by many as "worship," has an interesting history. It once meant to "work for hire or pay." It was the word used for one who gave himself into the employment of another, and is also used for the pay that the employer would give to the employed. It meant, not slavery, but voluntary work. The word then came to mean "to serve," but it also came to mean "that to which a man gives his whole life." The word then was used especially for "service to the gods." In the Bible it is always used for the service to and worship of God and is never used as service to man.

Then an interesting thought that comes from Paul's word. Spiritual worship is the offering of one's day and all that one does in that day to God. It is the offering of life instead of liturgy, ritual, and form. Having been inspired and supplied in church, it is demonstrated and performed in the world, in "my Father's world."

So the Christian has the opportunity to yield himself in cooperation, with God and God's children, to perform those tasks in the world that will bring God's kingdom into being.

Joy Through Pain

Rejoice with me (v. 18b).

Recall the haunting and beautiful words of George Matheson's hymn:

> O Joy that seekest me through pain,
>   I cannot close my heart to thee;
> I trace the rainbow thro' the rain,
>   And feel the promise is not vain
> That morn shall tearless be.

The joy that seeks through pain is a fitting subject for Paul's Letter to the Philippians. Professor A. T. Robertson called his book on Philippians, *Paul's Joy in Christ.*

We may feel that being a Christian should guarantee against pain. No! There are pains that are peculiar to Christians, pains that non-Christians would not have. Paul was in prison for Christ and the gospel's sake. He was saved not only by the cross, he was saved to the cross, its passion and pain.

Paul could have been occupying a place of honor and eminence; he could have been looked up to, admired, respected, and loved, had he not been a Christian! There were, too, the tensions and pain he experienced through knowledge of the pagan world. The ignorance, weakness, sin, inequalities, injustices, and cruelties that others saw and took for granted, Paul took to heart. Paul knew the "care of all the churches." It was given to him not only to live and reign with Christ but to suffer and die with him.

There was pain that was caused as a direct result of Paul's Christian faith. We sing about the comforts and security of the Christian faith; it is real, let us thank God for that! But Christianity has two sides: one, comfort and security; two, pain and agony. There is the joy that seeks through pain.

"On Speaking a Good Word"

Sirs, we would see Jesus (v. 21b).

Beside *the Bonnie Brier Bush,* which I have already mentioned, was published about eighty years ago, and it made the author, Reverend John Watson, famous. The author's pen name was Ian Maclaren. The book adorned thousands of sermons, as Edgar DeWitt Jones reminded us, on both sides of the Atlantic.

One of the finest chapters in the book is called, "His Mother's Sermon." That chapter is about a brilliant Scottish lad who was called to preach. His professors forecast great things for the youth. He was in his first church, small but renowned, because from it had gone some of Scotland's greatest preachers. It was the Lord's Day and his first sermon was approaching. He was filled with excitement and anticipation. He worked hard and long on his sermon. Being sure of his scholarship, being careful to quote unquestioned authorities, he wrote out his sermon most carefully.

With great pride he read it on Saturday night to his maiden aunt, with whom he lived. She listened carefully and said nothing. But he knew she was not pleased. He asked her what was wrong; she assured him that it was a good sermon, and it was not for her to criticize one who had such gifts. "Out with it, Auntie; what's wrong?" When he insisted, she finally reminded him that the people were humble folk and they needed comfort, for they knew hardship and great want. She ended by saying, "Oh, Laddie, be sure to say a good word for Jesus Christ." That did it. He tore up and burned his "brilliant thesis," and, with his mother's face before him, prepared another sermon in which the people saw Jesus in all of his love, compassion, and saving grace. The people saw the Lord and were glad!

Good News from Graveyards

That it may be a sign among you (v. 6a).

Professor Luccock once said that the best news about America was coming from graveyards! A graveyard in Springfield, Illinois, the grave of Abraham Lincoln, the news of what America might be at its best. He said that the best news in the international realm was coming from a graveyard—the Washington Cathedral—the grave of Woodrow Wilson, the legacy of a vision. Of course, Professor Luccock was thinking ideals and dreams, not of epitaphs written upon stone; although the dreams are frequently chiseled on the stones. Incidentally, it is surprising how much information can be gained of local and national history from epitaphs! Look at several of these:

On the banks of the James River in Virginia is a simple stone with the revealing words of what women meant to the pioneer years.

She touched the soil of Virginia with her little foot and the wilderness became a home.

The Reverend Samuel Hidden is buried in the town cemetery at Tamworth, New Hampshire. His epitaph,

He came into the wilderness
And left it a fruitful field.

In Wilmington, North Carolina, Oakdale Cemetery, is the grave of John Decatur Barry who died in 1867; he entered the service as a private and rose to brigadier general. His epitaph:

I found him a pigmy
And left him a giant.

Dr. George W. Truett, the great preacher, is buried in Hillcrest Memorial Park, Dallas, Texas; his epitaph,

My greatest desire is to help the people
And to magnify the matchless name of Christ.

He is not here, but has risen (Luke 24:6).

August 11   Read 1 Kings 19:9-13
"The Significance of the Insignificant"

And after the fire a still small voice (v. 12b).

Anyone familiar with the Bible knows something of the emphasis placed upon the small and the insignificant things of life. The Lord did not appear to Elijah in the great wind, the mighty earthquake, the consuming fire, but in the "still small voice." A small pot of oil was sufficient for Elisha's needs. And, when we come to the New Testament: five loaves and two small fish, the cup of cold water, the sparrow that falls, the flower that withers, the borrowed room, the kiss of welcome, the hungry fed, the prisoner visited, a call upon the sick, faithful in little—faithful in much. The Scriptures in general, our Lord in particular, seem to have had a different scale of values from ours. The emphasis is also made in proverbs and verses.

> Two little things, a match and a mouse,
> Kindled the fire that burned the big house.
>
> The massive gates of circumstances
> Are turned on the smallest things.

Wordsworth penned these lines:

> That best portion of a good man's life,—
> His little, nameless, unremembered acts
> Of kindness and of love.

The small things make the large things possible. Examples: A teakettle on a stove was the beginning of the steam engine. A shirt waving on a line was the forerunner of the Graf Zeppelin. A spiderweb strung across a garden path suggested the suspension bridge. A lantern swinging in a tower suggested the principle of the pendulum, while a falling apple from a tree spurred the discovery of the law of gravitation. Many physiologists have called attention to the human heart. It is no larger than your fist, but it pumps enough blood every day to fill a railroad tank car, and without that small organ life is impossible.

He that is faithful in that which is least is faithful also in much: and he that is unjust in the least is unjust also in much (Luke 16:10).

230

Read Proverbs 19:16-23   August 12
A School Lives by Its Appointments

Hear counsel, and receive instruction, that thou mayest be wise (v. 20).

James Archibald Campbell, the founder of Campbell University, gave great care to the selection of his teachers. He knew that the teacher makes the difference between a school and a school that is different. He sought three qualities in his teachers. First, he wanted committed Christians. He made no apology for that; he affirmed it and advertised the fact. Second, he sought teachers who were committed to boys and girls, believed in them and their possibilities. Third, and I think the order is as he would have put it, he wanted teachers who were committed to and competent in the area of subjects taught.

Academic proficiency was of tremendous importance to Dr. Campbell. He put it last because he believed that was where it belonged, not because he discounted its importance. He did believe that there were things in life more important than academic knowledge. He knew it was possible for an individual to be a useful citizen, a valuable member of society, a participating member of the kingdom of God without being a brilliant student.

One who knew Dr. Campbell well was present when a committee was sent to investigate the school in view of its accreditation in the junior college field. The committee chairman came to see Dr. Campbell as the group was leaving the campus. "Dr. Campbell," he said, "we shall write our report and you will, of course, be notified. We are kindly disposed to what you are trying to do here. We wish you well. But frankly, the members of your faculty have very poor academic preparation. Only one of your teachers has a Ph.D. degree."

Quickly Dr. Campbell responded, "You mean you do not think my teachers know enough?" The chairman smiled and said, "Well, I would not have put it in those terms but I guess it is about what I mean." Dr. Campbell's response was immediate, "Well, Sir, there may be a lot of things my teachers don't know, but most of what they know is so!" The school received accreditation.

Seek ye first the kingdom of God (Matt. 6:33a).

August 13   Read 2 Kings 6:11-17
"Your Breath About Him"

They that be with us are greater than they that be with them (v. 16).

Man is mortal; that means he is a sinner. The sin of pride and egotism are no respector of persons. God requires humility. Micah said that "to walk humbly with thy God" was one of the basic requirements. James and John, disciples of Jesus, sought places of preferment. The other disciples were angry with the two brothers. We probably can assume that most of the anger came from the fear that James and John would get there with "the fustest and the mostest." James and John were seeking outright and boldly what all the rest wanted but hesitated to seek—or, couldn't they get their mothers to plead for them?

Somewhere there is on record the deacon's prayer, to the effect that the pastor might always remain poor and humble. Then the deacon added, "Lord, you keep him humble; we'll keep him poor." Someone said to the father of Woodrow Wilson, a Presbyterian minister, "Dr. Wilson, your horse looks better fed and groomed than you do." "Yes," said Dr. Wilson, "you see I take care of my horse; the congregation takes care of me." But, deep within the conscience, pastors and laymen know the proper priorities.

When Charles Spurgeon was at his height as a preacher in London, the head of a lyceum offered him a thousand dollars a night, easily the equivalent of twenty thousand now, if the famous preacher would come to America and lecture for fifty nights. Spurgeon declined and said, "I can do better than that; I can stay in London and be used by God to win fifty souls."

And there was the wife of a dying man who knocked on the door of Henry Drummond one night, saying she thought her husband was dying, and that she did not believe her husband would be able to see or hear Drummond. "But," she said, "I would like for him to have the breath of you about him before he dies."

"Both And!"

My son, be wise and make my heart glad (v. 11a).

In *The Bible and World Evangelism,* A. M. Chirgwin pointed out how closely education in the Scriptures has gone with reform movements. He wrote:

> The facts seem to show that the rediscovery of the Bible and the Reformation grew up side by side, acting and reacting on one another. First one made a move and then the other followed suit. A glance at the dates show this happening. In 1516 Erasmus published his Greek New Testament and the very next year Luther nailed his theses to the church door in Wittenberg. In 1522 Luther translated the New Testament into German and a few years later German princes and cities began to call themselves "Protestant." Again, 1525, Tyndale translated the Bible into English and in two years time Reformation doctrines were being openly advocated in Oxford and Cambridge. Once more, in 1535, Olivétan translated the Bible into French and a year later Calvin published his Institutes and Geneva went Protestant. Every new step in biblical discovery or translating seemed to be the occasion, if not the cause, of another development in Protestantism. The biblical renewal and the Reformation moved forward together, with the biblical renewal generally taking the lead.[14]

Chirgwin points up something that needs to be remembered. Education for reform has to be the right kind of education, just as legislation has to be the right kind of legislation. Attention has been called to traffic laws. It is possible to educate children to break traffic laws. Reformation uses education and law; regeneration is essential to the right use of each.

> All education should be directed toward the development of character. Sound character cannot be achieved if spiritual development is neglected. I do not like to think of turning out physical and mental giants who are spiritual pygmies.

—WALTER COFFEY

Easy to Forget

I do remember my faults this day (v. 9b).

It is fearfully easy to forget great events and to live as if they never
occurred. So George Bernard Shaw in *St. Joan* has one who voted
for Joan's death say that it was an awful thing he had done, but he
never knew what cruelty was until he saw a young girl burned to
death. The bishop asks, "Must then a Christ perish in torment in every
age to save those who have no imagination?" And in his play, *Valley
Forge*, Maxwell Anderson has George Washington say, as he surveys
his starving, freezing, dwindling recruits, "Men will think lightly of this
liberty when they forget what it cost." It is so easy to forget great events
and to act as if they never occurred!

On Monument Avenue in Richmond, Virginia, along with many
other statues, is the monument to General Robert E. Lee. Thousands
pass the monument every day without so much as lifting an eye. But a
friend of mine once drove past that statue with Dr. John R. Sampey, an
erudite Hebrew scholar and seminary president. When they came near
the statue, Dr. Sampey became silent; then he asked if it was not
General Lee. When my friend assured him that it was, Dr. Sampey sat
at rigid attention, made a sharp salute, held the salute until they were
well past the monument, then, at ease, said, in a husky voice: "My
hero!"

Or again in Washington, you walk in the area of the Lincoln
Memorial. You seldom go that you do not see a group of small
schoolchildren, led and lectured by their teacher. The children are
quiet, their faces upturned, and their eyes aglow with adoration. Yet,
look closely and, unless the park workmen have done their work well
and recently, you will see trash, filth, cigarette butts, and beer cans at
the base of the statue. So easy to forget great events and to live as if
they never took place!

*Thou shalt remember all the way which the Lord thy God led thee these
forty years in the wilderness (Deut. 8:2).*

"Good Thoughts in Bad Times"

Teach us what we shall do unto the child that shall be born (v. 8b).

When a tourist inquired of the ancient native, "Any big men born around here?" the old man responded, "Nope, best we can do is babies. Different in the city, I suppose." No, it's no different in the city. This is one of the things that is entirely democratic between the country and the city; no "big men" are born in either, only babies. Edgar A. Guest's well-known line says that within the walls of the home there have to be some babies born and, then, the parents have to raise them up to be good women and men.

What the home does to and for the children, the children will do to the home, the church, and the nation. Of course, one always has to say that with reservations. There are exceptions. Thomas Fuller spoke of this in his *Good Thoughts in Bad Times*. He wrote:

> Lord, I find the genealogy of my Saviour strangely chequerd with four remarkable changes in four generations. Roboam begat Abia—a bad father begat a bad son. Abia begat Asa—a bad father and a good son. . . . Josaphat begat Joram—a good father and a bad son. I see, Lord, from hence that my father's piety cannot be entailed; that is bad news for me. But I see also that actual impiety is not hereditary; that is good news for my son.

Yet, the Bible, biography, psychology, observation, experience, and faith all tell us, "Train up a child in the way he should go: and when he is old, he will not depart from it" (Prov. 22:6).

The Department of Health, Education, and Welfare of the United States government announced that four hundred thousand newborn babies would be given the Guthrie test to detect illness which leads to mental retardation. If an error were found in a baby's metabolism, that child would be placed on a special diet to prevent "subsequent, irreparable mental retardation." Wonderful! Now we need to get on with the work of doing that in the field of morals and true religion.

August 17   Read John 10:7-18
At Lambing Time

I am the good shepherd, and know my sheep (v. 14a).

Halford Luccock once wrote of an incident in the life of Dr. Winnington-Ingraham, one-time bishop of London. The bishop was on holiday; out walking he fell in step with an old shepherd. The bishop said, "I am a kind of shepherd, too." They walked in silence for a bit and then the old shepherd said, "How many sheep do you have?" The bishop thought about his London diocese and said, "About a million." More walking and more silence—then the shepherd asked, "What do you do at lambing time?" Good question! The Bible and the Christian faith are always concerned about "lambing time" and what is to be done for the children.

There is poignant truth suggested in the lives of Rachel and her father, Laban. When Jacob secretly stole away from Laban, taking his wife, the daughter of Laban, it was learned that Rachel had taken her father's idols. Why would lovely Rachel take the household gods—idols? Could it be that she wanted something to remind her of those times when her family was closest; did she realize that those were the times when the family came together for worship, even false worship, worship of idols? She was going into a far country, among strange people and customs. She wanted that which had drawn her family together during the days of her childhood. So, she took the household gods, idols.

Is it not tragic that there was nothing in that household of Laban's that could better serve the lonely heart of a lovely girl than pagan idols!

But, easy does it. What do the young women and young men take when they leave our roofs for the foreign lands of school, marriage, and profession?

> The home is a lighthouse which has the lamp of God
> on the table and the light of Christ in the window,
> to give guidance to those who wander in darkness.

—HENRY RISCHE

236

An Unforgettable Experience

But Samuel ministered before the Lord (v. 18a).

Rufus Jones, the Quaker author, teacher, and mystic, told of an experience he had as a small boy. His parents were away for the afternoon; he was left at home to weed the garden. Just as the task was getting under way, some of his friends came by and persuaded him to go fishing. Young Rufus fully intended to get home and finish weeding the garden before his parents returned. But, fishing was so good that he did not return until after dark. His mother was waiting for him; he knew what was ahead, at least he thought he knew. His mother took him into another room; he made no resistance; he was ready for his punishment for he knew it was deserved. But punishment was not administered, at least not in the form that Rufus expected.

He was put in a chair and his mother kneeled before him, put her hands on him, and began to talk to God. She poured out her heart to God, told him about her son and the man she had always expected Rufus to be, and then how the boy had disappointed her. She prayed, "O God, take this boy of mine and make him the boy and the man he was divinely intended to be." Then his mother kissed him, arose from her knees, and went out of the room, leaving young Rufus alone in the silence with his thoughts and with God. Rufus Jones never forgot the experience.

A mother's love is indeed the golden link that binds youth to age; and he is still but a child, however time may have furrowed his cheek, or silvered his brow, who can yet recall, with a softened heart, the fond devotion, or the gentle chidings, of the best friend that God ever gave us.

—CHRISTIAN BOVEE

"Christians Never Lie"

Thou hast not lied unto men, but unto God (v. 4b).

The *Kiwanis* magazine reported on an exciting basketball game. It was an important game—tension ran high, the crowd was partisan, and gave the visiting referee a tough time. At one point in the game, a player on the visiting team passed the ball to his teammate but it ended up in the crowd. What the crowd did not see was that a member of the home team lunged for the ball and kicked it as it went out of bounds. The referee did see and called the ball "out of bounds" in favor of the visiting team.

At that point the roof fell in; the crowd went wild and would not be silenced. Poor sportsmanship, which seems ever just below the surface, overflowed. The crowd booed and jeered; the official was called all sorts of names. One old grad rushed onto the court; real trouble seemed ahead. The referee managed to get some sort of order, looked the players over until he found the boy who had touched the ball, called him over, and asked, "Son, did you or did you not touch the ball?" The boy looked the referee in the eye and said, "Sir, I touched it." Immediately the jeers were turned to cheers for the boy and the referee.

Dr. Robert Speer laid down two principles on truth and honesty. He stated that God cannot lie; second, God cannot delegate to you the privilege of lying for him.

E. Stanley Jones told of a Hindu doctor who asked the compounder why he did not give the two women who were waiting their slips of paper. The man affirmed that he had; the women said that he had not. The doctor turned to the man and said, "Get those papers. Don't you know who these women are? They are Christians. And Christians never lie." Stanley Jones said, "The doctor was right; Christians never lie; when we lie we are not Christian."

Shoulders and Holy Things

Comfort ye, comfort ye my people, saith your God (v. 1).

Some persons do not reveal the troubles they have known. Sir Malcolm Sargent seemed never to have known a serious tragedy. But just as he was beginning his brilliant career as a musician he was stricken with tuberculosis. For two years he fought the dread disease; it sapped his energy and tried to break his spirit. When he returned to his music, and life stretched out with promise before him again, his thirteen-year-old daughter, Pamela, was stricken with polio. For six years she fought her gallant battle. Sir Malcolm was constantly by her side or away seeking medical help.

One evening in Liverpool he was ready to direct a performance of Handel's *Messiah*. Just before the performance began he was given a note. He had better come at once; it was thought that Pamela was dying. With that news in his heart, he raised his baton and directed the orchestra in the recitative, "Comfort ye, comfort ye my people, saith your God." His biographer is quite sure that from this experience Sir Malcolm came to such a deep understanding of, and mystical communication with, his audiences.

Let me remind you of a dramatic scene in the seventh chapter of the Book of Numbers. Moses has portioned out the units of transportation to the Israelites. Then this word, "But to the sons of Kohath he gave none, because they were charged with the care of the holy things, which had to be carried on the shoulder" (v. 9, RSV). Now, run that out in any direction. The "holy things" always have to be carried on shoulders and wounded hearts. Mechanical inventions have their place. But there are some things which have to be carried in a more intimate, personal, and painful way.

August 21   Read John 10:40-42
Your Most Unforgettable Character

. . . all things that John spake of this man were true (v. 41b).

Who is your most unforgettable character? Allow me to nominate "Miss Cora." She was unmarried, worked as a clerk in a department store, and taught a group of ten-year-old boys in Sunday School. She did not have a car; she walked to church and to the homes of her "boys." Occasionally, if the weather were especially bad, I would ask someone to take her to the more distant homes. I have known them to come back in amazement, saying: "It's incredible; you wouldn't believe it! Do you remember that boy 'Blank' we used to have so much trouble with? Well, no more. I visited with Miss Cora in his home. He is a different boy now since she got hold of him. His mother is so grateful that she didn't want to let Miss Cora out the door."

A second nomination? For many years I went on a particular Sunday afternoon to a cemetery where I met a group of men; we gathered about a grave and had a brief service. The time was deep winter; I have been with the men when the snow lay deep upon the ground and was still falling. The men were middle-aged in those days. They represented business, labor, and the professions. I would lead the group in a brief memorial service. Frequently, if the weather were not too bad, I'd ask one of the men to speak briefly. The message was always the same, the words varied. "I was wild and reckless, headed straight for hell, when she got hold of me. She never gave up until my feet were on the straight and narrow path. Today I thank God for her!"

She was no genius or miracle worker, merely a normal, ordinary woman with an extraordinary love for boys who came to her Sunday School class. The only time we could remember her name being in the headlines was when she was killed in an accident.

I thank my God on every remembrance of you (Phil. 1:3).

Those Fifty-Eight Cards!

They recognized that they had been with Jesus (v. 13b).

Rummage in your memory, inquire of your minister, ask the evange-list, "Who are the most effective personal witnesses for Christ?" The answer will probably reveal a group of ordinary human beings who have shown an extraordinary devotion. In my youth I knew such an individual. He was "superintendent" of our Sunday School in the little country church where I accepted Christ as my Savior. This man could neither read nor write and had to put a cross mark on checks that were written on his account. He was a fine farmer, admired and respected by all who knew him, but severely limited in education. I have seen his radiance and deep love move young and old to accept Christ as Savior and Lord.

Once a secretary brought to me a package of fifty-eight cards. On each card was the name of an individual in our church. They were useful, influential, unselfish Christians, members of that church. It was difficult to see how that great church could operate successfully without those fifty-eight individuals. Yet, each of the fifty-eight, five years before to the day, had walked down the aisle of that church and given himself or herself, to Christ and his cause. It was a "regular" service; no revival was in progress. Explanation? Simple. During the past week a group of ordinary, run-of-the-mill folk had gone out and borne their witness. And when I gave the invitation on Sunday morning the group came.

> All hail the pow'r of Jesus' name!
>   Let angels prostrate fall;
> Bring forth the royal diadem,
>   And crown him . . . Lord of all.
>
> Let ev'ry kindred, ev'ry tribe,
>   On this terrestrial ball,
> To him all majesty ascribe,
>   And crown him . . . Lord of all.
>
> —EDWARD PERRONET

"Lantern In My Hand"

The law of the Lord is perfect (v. 7a).

Because the way was steep and long
  And through a strange and lonely land,
God placed upon my lips a song,
  And put a lantern in my hand.

—JOYCE KILMER

Look at that "lantern." "Thy word," said the psalmist, is a lamp unto my feet, and a light unto my path." The Bible has been exactly that to the people of God. It is in and through the Bible that God speaks redemptively to his people. The Scriptures are his appointed means of communication. The Bible is not God's only means of communication, of course. With Joseph Plunket we may see his blood upon the rose, his eyes in the glory of the stars, his face in every flower, and find his footprints in all paths. Still, it is in and through the Bible that we are able to see and hear him through such mediums; the Bible is God's code book. If you doubt that, investigate the lands and people where the Bible is not known and see if they are able to so interpret nature.

In 1849 Dostoevski, the Russian writer, was banished to Siberia. There, for four years, he was herded with criminals in what was known as the "House of the Dead." Everything in his sensitive soul cried out against that cruelty and inhumanity. But Dostoevski carried with him into that "House of the Dead," a little book, the New Testament. He read it over and over. The burning flames of anger died down in his soul; he became a follower of Christ.

After ten years of banishment, he returned to his home a new person. From henceforth he was known as a philanthropist, a helper of the helpless; a teacher of the Christian faith "once delivered to the saints." George Brandes affirms that Dostoevski's death brought grief to the nation, and even Nietzsche acknowledged the reality of Dostoevski's life in Christ. The New Testament became a "lantern" in Dostoevski's hand.

"When He Left—No Darkness"

His delight is in the law of the Lord (v. 2a).

Years ago the church of which I was then pastor gave me a sabbatical leave. I had been with the church for seven years; the year's leave was to be used for travel and study. I made use of two great universities, one on this side of the Atlantic and one on the other side. Never, "till death hangs his sickle on my garden gate" shall I be able to tell what that year meant to me.

During that year I was a student of some of the best, clearest, and most devoted teachers in the world. Yet, looking back upon the experience from the distance of years, I bear my witness. What meant most to me during that sabbatical year was the reading of the Word of God. I read it carefully, devotionally, lovingly, and patiently. I read it for great blocks of time on through the night hours. I read it not for sermon building but for soul building; not to meet a deadline but to meet a lifeline. It became a "lantern in my hand."

This Word is adequate. Like the famous magic tent of which we read when we were young, a tent that could be folded and carried in a man's hand or unrolled so that it would cover armies, so this Bible is a lamp for the feet of the individual and a light for the nation. Its light and truth are certain. Christ declared that heaven and earth would pass away but that his words would not pass away. Both prophecies have come to pass: the heavens and the earth, as they were known, have passed away; his words remain.

Under the picture of Peter Milne, in the church founded by him on Nguna in the New Hebrides, is a tribute that might be ascribed to the Word of God. The inscription reads:

> When he came there was no light,
> When he left there was no darkness.

"The Sail Is Spread"

My lovers and my friends stand aloof (v. 11a).

illiam Saroyan wrote the beautiful book, *The Human Comedy.*
There he gave us the lovable and unforgettable Homer. Homer
is a small boy who is sensitive to all the wonders and delights of a small
boy's world, when the boy is safe and secure in a home of love. Yet,
Homer has to grow up; growing pains are real pains. Homer says to his
mother, "I feel lonely—not like I ever felt before. . . . I'm lonely and I
don't know what I'm lonely *for.*" His wise and wonderful mother
smiled and waited to see if the boy had anything else to say. Then she
said, "The loneliness you feel has come to you because you are no
longer a child. But the whole world has always been full of that
loneliness. The loneliness does not come from the war. The war did
not make it. It was the loneliness that made the way. It was the despair
in all things for no longer having the grace of God." [15]

Man needs a feeling of "at-one-ment." Somewhere in his life he
needs to touch other human beings who have similar motivations,
goals, and purposes at the deep levels of life, the God level. Let a
group of individuals bow and stand and adore in the same place, at the
same time, to the same Person, in the same Spirit, and there will be an
experience of Christian community, and that will be Christian worship.

> What wind brings to the lagging sail,
> Rain to the drooping flower,
> Sweet fire
> And the broken bread
> And song's peace
> To the lonely hour,
> You bring,
> And blithely, to your kind
> You come, and lo!
> The sail is spread,
> The flower dances in the sun,
> And the heart leaps heavenward
> Like a flame—
> And God is in the broken bread. [16]

Freedom in Bonds

But now being made free from sin, and become servants to God (v. 22a).

E. P. Dickey told a haunting story of death on a slave ship. The ship was transporting men from their homes and freedom to the auction block and slavery. In the hold of the ship where the men had been driven and bound was a giant of a man, who day after day burned with anger and seethed for revenge. One day the giant's opportunity came. The guard in a careless moment came too close. With one mighty blow he was struck down, killed on the spot, and his keys taken. The murderer unlocked his own ankle irons and then released all his fellow prisoners. Quietly they crept to the deck, and almost before the crew knew what was taking place the captain and entire crew had been murdered.

Now, at last the once-bound men were free! The ship was their own; they could do as they pleased. No. For they did not know how to navigate the ship. They had been bound men; now they were lost men. They did not know where they were or how to get where they wanted to go. Their "last state was worse than the first." They had seen members of the crew studying a small instrument called a compass. The rebels decided that it was the ship's god; so, they fell down and worshiped it, asking to be guided to their homeland. The compass did not respond to their pleas; they smashed it.

All over the world men are rising in rebellion, as nations, groups within nations, and individuals. These rebellions are frequently understandable; they may even be applauded. However, the undeniable fact is that freedom calls for more than breaking the shackles of slavery; it also calls for forging the bonds of character, discipline, and government; it calls for a reliable compass. It is frightfully easy for men to destroy; it is more difficult, and it takes more time to create and to build.

Education makes a people easy to lead, but difficult to drive; easy to govern, but impossible to enslave.

—LORD BROUGHAM

On Learning to Worship

Lord, teach us to pray (v. 1c).

Stephen F. Winward has reasoned that it is necessary for one to be taught to do almost everything. We may possess something that is surpassingly valuable yet never get the best out of it if we have not been taught its proper use.

So, there is a technique and proper procedure for doing almost everything—using the dishwasher, vacuum cleaner, driving an automobile, and using a typewriter. What is more natural than breathing? One does not "learn" to breathe; one just breathes. Yet, doctors tell us that many of our physical ills spring from improper breathing. Walking is a simple activity, we assume. But we are assured by those who should know that most of us never learn to walk correctly. One of the first things a good "house of charm" does is to teach a young woman how to walk and sit! Talk? Who needs to be taught that art? Yet, one day we meet someone who is a skilled and competent conversationalist, and then we know how ineffective we are in communication.

Many educators are saying that a basic problem in education—child, youth, adult education—is the matter of reading. "Johnny can't read," we are told. What is more, we are assured that Johnny's father, mother, brother, and sister might learn to read. There are techniques, there are books, there are laboratories for correct reading habits. Once these correct habits are formed, reading becomes far more profitable and enjoyable; therefore, the person reads more and profits more by what is read.

Why, then, should we be surprised that it is necessary that we "learn" to worship, and that we can do so?

> The dullest observer must be sensible of the order and serenity prevalent in those households where the occasional exercise of a beautiful form of worship in the morning gives, as it were, the keynote to every temper of the day, and attunes every spirit to harmony.
>
> —WASHINGTON IRVING

Yes, but . . .

In thinking about formal acts of worship, it may be urged that God is more interested in what a man does on the job than he is in what the man does in his closet; that religion is more than what a man does with his solitariness—it is also what he does with his togetherness. It may be contended that there are those who spend much time in the prayer closet but are unethical in their human relations, while there are those who take little time for the closet, yet are just in their dealings with their fellows. We do have it on good authority that we are not heard for our much speaking.

That there is some truth in all this it may be readily agreed. But it is not all of the truth. Consider: since all of our time belongs to God, is it reasonable to suppose that he would be pleased if some of it were not given back to him in structured worship? If we are too busy to dedicate a reasonable amount of time to worship with him in the closet, is it probable that we shall honor him with a greater amount of time in the office, business, kitchen, or classroom?

If all of our hours are to be holy, we need to dedicate one hour to his holy presence; if all our days are his, then one day could best be spent in special honor to him. This is a point that we are prone to overlook. When we dedicate a small amount of time or a small sum of our wealth to him, in keeping with his teaching and in response to our sense of gratitude, this does not free us from honoring him with the rest of our time and the remainder of our wealth. The reverse is the case; God could not insist that we reserve a small amount if he did not have a right to the total. Think about it: when the owner of an orange grove sells his fruit with the understanding that certain types of fruit or certain trees are exempt from the bargain, he does so on the basis that he owns and controls the entire orchard. He could not exempt certain parts of the grove otherwise.

It is required in stewards, that a man be found faithful (1 Cor. 4:2).

Work Shall Be Prayer

Whatsoever ye do, do all to the glory of God (v. 31).

> Let us put some hour of every day
> For holy things—whether it be when dawn
> Peers through the windowpane, or when noon
> Flames, like a burning topaz, in the vault,
> Or when the thrush pours in the ear of eve
> Its plaintive melody; some little hour
> Wherein to hold rapt converse with the soul,
> From sordidness and self a sanctuary,
> Swept by the winnowings of unseen things,
> And touched by the White Light ineffable!

Those beautiful lines by Clinton Scollard surely say what many a heart echoes. Today, however, let us look a little more deeply at that "set-aside" hour. The purpose and end of the devotional life is the devoted life. We set aside a few minutes that the hours may be God's; we set aside one day that all days may be his; we come to the Lord's table that we may recognize his presence at all tables; we bow before him in the Lord's house that he may have preeminence in all houses; we pay the tithe of our income to the intent that he may have control of all income.

The individual who conscientiously reserves a quiet time needs to remember that these quiet times are not little islands cut off from the mainland of life; they are a vital part of the whole of life. We moor our ship to these quiet islands for a time that we may sail forth better mariners on the sea of daily living.

> Take my life, and let it be
> Consecrated, Lord, to thee;
> Take my hands, and let them move
> At the impulse of thy love.
>
> —FRANCES R. HAVERGAL

Families that Pray Together

Many were gathered together praying (v. 12b).

Richard Baxter, the seventeenth-century preacher, at whose disciplined thought and devotion many present-day preachers still kindle their fires, bore witness to the fact that when he came to Kidderminster to serve as pastor, in some streets there was scarcely a single family that worshiped. When he left there were streets where it was impossible to find a single family that did not have family prayers every day. We do not have to go back a hundred years to find examples.

Francis Carr Stifler went to Chicago to call on a Lutheran pastor, whose work, according to a newsmagazine article, was attended by unusual success. The accuracy of the report was borne out. Although the church members had recently built a new building—one they had felt would be adequate for many years—they now were having to conduct three morning services to take care of the crowds. There was a constant stream of people uniting with the church by baptism. The church was having no problems with finances. All of this in the face of the fact that this was an old downtown church.

When asked for the secret of such a phenomenon, the pastor attributed the success mainly to one thing: "I have persuaded ninety percent of my families to have regular family prayers." The church had twenty-nine hundred families in its local membership. This meant that about twenty-six hundred families in the membership of the church were having family worship. When asked how he persuaded such a large percentage of his people to do this, the pastor said that he had personally taught most of his families to do it; he had gone from house to house, as many times as required, until they were willing to continue with the experience.

The king's business requireth haste (1 Sam. 21:8).

August 31   Read Matthew 13:53-58
What He Would Not Do for Us

And he did not many mighty works there because of their unbelief (v. 58).

The strength of the Savior is revealed not only in what he was willing to do to redeem us, but also in what he refused to do to redeem us. Man is made in the image of God. Man is so valuable that God sent his Son to redeem man. Man was given "dominion"; he is so great that God would not coerce him. Persuade, yes, with the persuasion of Calvary, but let man be free to choose.

A few days after Douglas MacArthur's death, Billy Graham the evangelist reported a private conversation he had had with the general. MacArthur said that Emperor Hirohito of Japan had talked with him shortly after Japan's surrender and declared his willingness to make Christianity the official religion of Japan. MacArthur hesitated; the emperor asked him to think further about it. Later MacArthur had returned to the emperor with these words, "Never. No nation must ever be made to conform to any religion. It must be done voluntarily."

Freedom is both a privilege and a responsibility. It can be a weight as well as wings. Mass movements often flourish because individuals wish to escape individual responsibility. They desire *freedom from freedom.* The Nazis bitterly fought the idea that they were individually responsible for obeying orders.

This state of affairs is known in the religious realm. Any system of religion which promises to be responsible for the salvation of the individual in return for that individual's freedom of thought and will has a great advantage with multitudes. Many are glad to exchange freedom of choice in return for a "package deal" in the salvation market. This idea is a travesty of true religion! Christ would have none of it.

The cause of freedom is the cause of God.

—EDMUND BURKE

250

The Mind of Jesus

For the body is not one member, but many (v. 14).

Paul writes that we, as followers of Christ, "are the body of Christ." What part of his body would you like to be? His mind? The apostle wrote to the Philippians, "Let this mind be in you, which was also in Christ Jesus" (2:5).

Jesus had a sharp mind; his enemies were never able to trap him in an argument. His mind was profound; he was able to see through cloudy, and clouded, issues. His enemies wanted to know about paying taxes to Caesar and about wives in the judgment. The mind of Jesus saw the issues clearly and sharply. He had an understanding and sympathetic mind. Call the woman at Jacob's well to witness, or Zacchaeus of Jericho, or the woman who anointed his feet in Simon's house. He had an optimistic mind and spirit. He called on his followers to have faith in God, but he had faith in his followers, too. He told them that they should be perfect, even as his Father God is perfect. He told them that they would do greater things than he was able to do. He called on them to be "light," "salt," "branches," and "witnesses." And, he told them to go into all the world with his message.

The mind of Jesus was a humble and obedient mind. It was this which seemed to impress Paul the most. He said that even though Christ was in the form of God he humbled himself and became a servant, a slave. He did not "grasp" for the place of preference. His mind was attuned to joy; the words *peace* and *joy* were often in his teachings.

For nearly two years the church bells in England were silent; their glad sounds were reserved for the time when, possibly, fearfully, the invader might come to their shores. Then came the hour of defeat for the enemy, and the bells began to peal their joyous sound. We are told that strong men and noble women wept unashamedly for the joy! Would you like to be the mind of JESUS?

The Voice of Jesus

The officers answered, Never man spake like this man (v. 46).

Kahlil Gibran thought the speech of Jesus was unlike that of the orators of Athens and Rome! He noted that while their words had an art that would enthrall you, the words of Jesus had a power to make your heart leave you and go wandering into regions you had never visited. The orators spoke of life as the mind understood it; Jesus spoke of a longing that was caught in the deep recesses of the heart.

It has been suggested that the energy of every sound and voice ever uttered is retained in the atmosphere. And that it may be possible in the future for some instrument to search out, tune into, these voices of the past so that we shall be able to hear the voices of Abraham, Moses, Amos, the voices of Washington and Lincoln. Whose voice would you most like to hear? The voice of Jesus? Of course.

He had a voice that could calm the waves of an angry sea, but it was a voice so quiet and gentle that little children would come and serve as object lessons. He could speak words that would challenge rough fishermen, causing them to forsake their nets and follow him; he could speak so the broken heart of a sinful woman would find hope and healing. His voice demanded the attention of the dead. Would you like to be the voice of Jesus? Remember, Paul wrote that "ye are the body of Christ."

John Oxenham told the life story of an obscure French saint by the name of Jean Marie. Oxenham said that the old saint preached in a very loud voice, but when he prayed, his voice was just above a whisper. When asked why the difference, he answered that when he preached it was to people who would not hear unless he spoke in a loud voice, but when he prayed it was to a God who listened to his children's whispers.

Now ye are the body of Christ (1 Cor. 12:27).

The Eyes of Jesus

The light of the body is the eye (v. 34a).

Now ye are the body of Christ" (1 Cor. 12:27). What part of his body would you like to be? His eyes? What eyes the Master had! He saw God and the kingdom of God in plants and flowers and seed and fruit and sky, in the birds of the heavens, in business and commerce, in home and family.

Yet, he was strangely "blind" to much that others saw. When a woman was taken in the act of adultery, others saw only the sin; Jesus saw the woman and possible forgiveness. In the case of the woman at the well who had had five husbands and was then living with a man who was not her husband, Jesus saw a redeemed life and an effective evangelist. There is the legend of a crowd standing on the streets of Jerusalem looking at a dead dog lying in the gutter, ugly, vile, repulsive. Then the people heard a voice say, "But doesn't it have beautiful teeth?" And, without turning, they knew it was Jesus of Nazareth who had spoken. No one else could see the beauty there.

If we had the eyes of Jesus, we would be able to see the sleeping good and the dormant potential for helpfulness in persons we meet. Once when Gutzon Borglum, the sculptor, was carving the head of Lincoln for the Mount Rushmore memorial, the woman who cleaned his studio each morning became greatly concerned. Each day the head and face of President Lincoln became a little more clear and distinct. Day by day the cleaning woman observed the emerging head of Lincoln. One day she exclaimed, "Mr. Borglum, how did you know Mr. Lincoln was in that rock?"

The eyes of Jesus could see in the far distance; he was able to "read the signs of the time." He knew that the past, the present, and the future bore the imprint of his Father's presence and love. And he knew that one day every knee would bow and every tongue make its confession. Would you like to be the eyes of Jesus?

September 4   Read Luke 24:28-40

The Hands of Jesus

Behold my hands (v. 39a).

Remember, you are the body of Christ and individually members of that body. Would you like to be the hands of Jesus? He had hands that made an indelible impression on the disciples. The writers of the four Gospels refer either directly or indirectly to the hands of Jesus about fifty times. The hands of Jesus were clean hands; no one was ever able to convict him of sin.

His were hands of toil, hands that held the ax, saw, and hammer. It was said that Jesus puts to us the same test now that Thomas put to him, "Show me your hands." If we are to be the hands of Jesus in this world, our hands will have to bear the marks of service. And the hands of Jesus were strong hands; they could not only hold the ax and adz, control a colt on which no one had sat before, but they could, and can, hold onto the life that puts its trust in him with a loving strength that is the despair of the forces of evil. No power on earth or in hell is able to snatch from Christ's hands the life that commits itself fully to him.

Unselfishness is a characteristic of the hands of Jesus. His hands were always busy for the good of others. Your hands are quick to defend and protect your body from falling; your hands are quick to protect eyes and face from flying debris or a swinging limb, so the hands of Jesus are ever busy protecting those whom he loves, his church.

The hands of Jesus bore the marks of pain and suffering. It was this that Thomas longed to see; Thomas wanted to see the marks in his hands, authentic marks of pain and suffering. Would you like to be the hands of Jesus in a needy world?

Who shall ascend into the hill of the Lord?
* or who shall stand in his holy place?*
He that hath clean hands, and a pure heart (Ps. 24:3-4).

The Feet of Jesus

Nevertheless I must walk to-day, and to-morrow, and the day following (v. 33a).

> Judean hills are holy,
> Judean fields are fair,
> For one can find the footprints
> Of Jesus everywhere.[17]
>
> —WILLIAM L. STIDGER

Would you like to be the feet of Jesus, remembering that we are "the body of Christ?" If we are to be his feet we shall have to travel much! A. Ian Burnett says the feet of Jesus were the most-traveled feet in the world.

Once tiny baby feet that Mary, his mother cupped in her hands;

Once small feet that Joseph probably loved to tease and tickle as Jesus lay in his crib;

It was on the warm sands of Egypt where Moses played as a boy, that the feet of Jesus learned the fine art of walking;

Later these feet roamed the highland and vales of Galilee and explored the haunts of Carmel;

Those feet carried him to play and synagogue; to school and worship, to workshop and village store;

They were firmly planted on the good earth as he worked at the carpenter's bench;

They bore him gladly as he strode through the fields of wheat, rye and barley;

Those feet bore him from Nazareth to the Jordan to be baptized of John; on into the wilderness to be tempted of Satan and back to Galilee;

. . . .

And they finally took him along the Via Dolorosa to a skull-shaped hill, where Roman soldiers held his feet in a vice-like grasp and drove great spikes through them as they were nailed to the cross for "us men and our salvation";

The cross could not hold him; neither could Joseph's tomb; neither could Judea and Galilee, nor the East nor the West; those feet travel the highways and sea-lanes and air-ways of the world today and make themselves at home wherever a heart bids them rest.[18]

And you would like to be his feet?!

"If You Have Faith, Follow Me"

Looking unto Jesus the author and finisher of our faith (v. 2a).

In his story, *Jesus Christ in Flanders*, Balzac told a beautiful story of faith. There is a boat traveling from Walcheren to Ostend on the coast of Flanders. Just as the boat is ready to leave, a Stranger appears and enters the boat. The boat is scarcely under way before a dreadful storm breaks.

The passengers are beside themselves with fright. A young mother with a baby begs for someone to save her child; the Stranger assures her that she herself will save her child. A rich merchant cries out to the holy virgin of Antwerp, promising rich gifts; the Stranger reminds him the virgin is in heaven. A young cavalier assures a proud young woman that he can swim and will save her. The mother of the young woman begs the bishop for absolution; the bishop is blessing the waves and asking that they be quiet, but his mind is on his concubine who is waiting for him at Ostend. A ragged, old prostitute is begging to hear the words from a priest, "Your sins are forgiven"; the Stranger says, "Have faith and you will be saved."

When the ship is near shore it is driven back and begins to sink. The Stranger begins to walk on the waves. He turns and says to those in the boat, "Those who have faith shall be saved; let them follow me." Instantly the young mother with the child walks beside him. So does the soldier and the old prostitute, the peasant and his son. The merchant goes down with his gold; the young lady and her cavalier, the bishop and the woman who begged for absolution. Only those who have faith follow the Stranger, walking on the waves. When they come ashore, they see a fisherman's cabin with a light streaming from the window.

"Those who have faith . . . follow me," he had said.

Have faith in God (Mark 11:22).

Not Fruit, Only the Seed

Being born again, not of corruptible seed, but of incorruptible (v. 23a).

Leslie Stannard Hunter gives an imaginary but pertinent story. He says that with the shout of war and the dispossessed ringing in his ears, Western man fell into a fitful slumber and troubled sleep. In his sleep he dreamed. In his dream he saw himself in a vast storehouse where all God's gifts to man were kept. There was an angel behind the counter, and Western man spoke to the angel. He said that he had run out of the fruit of the Spirit and wanted to know if the angel could restock him. In the place of war, injustice, affliction, lying, stealing, greed, and lust he would like a supply of love, joy, peace, integrity, and discipline. The angel replied that they did not stock the fruit of the Spirit, only the seed. It is a deep conviction of the Christian faith that the heart must be soft and receptive before the seed of the Spirit can germinate and produce desired fruit.

Charles Spurgeon once spoke of his vast correspondence. He confessed that his mail would pile up and pile up until one day, the day of reckoning, would come. Then he would sweep batches of it into the wastepaper basket and burn it. But certain pieces which would be kept as long as he lived. Why? Those pieces bore the stamp, the unmistakable stamp, of the hand of love. The person might be dead or alive, but anything in that person's hand would be treasured and kept.

There will be a general "office cleaning" at the end of the way. God will look over his correspondence. Some of it will be burned in fire. But there will be hearts upon which are written his new covenant. God will look at that heart and say, "That is the writing of my dear Son; I shall treasure and cherish this heart through all eternity."

Ye are our epistle written in our hearts (2 Cor. 3:2).

"Your Pain in My Heart"

And he took the damsel by the hand (v. 41a).

The overpowering motive for the miracles of Jesus was love and compassion. We read, "He was moved with compassion. It was a great heart going out to a hurt world.

It is difficult to keep compassion fresh. Those who are constantly with those who suffer have to be on guard: doctors, nurses, pastors. A degree of objectivity is essential. The patient needs your strength and courage more than your tears and grief. But we have to guard against "professionalism."

One of the many stories I cherish about Gladstone, a notable English prime minister, is this. One day a pastor was visiting a sufferer who had a small shop on the street which led to the prime minister's office. Before the pastor left, the sufferer took from a small box a little book of devotional messages and showed it, saying, "Mr. Gladstone gave me this." The pastor was surprised; turning the pages he found, in the well-known handwriting of the prime minister, the words, "From her friend, W. E. Gladstone." The pastor discovered that the mighty statesman had gone again and again to visit this ill person.

One of the superb definitions of sympathy and compassion says, "Sympathy is your pain in my heart." But even better is this, "He was wounded for our transgressions, he was bruised for our iniquities; the chastisement of our peace was upon him; and with his stripes we are healed" (Isa. 53:5).

> That woman is a seismograph! She can record a shock all the way from a boy falling off his bicycle across the street to an earthquake in Japan.
>
> —AUTHOR UNKNOWN

The Meaning of Confession

But whom say ye that I am? (v. 29a).

Jesus was interested in what was being said about him. He also wanted to know what his disciples were thinking and saying about him. All deep matters of the spirit come back to this personal element. It is easy to think of friendship in universal terms. Read Emerson's essay on "Friendship." It is a beautiful and stimulating piece of writing, yet it falls short of the individual and personal experience of having a friend, of being a friend. So one's experience with, and confession of, Christ must be a personal matter.

Personal confession is more than speaking a few words. It involves at least these five areas of life. It involves the *witness of the tongue.* Christ asked for that; he wanted to hear his disciples confess with words. If we are required to give an account of every idle word spoken, and Christ says that we are; will we not be required to give an account of every guilty silence?

The confession of Christ calls for the *assent of the mind,* as well as the voice of the tongue. Christ says that we are to love God with all of our minds. The kingdom of God places no premium on ignorance and stupidity. Jesus prayed for his crucifiers' stupidity, "they know not what they do," he told God. The confession of Christ also calls for the *affection of the heart.* "Do you love me?" was the question Jesus put to Peter. It has been said that there are missionaries who have given everything for the cause of Christ in missions, everything but themselves. If the gift of confession is to be worthy, it must have the affection of the heart.

There are two other areas of life that are involved in our confession of Christ. They are: the *surrender of the will* and the *service of the hand.*

"No Enemies?"

How is it that he eateth and drinketh with publicans and sinners? (v. 16b).

According to Shakespeare, "Some men are nothing if not critical." The Romans had a proverb, "Not even Jupiter could please everyone." Dr. J. B. Gambrell, a memorable Baptist leader of a former day, used to say, "You can't walk around much without getting on someone's toes." Jesus said, "Woe unto you, when all men shall speak well of you" (Luke 6:26). There were those who said that Washington was little better than a murderer; they said of Lincoln that he was a low, cunning clown, the original gorilla. So,

> You have no enemies, you say?
> Alas! my friend, the boast is poor—
> He who has mingled in the fray
> Of duty, that the brave endure,
> Must have made foes!
>
> —CHARLES MACKAY

There are four main reasons for criticism. First, there is prejudice. A person is often criticized for his race, his class, or his group. No effort is expended to learn about the person as an individual; he is judged by other standards. I have experienced this as I traveled in different parts of the world. I have been in streets when my face was the only white face in the entire block; I was there to help, but I was judged on the basis of the color of my skin.

People are criticized because they are different in temperament and disposition. We like for people to fit into our mold; we do not like for them to be better or worse, smarter or foolisher, richer or poorer. The Greeks told of Procrustes who had a standard-size bed. If he had a guest too long for the bed, legs were chopped off; if a person was too short, he was stretched to fit the bed.

And there is plain outright jealousy; we do not like to see others succeed when we fail. Finally, we are ungrateful creatures; we forget the good and remember the bad.

"The Power of Preaching"

Jesus came into Galilee, preaching the gospel of the kingdom of God (v. 14b).

In the study of a great person's life it is good to give attention to his beginnings. We like to know when and where he began and we like to know what his emphasis was. Jesus began his work in Galilee just after the imprisonment of John the Baptist. Jesus began his work with preaching; he came into Galilee preaching. George Buttrick stated that preachers, not kings and warriors, have been the molders of history. The sermons of Isaiah and Micah outlast the pyramids, outweigh the cargoes of commerce, and cast in the shade all the acts of parliaments. Halford Luccock emphasizes the same truth. He writes, "Every great movement of history has been prepared for and partly, at least, carried forward by preaching." He cites some of these, such as the Christian churches, the Crusades, the abolition of slavery, the Reformation, the great revivals, the labor movement, and others.

On May 31, 1792, a preacher-cobbler named William Carey preached a sermon in Nottingham, England. His text was Isaiah 54:2-3. His sermon had two points: "First, Expect great things from God; Second, Attempt great things for God." The event seemed humble enough; not many people were present. The offering that day was small—thirteen pounds, one shilling, and sixpence, or roughly $52.30. One fact we must not forget, however. God's word had been preached by God's man. Result? Church historians know it marked the beginning of the modern missionary movement.

> A good sermon helps people in a couple of ways.
> Some rise from it greatly strengthened,
> Others wake from it refreshed!
>
> —Anonymous

Thou Shalt Find Me

Whatsoever good thing any man doeth . . . shall he receive of the Lord (v. 8a).

What are the rewards of a life spent in the kind of service that God approves, chooses?

A clear conscience: If one is to have a healthy, happy, mental attitude, one must have self-esteem. If you do not like your job, you can change jobs; if you do not like the neighborhood in which you live, you can move to another; if you do not like your name, the courts will allow you to change it, but your own inner self is another matter. You need to have respect for the person who looks back at you from the mirror.

Approval of others: Little persons desire flattery. Even Jesus desired recognition and approval for good done, "Were there not ten cleansed?" he asked, "But where are the nine?" When I was a pastor, I occasionally turned our mid-week service into a "Thanks-Service." I would invite the people to give expression of heartfelt gratitude for some person, present or absent, living or dead, whose life had been a benediction. Person after person would stand and in warm, moving expression, give thanks for some individual whom the world never thought of rewarding.

Praise of God: To hear God's "Well done, good and faithful servant" is life's highest reward!

> Well I know thy toil and trouble;
> often weary, fainting, worn,
> I have lived the life of labour,
> heavy burdens I have borne.
>
> Never in a prince's palace
> have I slept on golden bed,
> Never in a hermit's cavern
> have I eaten unearned bread.
>
> Born within a lowly stable,
> where the cattle round me stood,
> Trained a carpenter in Nazareth,
> I have toiled, and found it good.
>
> —Henry Van Dyke

"His Factory Bench an Altar"

Let thy work appear unto thy servants (v. 16*a*).

When is a vocation Christian? How can one know that the work that he or she is doing is work that fulfills God's will for life? Suggestions:

One must be honest. A Christian vocation is one in which the person involved can be honest. God does not, cannot lie; God does not call upon, or allow, his servants to lie for him or in his name. It is probably impossible for a person to be totally and completely honest at all times, but the position is clear enough. God may lead a person into work where the person is tempted to sin; temptation is not a sin; yielding is sin.

One must be useful. God does not call, lead, his children to useless, unproductive, futile, parasitical tasks. There is work to be done, hard work, useful work; work that will help, not hurt. Death is not necessarily tragic, it may be beautiful, but, to live a useless, wasteful life is tragic indeed.

God can bless it. A Christian vocation is one that you can conscientiously ask God to bless. You can ask God to bless it because you know it is in keeping with his will. Edgar Frank wrote:

> A man I know has made an altar
> Of his factory-bench,
> And one has turned the counter in his store
> Into a place of sacrifice and holy ministry.
>
> Another still has changed his office-desk
> Into a pulpit-desk, from which to speak and write,
> Transforming commonplace affairs
> Into the business of the King.
>
> A Martha in our midst has made
> Her kitchen-table a communion-table
> A postman makes his daily round
> A walk in the temple of God.
>
> To all of these each daily happening
> Has come to be a whisper from the lips of God,
> Each separate task a listening-post,
> And every common circumstance
> A wayside shrine.[19]

263

Full-Time Christian Service

If I had not come and spoken unto them, they would not have sin (v. 22, RSV).

Every Christian is called to "full-time Christian service." Only in this light can this world be made, in fact as well as in faith and prophecy, our Father's world. Consider:

Numbers involved—The majority of the people are not, never will be, and never should be in church-related vocations. The work of God's world must be done: creation, production, preparation, transportation, information, communication, etc. All this must be brought under the will and way of God.

Time Spent—Think of the time spent in these "secular" jobs. It is here that lives are spent. Obviously, much of what is done for God must be done in and through this work. A treadmill existence or on mission for God, that is the difference.

Decision-making places—It is at this level, not in the pulpit, nor on the mission field, that many of the destiny-determining decisions of the world are made: war or peace, freedom or slavery, feast or famine, capital, labor, race, crime, moral standards, name it; it is all dealt with in the marketplace.

Time dimension—Lay people are at the decision-making spots; they are on the decision-making teams, and they will be at those places long enough to make their influence felt for God and good.

Acceptable ground—The layperson is often accepted when a minister of the gospel is not. The layperson is already a member of the special fraternity of mutual problems and concern and involvement. So, let the Christians in these "secular" jobs realize that they are on full-time Christian service for the Master whatever and wherever they are, and we have a chance to make this world into the kingdom of our Lord and his Christ!

"No Last nor First"

Ye are a chosen generation, a royal priesthood, an holy nation (v. 9a).

There are basic truths in the realm of vocational choice. The Christian owes his life to God; he owes all of his life to God; there is no part of his life that he does not owe to God. This is God's world, all of it. All persons are called to God's love, forgiveness, salvation, fellowship, resources, and service.

The dedication and stewardship are required of Christians whether in the pulpit, on the mission field, at the bank teller's window, behind the secretary's desk, in the cornfield, behind the wheel of a truck, in the kitchen, nursery, or the policeman's beat.

When the dedication and the stewardship are the same, the rewards are equal, no matter where a person's lot is cast. Browning wrote,

> All service ranks the same with God: . . .
> There is no last nor first.

The truth would be breathtaking were it not so familiar. It calls for and emphasizes the doctrine of the priesthood of all believers. All Christians have equal access to the Father's throne, to his ear, and to his heart. This does not mean that no one is called to stand before God for others; it means that every Christian is called on to stand before God for others! Every believer in Jesus Christ as Savior and Lord becomes a priest. He can go to God for himself; he is required to go to God for others.

Remember the old song we used to sing:

> Others, Lord, yes, others,
>   Let this my motto be,
> Help me to live for others,
>   That I may live like Thee.
>
> And when my work on earth is done,
>   And my new work in heaven's begun,
>   May I forget the crown I've won,
> While thinking still of Others.

> —C. D. Meigs

"How Grandly It Had Rung"

If any man offend not in word, the same is a perfect man (v. 2b).

There is great power in words. In the drama, *The Terrible Meek,* Charles Rann Kennedy wrote, "All the things that ever get done in the world, good or bad, are done by words."

We are prone to make light of words; it shows in our proverbs folklore: "Mere words"; "Talk is cheap"; "Put your money where your mouth is"; "Practice what you preach"; and, "Words are the daughters of earth; deeds are the sons of heaven." We are told that the average person speaks about 30,000 words each day. If all these words were published, they would form a book of more than one hundred and fifty pages!

How frightening, then, to hear the words of Jesus, "But I say unto you, That every idle word that men shall speak, they shall give an account thereof in the day of judgment. For by thy words thou shalt be justified, and by thy words thou shalt be condemned" (Matt. 12:36). It helps one to appreciate Will Rogers's words, "One should so live that he would not be afraid to sell the family parrot to the town gossip!"

Did you ever consider what Jesus accomplished with words? With words he banished disease, calmed the insane, brought the dead back from the grave, forgave sinners, comforted the brokenhearted, rekindled faith in the doubting, sent his disciples out to proclaim his gospel—all by the spoken word!

We have been amazed at the power of a mother's words, quieted by a lover's words, encouraged by a friend's words, challenged by a statesman's words, moved by a patriot's words, inspired and stirred to repentance by a preacher's words. Words have produced wars and brought peace.

> *The word we had not sense to say,*
> *Who knows how grandly it had rung?*

"A Christt Distance Away"

Faith, if it hath not works, is dead (v. 17).

James writes that a man's faith will show itself in his love for his neighbor. *Neighbor* once meant a nearby farmer. The word's meaning has changed with the years and now means not merely a farmer but anyone who lives near. So, today every person in the world is a neighbor, for the world is in our yard. In a Christian sense, every person in the world is a neighbor. Jesus taught us in the parable of the good Samaritan that neighborliness is a matter of need—anyone who is in need is my neighbor.

Edna St. Vincent Millay wrote many hauntingly beautiful works, many disturbing things, too. In one of her poems, she spoke about need and that she felt a starving beggar's gaze and heard his moan. She wrote of a tragedy being "only a Christ distance away." Lovely, poignant, disturbing phrase, "only a Christ distance away." That means the tragedy was very near. Do you know of some neighbor who is "only a Christ distance away"?

James was sure that the matter of poverty must not keep a person from being a neighbor. There is to be no respecter of persons. It has been said that whether an action is crazy or eccentric depends upon whether the person performing the action is poor or wealthy! No respecter of persons, please!

Thomas Lamont, partner of J. P. Morgan the banker, once visited a small church where he worshiped as a boy. The pastor of the church was deeply concerned about a leak in the roof of the church. He prayed fervently, "O Lord, send us succor." When the plate was passed, Mr. Lamont dropped in a hundred dollar bill. Looking over the pulpit, into the collection plate, the pastor announced, "The succor has been provided!" We like to provide "succor"; we do not like to be taken as "suckers." But remember, no respecter of persons!

"Won Easily in Eighty-four Rounds"

The trying of your faith worketh patience (v. 3).

I was interested in how an eighty-year-old man had spent his time. He had kept a diary of his activities carefully all his life; this is how he had spent his time: twenty-six years in bed, twenty-one years working; eating had taken six years; being angry had taken another six years. He spent five years waiting for people who were late, spent 228 days shaving, twenty-six days scolding his children, eighteen days tying his neckties. Would you believe it, the man reported that he spent eighteen days blowing his nose? Lighting his pipe took twelve days. And this: the man wrote that he had laughed only forty-six hours in eighty years! Amazing. Care to check the next twenty-four hours of your life? That record of the eighty-year-old man would not please James; he believed in work and service.

And he believed in patience and perseverance, too. James does not want us to be weary in well doing. As the farmer waits for the harvest, so, we must wait for the fulfillment of hopes and dreams.

The worthwhile things take time. We would like to send an army to take over; God sent a baby—that takes time. We would like to board a jet and zoom to Christian character; God permits pain and suffering to do their perfect work—that takes time. We would like for all persons to have an opportunity to accept or reject Christ; God waits on the willingness and generosity of his people—that takes time. We would like to write a check for our son's education; but he has to attend classes, do homework and visit the library—that takes time.

Halford Luccock tells of a boxer in Australia many years ago. The boxer knew that his father would be anxious about the fight so, as soon as possible, he sent the following telegram to his father: "Won easily in eighty-four rounds." Winning is easy; the eighty-four rounds are hard, and it takes time!

Others Up Front

There is a lad here (v. 9a).

In three areas of missions and evangelism Andrew excelled. He was good as a home missionary; he brought his brother to Jesus. That is seldom easy. Jesus said a prophet was without honor in his own country; in Jesus' case, he could have said in "his own home." The family of Jesus, it seems, did not believe in him until after the resurrection. To win a member of your own family calls for courage, character, and Christ. Andrew had all three.

Andrew, in the second place, was a missionary to children. He had a sharp eye for lads with small lunches! Years ago an old minister walked into a churchyard in England and wept. He had just been informed by the leaders of his church that he must relinquish the responsibilities of pastor and give them to a younger man. They said the church was not making the progress it should under his leadership. The old man looked up and saw a boy coming down the road. The old man loved boys; boys trusted the old man. He called the boy to him and told him about Jesus and the way of salvation. The boy listened, understood, and responded. Soon the old man went on his way to his eternal reward. What of the boy? His name was William Carey.

And in the third place, Andrew was a foreign missionary. He brought Greeks to Jesus. Others might stand on custom and ceremony; Andrew knew to cut through all that obstructed and put people directly in touch with Jesus, no matter their origin or background. Home, child, and foreign missions. Some believe in one and some two; Andrew believed in all three. So far as we know, he had no formal training for the task. He made no long speeches, but he performed his task and was content to let others go "up front." Can you imagine what Andrew's thoughts were on the day of Pentecost as he listened to Peter preach?

> Is your life a channel of blessing?
> Is the love of God flowing thro' you?
> Are you telling the lost of the Savior?
> Are you ready his service to do?

> —HARPER G. SMYTHE

September 20   Read Acts 9:36-43
"The Dorcas Heart"

Shewing the coats and garments which Dorcas made (v. 39b).

Dorcas was the founder of the International Ladies' Garment Workers' Union, one of the greatest labor unions of all time, with branches in all lands. The rate of pay has been small, the hours long, but the union has never gone on strike. Otherwise it has been a highly successful craft union in the needle trades. Professor Halford Luccock wrote those delightful words in his book *The Acts of the Apostles in Present-Day Preaching.* "The pay has been small"; "The hours have been long"; "never gone on strike"; "branches in all lands." True words!

There is drama in the words, "And all the widows stood by him weeping, and shewing the coats and garments which Dorcas made, while she was still with them." What if all the coats and garments that have been made by the "Dorcases" from that day until now could be brought out and shown? There would be all shapes and sizes, lengths, styles, materials, weights, and textures. There are few people who have not been the recipients at one time or another of the "good works of charity" of Dorcas.

The Dorcas heart. Most anyone can work up an enthusiasm of "good works and charity." It takes heart to keep at it. Indeed this is where the work really starts. It was so in the case of Elizabeth Fry, the Quaker prison reformer of nineteenth-century England. She recorded her first stirrings of conscience on the matter. She wrote, "I feel like a contemptible fine lady, all outside and no inside." There is the Dorcas heart!

In describing Edna St. Vincent Millay and her poetry, a critic said that she had a "vulnerable heart." He meant that she had marvelous capacity for feeling. He said, "Her devotion to her mother and her sister was far finer than most family relationships. Her friendships were as emotional as love affairs." To a friend she wrote, "Never say to me again, 'Anyway, you can make a trial of being friends with me.' I can't do things that way. I am not a tentative person." The Dorcas heart!

270

"He Ate Victuals"

Jesus therefore being wearied with his journey, sat thus on the well (v. 6b).

A sparkling romanticism clung to the character of Richard the Lion-Hearted and the Crusades. It was difficult for the historian to get at the real man and soldier. Thomas Carlyle was one who tried. Finally he loosed his Scottish blast: "Coeur de Lion," he wrote, "was not a theatrical popinjay with cap and steel greaves; he was a human being who ate victuals!"

It has been difficult for the followers of Christ to realize that he was a man who ate "victuals." It has been almost as difficult for his followers to accept him as human as it has been for the world to accept him as divine. The heresy trials of history have frequently been at this point: his professed followers did believe he was divine. It was hard for them to believe that he was human. The Bible is very clear; it is not a case of "either or but of both and."

As a man he was the greatest of men. The Gospel writers are strangely silent about his physical appearance. He probably looked about like other men in his day; otherwise the writers would have described him. He had quickness of wit and sharpness of mind; he loved to be with men and women; he did not withdraw as an ascetic. He went into the homes of the rich and poor, the learned and the uninformed. The children loved to be near him; the women followed him; the men could not resist his challenge. His courage was amazing. In the face of storms, earthly power, criticism, loneliness, rejection, he was calm and assured. He had surprising reserves of strength; he could preach and teach all day, pray all night, and be fresh and eager in the morning! His confidence in himself, his followers, and in God was amazing!

Behold the man! (John 19:5).

How to Keep Correct Time

To every thing there is a season, and a time to every purpose . . . (v. 1).

Someone gave the story of timekeeping in a certain New England town. Each morning the local telephone operator received a call asking for the time. This went on for weeks and the operator became curious. She knew it was the same voice; the call came every day, at the same time each day. She finally asked the caller just why each morning he called for the time. The caller explained that he was the man who blew the twelve o'clock whistle every day; he called so he would be sure to have the correct time. The operator was quiet for a moment and then said, "Well, that is interesting; did you know that I set my clock by your whistle every day!" It is so easy for individuals, groups, and, even nations to take the time from each other. We need a more reliable timepiece than that.

Andrew Blackwood wrote about Robert Murray McCheyne. When the preacher was at home in Dundee, his watch kept perfect time, but when he was away his watch was utterly unreliable. The explanation was that every day, as the preacher passed the church, he would regulate his watch. That is a good story, a parable of life. Churches ought to get their timing from the stars, the heaven. If this is done, persons can well set their timing accordingly.

Of course, "the sky" is the only place to go for accurate time. This is how and where the Naval Observatory in Washington goes on behalf of the thousands of clocks that depend upon it for perfect timing; it goes to the "heavens," to the sun, the moon, and the stars.

It has been reported that when Charles V, the Holy Roman Emperor who reigned in the sixteenth century, retired, he spent his time, six years of it, in a monastery in Spain, trying to make six clocks tick together, keep perfect time. He couldn't do it. He did not depend upon the "heavens."

What One Vote Can Do

Follow thou me (v. 22b).

Let us hear again Christ's words to Peter when the impetuous disciple became too concerned about another. In essence Christ said, "That is none of your business, Peter; you follow me." You cast your own vote!

"Every man shall bear his own burden," said Paul (Gal. 6:5). "The soul that sinneth, it shall die," wrote Ezekiel. There is truth in the homey saying, "Every tub must sit on its own bottom."

One may surmise that both Paul and Ezekiel would cherish the story that is told of the New England preacher, Lyman Beecher. He and a neighboring pastor had agreed to exchange pulpits on a certain Sunday morning. They met on the road, each going to the other's church. The man for whom Beecher was going to preach said, "Dr. Beecher, I would like to point out to you that before the creation of the world it was decreed that you would preach in my church today and that I would preach in yours, and there was nothing that either one of us could do about it." "Is that so?" roared Beecher. "Then I won't do it!" And he turned his horse and went back to his own church.

Channing Pollock, the writer, and a friend were in a restaurant when a woman at the next table said to her companion that a certain situation was bad and there was nothing one individual could do about it. The friend leaned over and said, "Channing, shall we go over and tell her that everything in this world that is worthwhile started with one person?" He might have added, for instance, that one vote elected Governor Morton of Massachusetts, one vote added Texas to the Union, one vote made California a state, one vote put Cromwell in the "Long Parliament," and one vote was responsible for King Charles losing his head. God gives us some choice as to where we preach, and what we shall do about evil situations. We are free to cast one vote.

"People Who Can Do Things"

The lines are fallen unto me in pleasant places (v. 6a).

People are more interesting than any fiction that they can create. The young Michael Pupin is a case in point. Standing before an immigration officer in New York, he was asked if he had any friends in America. Young Michael affirmed that he did. Who? "Benjamin Franklin, Abraham Lincoln, and Harriet Beecher Stowe." The official thought that over and decided that any young immigrant who could claim these great Americans as his friends deserved to be an American himself.

And there was Ralph Waldo Emerson giving one of his learned lectures in Middlebury, Vermont. The presiding officer called on a local minister to offer a prayer at the close. "We beseech thee, O Lord, to deliver us from ever hearing any such transcendental nonsense as we have just listened to from this sacred desk." Later Emerson asked who the minister was. On being told, Emerson remarked that the fellow seemed to be "a very conscientious and plainspoken man."

Emerson and his son faced a stubborn calf they wanted to get into the barn; the calf had other ideas. The father got at one end of the calf, the son at the other; one pushed and the other pulled. No progress. They exchanged ends of the calf, still no progress. An Irish maidservant looked, giggled, and took charge. She extended a finger into the calf's mouth and the calf followed her willingly into the barn. That night Emerson wrote in his journal, "I like people who can do things!"

"They said it couldn't be done," is an old expression. When you hear that, watch somebody do it. The life motto of Charles W. Eliot, president of Harvard in a bygone day, was:

> It can't be done;
> It never has been done;
> Therefore I will do it.

Dear and ever-blessed Lord, keep us young at heart, we pray. Amen.

"Call the Roll of the Great"

Who is weak, and I am not weak? (v. 29a).

Call the roll of those who have left their mark on life, and you will find men and women doing their work in spite of handicaps: Byron and Scott both had club feet; Alexander Pope was such an invalid that he had to be sewn in rough canvas every morning before he could stand; Dante failed as a statesman before he wrote the *Divine Comedy*. Emile Zola got a zero in literature; a famous editor wrote across Robert Browning's first poem, "Froth, foam, nonsense, trash"; the director of the Imperial Opera House in Vienna advised Madame Schumann-Heink to buy a sewing machine and make dresses, for she would never be a singer. F. W. Woolworth was twenty-one and working in a store, but the owner made him work in the stockroom because, according to his employer, the young man didn't have sense enough to wait on customers.

Beethoven composed his *Ninth Symphony* after he was so deaf that he could not hear a note of it. Thomas Edison was so deaf when he invented the phonograph the only way he could detect the sound was by biting his teeth into the edge of the cabinet when a record was being played. All of Milton's best work was done after he was blind; Handel had one hand paralyzed; Rubens had gout and neuralgia; Molière had weak lungs; Loyola had a leg smashed by a cannon ball and went through two terrible amputations without anesthetics.

> Are you sheltered, curled up and content
>   by the world's warm fire?
> Then I say that your soul is in danger,
> The sons of the Light, they are down with
>   God in the mire,
>   God in the manger.

> —EDWIN MARKHAM

And, do not forget, Christ was crucified on a cross; yes, he was.

September 26　　　　　　　　　　　Read Matthew 25:14-30
"Into Flesh and Blood"

His lord said unto him, Well done, thou good and faithful servant (v. 21a).

Once my wife studied religious dramatics with Fred Eastman of the consolidated faculties of the University of Chicago. One morning Dr. Eastman announced to the class that an official invitation had come for the class to present a religious drama. Great care was given to the selection of a play. The one chosen had as its main character an old Southern mountain woman. Casting began. Every woman in the class who had ever been in any kind of production, tried out for the mountain woman character; they couldn't get it. Finally, Dr. Eastman had every woman in the class to read lines. When my wife's turn came, she stood and read, "doing what comes naturally." For Winnie was "born and bred in them thar hills." Anytime she does not sound like a Southern mountain woman she is "putting on airs." When she had read a few lines, Dr. Eastman said, "Could you do that again?" Winnie did; Dr. Eastman said, "Class, . . . that is real art!"

The opening night of the play was an unforgettable experience for Winnie. Just before curtain time, when every member of the cast was nervous, knowing that anything might happen, and probably would, the plump face, cherubic cheeks, smiling eyes of Fred Eastman appeared. He said, "I thought you might like to know that the author of the play has just arrived; he is in the center, near the front. Good luck!" And, he was gone; the curtain was going up. Winnie was on and, for the life of her she couldn't remember her first line! Fortunately, there was no time to faint or to flee.

At the close of the performance Dr. Eastman brought the author of the play backstage. He was kind and gracious in spirit and in words to every member of the cast. When he came to Winnie, the "mountain woman," he took both of her hands in his and said, "My dear, tonight you put into flesh and blood the woman I dreamed on paper. Thank you very much!"

And, God dreams his dreams for us; we have the privilege of putting them into "flesh and blood."

Read Ephesians 6:1-4   September 27
"My Mother's Kiss"

Bring them up in the nurture and admonition of the Lord (v. 4).

It is sad, but true, that many parents do not have confidence in their children. There are, also, parents who have confidence in their children but never voice the confidence. Few things are more important in the development of a child than knowing that his parents believe in and trust him. The child may fall below the parents' expectation; yet, the chances are he will do so less frequently if there is confidence on the part of the parents.

The parent who is generous with approval and praise will not be resented when reproof is in order. Ultimately, many of the decisions of life have to be made by the child. There are not enough guides and counselors in the world to guard the child against all mistakes. There must be a built-in counselor. The child must learn to be true to the royal within himself. The parents need to cultivate that potential.

Family pride and solidarity are tremendous forces in the area of discipline. "Everybody does it" are words that are often heard. Not true, of course. But it is possible for the home to build a bulwark against the "everybody does it" cult. The child can have a conviction that leads him to say, "No one in my family does that sort of thing."

Real family stability requires that parents behave, too! No discipline will be ultimately effective unless the child sees that the parent thinks enough of the discipline to practice it himself.

William Barclay told the lovely story of how Benjamin West became a painter. One day West's mother left him to baby-sit his little sister. The boy found some bottles of ink and began to paint his sister's picture. Soon the floor was a mess. When his mother returned, she saw the situation; she did not scold. She said, looking at the piece of paper, "Why, it's Sally!" Then she stooped and kissed the boy. Later when fame and fortune had come his way, West said, "My mother's kiss made me a painter."

"She Thinks I'm Real"

Beloved, if God so loved us, we ought also to love one another (v. 11).

The church sees individuals as persons, not as things or objects or means to an end. In his book, *Love Is Something You Do,* Frederick Speakman tells a delightful story of a boy, his family, and a waitress. The waitress was one of the useful and efficient creatures who was never disrespectful to her customers but who, all the same, had a way of quietly letting them know that she was in charge of the situation and that she feared no mortal man or beast!

She made jottings on her pad as the father and mother gave their orders, suggestions, substitutions or changes in sauce, dressings, and so on. Having finished with the parents she turned to the boy; he began with a sort of fearful desperation: "I want a hot dog." That was as far as he got. "No hot dog!" barked both parents at once. Then the mother, "Bring him the lyonnaise potatoes, the beef, and two vegetables, a hard roll and . . . "; the waitress wasn't even listening. She said evenly and quietly to the youngster, "What do you want on your hot dog?" The boy flashed a wonderful smile, "Ketchup, lots of ketchup, and bring a glass of milk." "Coming up," said the waitress, as she turned from the table, leaving behind her the stunned silence of the parents. The boy watched her go, turned to his father and mother, and in tones of awe and appreciation said, "You know what? She thinks I'm real!"

The church is the most redemptive society known. What other group is so interested in the sole welfare of the individual? What other body stands so firmly and persistently for the things that time and death cannot destroy? What other body says to man, in season and out of season, "Thou art immortal"; or stands on the parapets of man's soul and says to him, "Beloved, now are we the sons of God, and it doth not yet appear what we shall be: but we know that, . . . we shall be like him" (1 John 3:2).

Performance Words

For by thy words thou shalt be justified, and . . . condemned (v. 37).

Words and actions frequently merge into one. This can be seen in the work of the linguistic philosophers as they talk about that they call "performance words." These scholars (J. L. Austin is one of the best-known) say that the old idea of words being for the sole purpose of describing a situation as either false or true is inadequate. There are words that actually perform, and accomplish things simply by being spoken. Examples:

In the marriage ceremony, the bride and groom say, "I do." Those two words do not describe the wedding; they are a part of the very act by which the marriage becomes binding. The minister says, "I pronounce you married." The words actually perform. You step on your neighbor's toe and say, "I apologize." The words are the apology. Swing a bottle and strike a ship, "I christen you *Voyager.*" When the words are spoken the act is done. You come into my house and I say, "I welcome you." It is the spoken word that gives the welcome. A judge says, "I sentence you to thirty days in jail." A will is read and you hear, "I leave all my flat silver to Betsy." In each case the spoken words actually perform the act.

Words are often more revealing than actions. Many of the things we do are done so mechanically that there is little meaning attached. But to the discerning person, the spoken word reveals the person speaking: nationality, education, culture, vocation, place, and abode. It is this that makes certain spots in the musical, *My Fair Lady,* so delicious! The professor says that he can place a person within six miles of his home, that he can place him within two miles in London.

If any man offend not in word, the same is a perfect man (Jas. 3:2).

The Ways of Love

Wherefore? because I love you not? God knoweth (11:11).

In case your schedule will allow you to read the lengthy passage suggested for today, you will find something very different. Here is Paul's "severe letter." Here Paul defends himself, his ministry, his apostleship, his stay among them. He shames the Corinthians; he scorns them; he laughs at them; belittles them; threatens them. He fumes and weeps and boasts and shouts!

We need not maintain that Paul always, and without exception, exemplified the spirit of Christ. He admitted once that he spoke "in my folly"; another time he said that he was speaking on "his own authority." Yet, when we understand that, let us go on to say that there is a place and a time for rebuke. Jesus rebuked; Paul rebuked; good parents rebuke. There is nothing contrary to the spirit of Christ in doing so.

Severity and rebuke have a place in the way of love, because love seeks the welfare of the object. When the welfare of the person calls for rebuke, to do less than rebuke would not be kindness to the person. When surgery is called for, to be kind the doctor has to use the knife; to do less would not be for the patient's good.

There is a place in the way of life for discipline and punishment. Ask the good father and the good mother. Ask the child that has been disciplined and punished within the bonds of love. Whom God loves he chastens. If we are left without being chastened, then we are illegitimate children and not true sons of God.

Let the redeemed of the Lord say so (Ps. 107:2).

A Chest of Old Books

Blessed is he that readeth (v. 3a).

L et my wife tell her own story: "A long time ago there came from
England in a much-battered ship, a little family group; the family
brought a chest of books. The books were in Pennsylvania for a time
and then the family moved to 'the wilds of Buncombe County' in
western North Carolina. The family settled near the present Asheville
Airport. In 1840, according to a note on the flyleaf of one of the books,
a note came to the family saying that the Bible had been translated into
forty languages! The family was excited about that. Then, the family
moved further west, the chest of books among the few possessions
carried. That trek ended in what is now Cherokee County. Later, when
the Indians were driven out, the family bought the valley, with the
Valley River running through it. There came the day when my mother
became a part of that family. She grew up in the valley, married my
father, and went forth to establish her own home, on top of an old
Indian mound. As a part of her small dowry, she was given a few of the
books from that old, much-traveled chest.

"I was one of three children. Early my mother began to read to us.
One of the things my mother read to us at the foot of Snow Bird
Mountain was *The Pilgrim's Progress*. Feeling that the book was a little
over our heads, she took us and climbed the mountain, where we
acted out the story—I remember I requested that I be allowed to carry
'the burden'; it was very special.

"One of the memories I have of how I came to love reading is
hearing the sound of my mother's voice and then trudging up the
mountain to act out the story. Not a church recreation department, not
the drama department of a city summer program, but it was a home
that knew the value of books. The knowledge was contagious; I caught
it; I learned to love books."

> Show me the books he loves and I shall know
> The man far better than through mortal friends.
>
> —WEIR MITCHELL

October 2   Read Job 4:1-4
The Author's Prayer

Your words have kept men on their feet (v. 4a, Moffatt).

Can you imagine a world without writing, without books, a Christian faith without the Bible? If so, your imagination is better than mine.

At a conference for writers several years ago Dr. Benjamin P. Browne said, "Perhaps that which we all need most is a renewed faith in the greatness of the written word. We need to remember that though the temples and forums of Greece and Rome are in ruins, and though the Temple at Jerusalem 'has not one stone left upon another,' the writings of these rich civilizations—Grecian, Roman, and Hebrew—endure and remain forever with us in all their eternal vitality. Let us recover for ourselves the majesty and the enduring life of the words which we create from the inspiration of our spirits by the grace of God, and let us believe that to write one page that shines with the brilliance of eternal truth is a greater achievement than to create an atom bomb or to march an army across a continent."[20]

We have been reminded that by words Demosthenes struck the Greeks and the Greeks struck the king of Macedon. By words Peter the Hermit struck Europe and Europe struck the Turks. With words Wendell Phillips struck the conscience of the North and the North struck off the shackles of slavery. Through the use of words, written and spoken, Martin Luther struck at the evils of Romanism and hungry hearts threw off the yoke of spiritual oppression.

In the light of such examples, the "Author's Prayer" by Arthur Guiterman is understandable:

> Help me to hold the vision undefiled,
> To love, and, taught by love, to understand;
> Lord, as a father with a backward child,
> Guide thou the pen within my wavering hand.[21]

A Lap to Sit On

How sweet are thy words to my taste! (v. 103).

Parents, a soft light, an open book, and children's eager faces! Precious, enduring, and creative scene!

Melinda, the small daughter of Howard Maxwell, developed an obsession for *The Three Little Pigs* and wanted it read to her every night. Then Mr. Maxwell's ingenuity took over. He made a tape recording of the story. The next night when Melinda asked for the story, her father simply switched on the recorder. This went on for several nights; then one evening the child handed the storybook to her father. He said, "Now, dear, you know how to turn on the recorder." "Yes," said Melinda, "but I can't sit on its lap."

It is the privilege of the home to furnish a warm atmosphere, a "lap" for reading aloud to children. If there are several children, they cannot all sit on the lap. But by sitting on the floor with the children or in a large chair with arms or on a sofa, the children can drape, lean, hover, or snuggle, so that each can see the picture and become a part of the response. For a story well read is intimately connected with the twinkle in the reader's eye, the color tone of the reader's voice, the facial expression, and total body reaction. The voice is exceedingly important, for it becomes a contributing factor in carrying the listener along. The humor or tragedy is often announced in the tone of voice before it is conveyed in words.

If the child becomes restless, often a lowered tone will bring the attention back to the reader. The poet Whittier must have had a mother who observed such good reading habits. For in writing about the Bible he penned that while we search the world for truth, we finally come back "laden from our quest to find that all the sages said is in the book our mothers read."

> You may have tangible wealth untold;
> Caskets of jewels, and coffers of gold.
> Richer than I, you can never be—
> I had a mother who read to me.
>
> —STRICKLAND GILLILAN

"Note It in a Book"

Note it in a book, that it may be for the time to come for ever and ever (v. 8).

On the shelves of my library are thousands of books, all kinds of books. And as certainly as I discard one today I seem to need it tomorrow. However, there are a few shelves that hold special treasures—most of these are old books; some are new. But, new or old, they are the books that we come back to again and again; we seldom go on a trip of any duration that some of these do not go along with us. Have you ever read William Hazlitt's essay about old books?

> When I take up a work that I have read before (the oftener the better) I know what I have to expect. The satisfaction is not lessened by being anticipated. When the entertainment is entirely new, I sit down to it as I should to a strange dish—turn and pick out a bit here and there, and am in doubt what to think of the composition. There is a want of confidence and security to second appetite. . . . Besides, in turning to a well-known author, there is not only an assurance that my time will not be thrown away, or my palate nauseated with the most insipid vile trash—but I shake hands with, and look an old tried and valued friend in the face— compare notes, and chat the hours away. . . . In reading a book which is an old favorite with me (say the first novel I ever read), I not only have the pleasure of imagination and of a critical relish of the work, but the pleasure of memory added. It recalls the same feelings and associations which I had in first reading it, and which I can never have again in any other way. Standard productions of this kind are links in the chain of conscious being. They bind together the different scattered divisions of our personal identity. They are landmarks and guides in the journey through life. They are pegs and loops on which we can hang up, or from which we can take down, at pleasure, the wardrobe of a moral imagination, . . . of our happiest hours.

Of course, to wear well and to invite us back to them again and again, they have to have something suggestive of the *Book* that as often as we come back to it becomes "A lamp unto my feet, and a light unto my path" (Ps. 119:105).

> To produce a mighty book, you must choose a mighty theme. No great and enduring volume can ever be written on the flea, though many there be that have tried it.

—HERMAN MELVILLE

The Legacy of Influence

As I was with Moses, so I will be with thee (v. 5).

Recently I saw a miracle take place; it happened to a student of mine in a course called "Preachers of Power." Each student was to select a preacher of power and usefulness and study the life and work of that preacher for the entire semester. A list of acceptable names was submitted to the class. This particular student had heard of only two men on the list, Henry Ward Beecher and Phillips Brooks; each of these names was chosen before the student had an opportunity to choose. He had no further preference. I suggested John A. Broadus, scholar, statesman, author, educator, and preacher. The student was totally unfamiliar with Broadus, but he was willing to follow my suggestion, he would study John A. Broadus for a semester.

Until that time this student kept to himself; he was a loner; no one would ever have thought of calling on him for leadership. He began to read about Broadus; the miracle began to take place. Moffatt translates Ecclesiastes 12:11: "They put the mind of one man into many a life." That is what I saw!

The mind and spirit of John A. Broadus began to take possession of my student. He walked with a purposeful stride; there was a flash in his eye, a ring to his voice. He called for more and more materials on Broadus. When he gave me his term paper it was twice the length that I had required. When he took a full class period to tell the class about Broadus, the class was electrified! When opportunity was given to choose two students from the class to speak in chapel, to the student body, on the life and work of the person studied for the semester, the entire class, without a negative vote, elected this student as one of the two. That young man will never be the same again!

> Lives of great men all remind us
> We can make our lives sublime,
> And, departing, leave behind us
> Footprints on the sands of time.

—HENRY WADSWORTH LONGFELLOW

The Way to Understand History

Who is the greatest in the kingdom of heaven? (v. 1b).

One of the frustrating things for the serious student of life is the divisiveness of it. The pieces do not seem to cling together, and schools do not seem to do a very good job of promoting wholeness. We are turning more and more to specialists. Recently a friend of mine was asked to give the invocation at a religious service; as a special favor he thought he might be able to do that; however, he wanted it understood that he was specializing in benedictions! If we would only study the lives of key persons for any era! For example:

The last half of the nineteenth century—the Victorian era—was one of the great periods of history. It was a time of peace for Britain, but it was a time that was bounded by wars, the great French wars at the beginning and World War I at the close. It was a time of expansion, industrialization, colonization, reform, benevolence, and missionary advance. How will you study to understand all that? It can be done; and it can be a delightful undertaking. Take at least one good book on the life of each of the following key persons in that period.

Three statesmen: Queen Victoria, Gladstone, and Disraeli;
Three Philanthropists: Elizabeth Fry, Sir Thomas Powell Buxton, and Lord Shaftesbury;
Three literary persons: Robert Browning, Charles Dickens, and William Wordsworth;
Three Religious leaders: David Livingstone, Charles Spurgeon, and William Booth.

No special plea is made for every individual in these four trilogies; obviously others would choose different individuals. I do affirm, however, that to understand the period you will have to consider these twelve individuals and, if you know them and their contribution, you will understand the Victorian age. And you will better understand Thomas Carlyle's conviction: "The history of the world is but the biography of great men."

Let us now praise famous men, and our fathers that begat us
(Ecclesiasticus 44:1).

Guest List for a Banquet

Jesus saw Nathanael . . . and saith, . . . Behold an Israelite . . . in whom is no guile! (v. 47).

Banquets, as a rule, are not my favorite form of entertainment. However, Hendrick Van Loon staged a series of imaginary banquets that I would like to have attended. To tell the truth, in imagination I did attend these banquets. Van Loon invited the famous to his banquets. The centuries were no barrier. His guests came from far and near; they came in their period costumes, with their predilections and prejudices, with ideals, philosophies, and Christian faith— Beethoven, Shakespeare, St. Francis, Napoleon, Washington, and many others. Van Loon drew back the curtain of time and allowed his readers to attend the banquet and hear the characters tell their own stories. It was a delightful way of letting us know these personalities.

There are other ways of learning about people. You can get at an individual's character through a good portrait. Marchette Chute once called attention to the contrast between a portrait and a biography. He said that a good portrait could go far toward bringing a person back to life. If it is a good portrait, the character "will out." Someone, on looking at a certain politician, said, "If that man is not a scoundrel, God doesn't write a legible hand!" Of course, even in the best of portraits you catch only one pose, one moment of time, one costume. Can you imagine Longfellow without his beard, Whistler's mother without her bonnet and rocking chair, Napoleon without his three-cornered hat and his hand thrust across his chest and inside his coat, Adolph Hitler without his clenched fist and chopped mustache?

The biographer removes the costume and lets us see Queen Elizabeth without her starched collar, Richard the Lion-Hearted without his armor, and Abraham Lincoln without his beard.

What Was He Like?

And Jacob blessed Pharaoh (v. 10a).

The world is filled with interesting people. Would you like to know many of these? How can you do that? Travel is expensive. Frequently there are language barriers; walls and curtains sometimes divide. These people are busy; they do not grant interviews to strangers. Too, there is the matter of time on your part, as well as theirs.

But there is a way you can know great numbers of these people. You can know them as well, even better, than you know your next-door neighbor, better than you know the person who lives in the high-rise apartment above you, better than if you could have a personal interview with each of these. You can know them through books, biographies, and autobiographies.

In the personal interview your time would be limited, probably to an hour at most. Suppose you had prepared carefully for the interview, you had your questions all arranged, you had canceled out all the questions that had to do with information you already knew about the person. Still, you would be limited to shaking hands and asking a few questions to get the famous person's reaction to certain major subjects.

But in biography we can do much more. We can learn what motivates the person's life, what goals were sought, what and who opposed him, what and who aided him in reaching his goals. We can know who his friends were, what and who influenced him in his spiritual quest. Is he a man of God? How has life proved his profession? What contributions has he made to God and to others?

> When the high heart we magnify,
>   And the clear vision celebrate,
> And worship greatness passing by,
>   Ourselves are great.

> —JOHN DRINKWATER

"The Mighty Democratizer"

The kingdom . . . is like . . . a merchantman seeking . . . pearls (v. 45b).

If a fire destroyed everything you possess that is not five hundred years old or older, what would you have left? You may be an avid collector of antiques, but chances are that all you would have left would be a few books, possibly a Book.

These precious antiques would not be limited to the homes of the wealthy. It would be interesting, if painful, to walk over the ruins of the fire and see who was rich and who was poor after the fire destroyed all that was not at least five hundred years old. Some modest homes would have a large collection of these precious volumes, while the inhabitants of many a country-club estate would be left in the ashes without a volume to console, ennoble, and inspire.

Books are the great levelers, the mighty democratizers. They make their home with the prince; they never spurn the pauper. All who fervently love and faithfully use great books are blessed by the presence of the noblest spirits of the race.

Of course, the one ancient book which would be found in more homes would be the Bible. If that imaginary fire were to sweep the world, leaving only those items that are five hundred years old or older, probably no other single item would be seen as often as the Bible. John Quincy Adams wrote:

> I speak as a man of the world, and I say to you: search the Scriptures. The Bible is the Book of all others to read at all ages and in all conditions of life; not to be read once or twice or thrice through, and then laid aside; but to be read in small portions of one or two chapters a day and never to be omitted by some overwhelming necessity.

"What God Hath Joined"

They saw no man any more, save Jesus only with themselves (v. 8b).

Jesus once said that what God joined should not be separated by man. Those words may be applied to work and worship; the two should never be separated. Yet, the meditative, reverent, mystical person often feels that work is an intrusion, and the active, practical, busy person feels that worship is unnecessary.

Jesus was worshiped and adored on the mountain. The record reveals that they, the three, saw him clearly, that there was no one between them and Jesus. Peter saw Jesus and he felt the emotional impact of the hour, felt it and gave expression to it. Peter felt that this was the ideal situation. "Nothing between my soul and the Savior," as the song has it. Isolated, apart, on top of a mountain, alone with the Master, no intrusion of morals or ethics or work, only adoration and worship. Ideal! No, not quite.

Peter saw no carryover, no connection between being alone with Jesus on the mountain and the needs of men at the foot of the mountain. Peter's blind spot has always been a problem with the devout.

Sir John Bowring had that difficulty. He was governor of Hong Kong for the British. While serving in that capacity he had sweet and devout experiences with Jesus. While there he wrote the lovely hymn:

> In the cross of Christ I glory,
>   Tow'ring o'er the wrecks of time,
> All the light of sacred story
>   Gathers round its head sublime.

But Sir John was an agent for the British, and many of the British were engaged in the opium traffic, selling opium to the Chinese. Yet, this did not seem to disturb Sir John deeply.

> Whose life laughs and spits at their creed,
> Who maintain thee in word, and defy thee in deed!

—ROBERT BROWNING

Where to Find Rest

Rest in the Lord, and wait patiently for him (v. 7a).

A little girl had to undergo a serious operation. Everything was new and strange for her in the hospital; she was frightened and cried for her mother. One of the nurses came close and consoled her, "It's all right dear; we will not hurt you; I'll hold your hand." The child asked, "What are they going to do to me?" The surgeon heard and came, "My dear, we are going to put you to sleep gently, just like you go to sleep at home." The child: "And what are you going to do to me while I am asleep?"

The surgeon replied, "Well, you know how you have been hurting from that mean old pain; we are going to take it away so you can run and play like other children and your side will never, never hurt again. And we are going to do that while you are asleep so you will not even know about it." The child was comforted and was ready for sleep. Then suddenly:

"Why doctor, I never go to sleep at home without saying my prayers on my knees by the side of my bed." So, the child had to be lifted from the cot to the floor, and down on her knees, she prayed the childhood prayer, "Now I lay me down to sleep. . . . If I should die before I wake. . . . "

When she was finished with her prayer, the nurses, with misty eyes behind their white masks, helped the little girl to the operating table. There, with a sweet, composed, trusting smile she breathed deeply. Soon the awful pain that had kept her from playing with other children was removed.

A New Man Is the Proof

If any man be in Christ, he is a new creature (v. 17a).

If we are to find Christ "where cross the crowded ways of life," we must first learn to recognize him in the place where cross the lines of prayer. First the perpendicular, then the horizontal.

We lose Christ by being preoccupied with the petty cares of everyday existence. True, Christ went where the people were; he did "come eating and drinking." He did not isolate himself from his brethren.

Let us remember, however, why he went among his brethren and what he went there to accomplish. He went because he was sent by God to bring his brethren home to God. He entered into the joys and sorrows of his brethren to sanctify that which was good, to rebuke and forgive that which was bad, and never to lose himself simply to satisfy his physical needs.

When Columbus returned to Spain after discovering a new world, the Spaniards demanded proof of his discovery. How did they know that he had discovered a new world? Columbus gave many proofs, strange and different plants, fruits, and growth from the fields. However, the explorer's crowning proof, was a new and different man. He showed them an Indian. Then the Spaniards believed that Columbus had discovered a new world! It is the "new man" that is the final proof of all new worlds!

> Just as I am, thine own to be,
> Friend of the young, who lovest me,
> To consecrate myself to thee,
>   O Jesus Christ, I come.
>
> . . . .
>
> I would live ever in the light;
> I would work ever for the right;
> I would serve thee with all my might;
>   Therefore, to thee I come.
>
> —MARIANNE HEARN

Whose Hand the Pitcher Shaped

So he made it again another vessel (v. 4b).

The late George W. Truett had a famous sermon on the passage for our today's reading. It was an expository sermon and the outline grew out of the passage of Scripture.

First, God has a plan and a purpose for every life. The potter had a dream, a plan, and a purpose. Jeremiah, Paul, Peter, Martin Luther, William Carey were not accidents; they were within God's plan and purpose. But he has a plan for our lives, too. And God dreams no little dreams.

Second, the plan and purpose of God for our lives may be marred. "The clay was marred in the hand of the potter." Of course, the picture is not perfect; the clay was pliable; we have wills of our own; God gave them to us. We can say yes or no to God. Nations can, churches can, and individuals can and do; in fact, it is only individuals ultimately who do say no to God.

Third, life can be made over again. "So he made it again another vessel." God can make life over again. What he makes the second time may be different from what he would have made the first time, but if we let him have his way the second time it may be so good and great that we are unable to think of anything finer! Two thoughts follow: one, be careful not to mar God's plan for your life; two, if the plan has been marred, do not despair; he can make your life over.

> Have thine own way, Lord!
>   Have thine own way!
> Thou art the potter,
>   I am the clay!
> Mold me and make me,
>   After thy will,
> While I am waiting,
>   Yielded and still.

> —ADELAIDE A. POLLARD

Five Brothers of Yours

Lord, how oft shall my brother sin against me, and I forgive him? (v. 21a).

There are a few more than four billion people in the world, lots of people! But Samuel S. Drury and Homer Miller have helped us deal with the problem by thinking in terms of individuals. Imagine those four billion people as five individual brothers of yours.

First, the brother you will never see. This brother represents by far the largest percentage of the world's population. Yet, we depend upon this brother and he depends upon us. And, as followers of Jesus we have a Christian responsibility to this brother.

Second, think of the brother whom you will meet only once. I have traveled around the world and spoken to large groups of people in far-off lands. It was my one opportunity to look in their faces and tell them of One who loves them "with an everlasting love."

Third, there is the person you do not like. Of course, this ought not to be. Of course, we like some people more than we like others; we should not dislike anyone. But we do. One time Charles Lamb, the essayist, was berating a person; he was asked if he really knew the man. Lamb exclaimed, "Know him? Of course, I do not know him. I could never hate anyone I know!"

Fourth, there is the brother we do like, the brother who is a friend. The lady of the house said, "Bridget, I don't want you to have so much company calling on you; you have more callers in a day than I have in a week!" Bridget: "Well, Madam, if you would try to be a little more agreeable you might have as many friends as I have."

Fifth is the brother or sister across the table from you. This "brother" should receive our best, gentlest, and loving selves.

"All Alike Here"

I have received of the Lord that which also I delivered unto you (v. 23a).

Let me begin with the oft-told story of the Duke of Wellington at communion; who, when one hesitated through a feeling of unworthiness to kneel beside the "Iron Duke," insisted, "No, No, we are all equal here." We are. At the table of the Lord we are all equal.

There is no difference because we are all alike in our spiritual origin. In the image of God created he us, male and female. "For good you are and bad,/And, like to coin, some true and some false,/But, every one of us stamped with the image of the King."

There is no difference because we are all alike in our sin. This does not mean there is no difference in the way we live; there are differences there. But we all have sinned before our Heavenly Father—"none righteous, no not one."

There is no difference because we are all, and each, the recipients of God's love. The great Hebrew scholar of Scotland, "Rabbi Duncan," was an elder in the Kirk of Scotland. As he passed the cup to a poor woman who was weeping, he whispered, "Take it, Lass, it's for sinners!"

There is no difference because we are all needed and there is a place of service for each, and what is given will be treasured and remembered. Have you seen a bride show her gifts? Or a couple proudly display their tributes from a wedding anniversary? Christ may have his treasured gifts: a coin given by a poor widow, a bottle of costly perfume given by a young girl, a donkey used in a parade, an "upper room," a seamless robe, and your gift to him!

> Bless Thou the gifts our hands have bro't;
>   Bless Thou the work our hearts have planned;
> Ours is the faith, the will, the tho't;
>   The rest, O God, is in Thy hand.

> —SAMUEL LONGFELLOW

October 16   Read Luke 12:22-40
"Surprise Cash Audit"

Be ye therefore ready (v. 40a).

Recently I asked a friend of mine, an auditor by profession, to explain the term, "Surprise Cash Audit." He said, "A surprise cash audit takes place when an auditing firm steps into a place of business unexpectedly, a business that the auditing firm has been employed to audit, places a seal on all cash registers, boxes, and calls for the financial records of the firm. The auditors may be, or they may not be, satisfied with what is showing on the books. The auditors insist on seeing just what the pluses and minuses are." *Surprise cash audit.*

Life has its "surprise cash audits," too. "Be ye therefore ready also," advised Jesus; he said that we would not know the day nor the hour when the great "Auditor" would come to check the records of our life. He said that if the good man of the house had known what hour the thief was coming he would have been ready. He told a parable about a rich man to whom God said, "This night thy soul shall be required of thee." He said that the house built upon sand would be tested, "the rains descended and the floods came." Surprise cash audit.

But, even if the Master had not warned us, life would have taught us about the surprise audits in life. For testing time comes to each and to all. The unexpected temptation, the loss of friends, a blasted ambition, the dissipation of financial resources, illness, death of a loved one. Shall we have enough "cash in the till" to cover the obligations?

Of course, if we are prepared, many of these "surprise cash audits" are opportunities. In the parable of the wise and foolish virgins, the cry, "The bridegroom cometh; go ye out to meet him," (Matt. 25:6), was a crowning moment; that was what the party was all about! Jesus said the Son of man would come unannounced; but for those who are ready to meet him, it will be the chief of all moments!

296

How Many Gods Have You?

I perceive that in every way you are very religious (v. 22b, RSV).

We smile at the polytheism of the ancients; their belief in many gods is hard for us to comprehend. They should have known better. We certainly are far beyond that; we know there is only one God. And, one might answer, "Do we now?" For a person's god is that thing, person, or cause that gets his ultimate allegiance.

What about Bacchus, the god of strong drink? Can we say that he no longer lays claim to fortunes and lives? Think of the drunken drivers, deaths, crime, and disease. And there is Venus, the goddess of physical beauty. True, we no longer call her statues by name, but what a following she has! It is no wholesale blast at the entertainment world to claim that it is based largely upon the Venus cult of flesh and sex.

Take a glance at Mars, the god of war. We no longer build temples in his honor, by name at least. The nations are a monument to him. The giant share of the budgets of nations go for his keep. That is no word in favor of pacifism, which can be made into a god no less than Mars. They are both false gods.

Consider, too, the god mammon. We cannot afford to leave him out, for without his worship few of the above gods would be strong. A long time ago Jesus said, "You cannot serve God and mammon." He was sure that if we tried, a civil war would erupt within, hating one and cleaving to the other. The apostle Paul stated it quite clearly, "Other foundation can no man lay than that is laid, which is Jesus Christ."

> On Christ, the solid Rock, I stand;
> All other ground is sinking sand.
>
> —EDWARD MOTE

What Were They Like?

And Jesus said unto them, Come ye after me (v. 17a).

These early followers of Jesus were a strange mixture! James and John were boisterous as a thunderstorm. Peter was quick like mercury and as hard to hold; he was hot-tempered, yet he had sharp insight and unflagging enthusiasm. Andrew was quiet and retiring, but he was constantly on the lookout for persons he could bring to Jesus. Matthew was a close and accurate observer. Thomas always had to contend with his doubts as if they were a "swarm of gnats"; however, once he was convinced, no one of the disciples was ready to lay more upon the line. There was a Zealot in the crowd, Simon. He had a hot heart inclined to impatience and rebellion. Each was different; each was an individualist. Jesus chose them with this in mind for "he knew what was in man." He knew that his cause would prosper from unity in diversity.

These men were capable of great loyalty; they were not ashamed of enthusiasm; they were idealists. They were neither afraid to be the first to try the new nor anxious to be the last to lay the old aside. They could, would, and did do a daft thing, like giving up a safe living and a comfortable homelife to go traipsing off after a Dreamer who had not where to lay his head. They did not know much about the Nazarene—they knew less about his intent. They could not have passed any kind of entrance examination for a theological seminary.

Jesus accepted them on that basis. They responded to him; they were willing to follow him, and they were willing to pay for that following. Jesus was satisfied with that. They were known as "disciples," that is, pupils or learners. They were willing to accept Jesus as their teacher; he was willing to accept them as his students. He would teach; they would learn. They were willing to give high loyalty; he was willing to give intense love and sacrifice. That is how it all began.

No Clear Title

And the devil said unto him, All this power will I give thee (v. 6a).

Satan offered the world to Jesus if only Jesus would fall down and worship Satan. Jesus refused because he knew that Satan could not offer a clear title to the world. Satan said that the world had been given to him and he could do with it as he pleased. There was an element of truth in that; there is usually an *element* of truth in what Satan says. Satan owned the Roman emperor; the emperor owned the Roman empire; the Roman Empire controlled the world. But it is one thing to have *temporary* control of something, another thing to own it so you can give a clear title. It is the Christian's belief that "The earth is the Lord's, and the fulness thereof" (Ps. 24:1). Man is only a trustee and will be held responsible. Yet, in evil pride man continues to boast of his ownership. Centuries ago Ezekiel taunted Pharaoh for saying, "My Nile is my own; I made it" (29:3, RSV).

There is an old rabbinical tale of two wealthy men arguing over who owned a certain piece of land. They asked the rabbi to settle the dispute. The rabbi said he would ask the land. Putting his ear to the ground and listening closely, he then stood and said: "The earth says it does not belong to either of you; you belong to it. Dust thou art and to dust returnest."

It sounds like what Dudley Zuver wrote, in *The Universe Is My Hobby,* about the white man and the Indians. The white man was still smiling over the fact that he bought all of Manhattan Island from the Indians for only twenty-four dollars. Zuver said that the Indians felt the white man was a fool for giving money for what was not man's to sell in the first place.

Only God can give clear titles.

Read Matthew 6:19-24
God Can Wait, He Thought

Behold the fowls of the air (v. 26a).

We sometimes mistake pity for love, compromise for forgiveness, and desire for aspiration. Graham Greene saw it clearly in his novel, *The Heart of the Matter.* It is the story of a man, Scobie, who built his life on pity and compassion for the unfortunate. But in Scobie there was no unyielding loyalty to God. Putting others before God or himself, he not only failed God and himself, he failed the very persons whom he sought to help.

Scobie was a religious man. He believed he could love God only by loving others. From that he came to feel that love for God was a by-product of his love for others. Failing to give God his highest allegiance, he was left to his own wisdom as to what was best for his neighbor. Instead of being responsible under God to his neighbor, he became responsible for his neighbor.

Through his great love for his wife, he compromised as a police officer; he began to borrow money from a smuggler. He did this to satisfy the expensive tastes of his wife. His compassion for a sea captain who did business with enemies of his country caused Scobie to withhold a report that it was his official duty to file. Through pity and compassion for an unfortunate widow, Scobie became an adulterer. He was led into the situation because, in his confused state, he honestly felt that he had an obligation to alleviate Helen Roth's loneliness.

In every instance, Scobie acted on the principle that his first and highest duty was to others. In every instance, what he actually did was to confuse and injure the persons he sought to help. In a letter to Helen Roth he wrote, "I love you more than myself . . . more than God, I think . . . I want more than anything in the world to make you happy." Later he said to her, "I'll always come if you want me." *God can wait,* he thought.[22]

You May Not Do That

Strait is the gate, and narrow is the way which leadeth unto life (v. 14*a*).

There are some things one may not do even to help one's neighbor. If that be treason, those who worship man will have to make the most of it. Jesus never said the First Commandment was to love man. He said the First Commandment was to love God and that the Second Commandment was that one must love one's neighbor as one loves oneself. A person may not love his neighbor as much as he loves God; he may not love his neighbor in the place of his God; he may not love his neighbor as his God. He or she must love God with all his heart, his soul, his strength, and his mind. Then, and only then, can one love one's neighbor intelligently. From this intelligent self-love, based upon and growing out of supreme love for God, will come one's basis and standard for loving one's neighbor.

The Scriptures affirm that "God is love" (1 John 4:10). The Scriptures do not affirm that "love is God." There is a difference; the difference is vital. Love is of God. It originates with him, not just our love for God but all worthy love. But God is not the product of love, nor does he have his being in love. God is self-sustaining. We cannot love God and hate our brothers. That does not mean when we love our brothers we necessarily love God. When a person trusts God, that person must work for God and his kingdom. But that is not to say that one gains God by one's works.

"Thou shalt have no other gods before me" (Ex. 20:3). The commandment stands not as an edict of an angry God but the wisdom of a loving Father. We may not put neighbor, father, mother, wife or children, brothers or sisters, or even our own lives, before our love for God in Christ. Idolatry does not depend upon a graven image; it begins when we allow anything, or anyone, to take first place in our lives.

Reminiscing

But thou shalt remember the Lord thy God (v. 18a).

A few days ago, I reread the old Greek myth of Charon, the kindly boatman whose job it was to ferry spirits of the departed across the river Styx into the future world. The story tells of a woman who came to be carried across the river, and Charon reminded her that she might drink of the waters of Leathe and forget all her past. The woman exclaimed, "I shall drink and forget all that I have suffered!" "Yes," the old boatman reminded her, "and all that you have enjoyed." "I shall drink and forget all of my failures!" "And all of your victories," he said. "I shall drink and forget all who have hated me!" "And all who have loved you." After a little thought, the woman entered Charon's boat without drinking the waters of forgetfulness.

But we can choose our memories. We have that power. Our life's review need not be a photograph, an exact duplicate in which every external detail and line is recalled. Memory can be more of a painted portrait in which selected thoughts, feelings, experiences, episodes, are recalled that will give depth of meaning to the past. It does not mean that the portrait is less true than the photograph which gives the exact surface accuracy. The painted picture may be more true for it reveals something of the inner life as well as the surface appearance.

In retirement, I have come to understand that memory builds and reveals character. There are maxims that seek to put life into a single sentence: "Clothes make the man" (and reveal the woman, some may add). "A man is what he eats." "A man is what he reads." All too simplistic, of course. But, if you say, "A man is what he remembers," you come about as close to the truth as a single sentence can state it.

> The faith that life on earth is being shaped
> To glorious ends, that order, justice, love,
> Mean man's completeness, mean effect as sure
> As roundness in the dew-drop—that great faith
> Is but the rushing and expanding stream
> Of thought, of feeling, fed by all the past,
> Our finest hope is finest memory. . . .
>
> —GEORGE ELIOT

Offside

Every one that heareth these sayings of mine, and doeth them not (v. 26).

F. Scott Fitzgerald, recognized spokesman for the jazz era, said there were those in the 1920s who thought that life was a game in which everyone was offside, the referee had been chased from the field, and there were no rules. That is not a bad description of Satan's leadership.

Can any fair-minded person look at today's world and believe that evil has enough wisdom to direct this world to any creative end? Look at crime, gambling, drugs, race, communism, graft, greed, illicit sex, broken homes, confused education, rudderless politics. On the cross Jesus prayed for his crucifiers not only because they were bad, but also because they were stupid. He said, "Father, forgive them; for they know not what they do" (Luke 23:34). Evil gives to man what he thinks is the Rachel of his heart's desire; but he wakes to learn that he has Leah instead! Wise is the person who can detect the difference between the devil's promise and his ultimate product.

In those tragic days following World War I, when the government in Washington was all but paralyzed because of the illness of President Wilson, Senator Albert B. Fall of New Mexico managed to get an interview with the President. Earlier, Senator Fall had declared on the floor of the Senate, "We have a petticoat government! Mrs. Wilson is President." Fall had also tried to have the president declared insane, unconscious, or paralyzed—even a prisoner in the White House. So, when he called on the President, he was far from being a welcome guest. At the close of the brief interview, at which Fall had been the loser, as if in an effort to salvage something from the meeting, the senator said, "Mr. President, I am praying for you." The sick but discerning President responded, "Which way, Senator?" And Fall fled from the room. Beware when evil offers concern and prayer!

October 24   Read Mark 8:34-38
Mixing Ends and Means

Whosoever will come after me, let him . . . take up his cross (v. 34b).

Ends and means must merge into one. "I will be unanimous," announced Henry David Thoreau, when someone asked what he was going to be when he grew up. Most of us can't say that; we are divided. We want right things for wrong purposes. We work to achieve the good but use wrong means.

Yet, we can never be quite sure which are ends and which are means in our service for Christ. You minister to a sick body hoping you will have an opportunity to tell the person about the love of the Savior; later you learn you were ministering to Jesus in the first place! You fight your way through a storm in order to help someone and later find that fighting through the storm was of the most help. A "Borden of Yale" surrenders and sacrifices, studies, and disciplines himself in order to glorify Christ in mission work; just as he is ready to go on that mission he dies. Then you learn that the study, the discipline, and the death are what touched thousands of college students and caused them to become involved in missions. Just where will you draw a line between means and ends for a "Bill Wallace of China"? Missionary Wallace died in a Red Chinese prison.

Van Wyck Brooks said, "No good writer has ever liked drudgery, nor has any good writer ever permitted anyone else to do his drudgery for him." So much of life, even the Christian life, is drudgery. Yet, the routine tasks are necessary; they cannot be avoided. They must be invested with the Spirit of Christ.

> It is a calumny to say that men are moved to heroic action by ease, hope of pleasure, recompense—sugarplums of any kind in this world or the next. . . . It is not to taste sweet things, but to do noble and true things, and vindicate himself under God's heaven as a God-made man, that the poorest son of Adam surely belongs. Show him the way of doing that, the dullest daydrudge kindles himself into a hero. . . . Difficulty, abnegation, martyrdom, death are the allurements that act on the heart of man.
>
> —Thomas Carlyle

Well, yes, the cross is a rather dirty business.

"A Hard Lesson"

That they may all be one (v. 21a, RSV).

On the bottom of the swimming pool at Monmouth, Illinois, the builders placed, at the center of the YMCA triangle, the Bible reference, "John 17:21." A boy observed the reference, dived, and swam to the bottom. When he came up, he asked his coach what the reference meant: "It says, 'John 17:21,' but what does that mean?" His coach answered, "That they may all be one." The boy's response: "You sure have to go through a lot to find that out!" Yes, we do, but if we really learn that, it is worth the effort.

On Christmas Eve, 1968, the Apollo astronauts flew over the surface of the moon. The earth was listening. The crew commented on the beauty of the earth as they saw it from that distance; they read the opening verses from the Book of Genesis and invoked God's blessings on our sphere. Those words and that action caused Archibald McLeish to write this observation which was released on Christmas Day:

> To see the earth as it truly is, small and blue and beautiful in the eternal silence where it floats, is to see ourselves as riders on the earth together, brothers on that bright loveliness in the eternal cold—brothers who know now that they are truly brothers.

As the boy in the swimming pool said, we "sure have to go through a lot to find that out!" But we will not be able to go much deeper, higher, or broader until we act on that discovery. If we are to travel safely into the future, we shall have to go on "ships": membership, fellowship, stewardship. We sometimes sing about, "We are one in the bond of love." We claim that we are one in the Spirit. And "That's nice work if you can get it." However, it will take more than trying on our own resources; that is a task which only God can accomplish. He will not accomplish it without our help and cooperation. All together now!

The multitudes who require to be led, still hate their leaders.

—WILLIAM HAZLITT

October 26   Read Joshua 6:1-6

"On Seeking the Promised Land"

The wall of the city shall fall down flat (v. 5c).

Moses was not allowed to lead the Hebrews into the Promised Land; Joshua was appointed to do that. His first major task was to capture Jericho, and he was told how to do it. The Hebrews marched around the city once each day for six days. On the seventh day they marched around the city seven times; then the priests blew their horns and the walls of Jericho fell—"came a-tumblin' down."

That scene has captured the imagination of the world. Why? Well, it's a good story; it's Bible history; Joshua was a great leader. But it is more—the story is a parable of life. This is what the children of God always experience. There are three major truths in the story:

First, every life has its promised land toward which it moves. And this Promised Land is what sustains us; it is the vision which lifts our eyes above present experiences to future realities.

Second, there is a Jericho blocking the entrance into every person's Promised Land. Jericho was the gateway into the Promised Land from the south and the west. It was a walled city astride the entrance into the Promised Land: you couldn't go around it, climb over it, dig under it; you had to capture it if you were going to enter the Promised Land. Now, isn't that life? Our Jerichos may take the form of grief, broken health, financial ruin, domestic tragedy, political misfortune, but it is there and it has to be conquered, or there is no entrance into our promised land.

Third, help from unseen, unexpected sources comes to our aid. It may be as strange as torches and trumpet blasts! Frequently we are not able to explain, not even understand, how we are able to capture and conquer these Jerichos. But if we are in obedience to the will and way of God, in time—usually God's time, not our own—Jericho's walls will come tumbling down.

"Ye May Not Enter"

The Lord hath said unto me, Thou shalt not go over this Jordan (v. 2b).

After more than four hundred years of slavery in Egypt the Israelites were led out of bondage by Moses. Moses was eighty years old; this was the crowning achievement of his life. It was as if everything Moses had experienced and known before was preparation and prologue. His studies in the universities of Egypt, hot-headed outbursts of temper in the brickyards, tending sheep on the backside of the desert, listening for God's voice in the stillness, and waiting for his giant hour.

The hour arrived. He received his orders. He went to Egypt, faced the Pharaoh, performed his miracles, organized, and led the children of Israel out, out across Goshen, through the Red Sea, on into the desert, and on toward the Promised Land. Moses did!

But he was an old man. His strength was not as it had once been. His nerves were taut; his patience was worn thin, and he did not always give God the glory due him. So, God allowed Moses to get within sight of the Promised Land but would not allow him to enter it.

Moses was not the last military leader who had the ability to break the shackles of slavery but was unable to forge the bonds of freedom, to lead the people from bondage but not into liberty, to throw off one yoke but not put on another, the ability to break but not to build, to prepare but not to consummate.

And yet it is a sad picture, tragic and very true to life. So often we give our lives for something and then, when it seems almost within our grasp, we can see it just "beyond the river," as Moses was allowed to see his Promised Land; then we hear God say, "Thou shalt not go over this Jordan." Dreams, like Moses, are frequently buried on the east side of Jordan.

"We Get Help"

Thou, Lord, hast helped me and comforted me (v. 17b, RSV).

We need not fight alone. When Joshua was planning his campaign against Jericho, he had a vision of an armed soldier standing with sword in hand. Joshua faced the Being with this question, "Are you for us, or for our adversaries?" To which the Being replied that he was neither for Joshua nor for his enemy; instead he was captain of the armies of the Lord. As if to say, the Lord will not be commanded by you or by your enemy. The Lord is concerned and involved in this mission. If you wish to enlist in his army and under his leadership, well and good. At this Joshua fell on his face and inquired, "What does my Lord bid his servant?" And the Presence said, "Put off your shoes . . . for the place where you stand is holy."

We need not go forth to fight our Jerichos alone; we may have divine assistance. But to secure that assistance, we must recognize who God is and what his rights are. We must get our marching orders from a divine command post, knowing that God is at least as interested as we are.

Joshua's experience is not unique. People have always had God's help in attacking the Jerichos of evil. Joseph was sold into Egypt, but the Lord was with Joseph. The Hebrew children were thrown into the furnace of fire, but there was a fourth Person in the flames, and his countenance was like that of the Son of God. The disciples were in the midst of the storm, but the Master of the storm came to them. The two on the road to Emmaus were joined by a Third, and the disciples' hearts were warmed as that Third opened the Scriptures to them. Stephen was stoned, but he was aware of the Christ; Paul experienced the loss of all his friends, but he testified, "The Lord stood by me." John was exiled to Patmos, but he "was in the Spirit on the Lord's day" (Rev. 1:10).

We get help.

What God Entrusts to You

Son of man, I have made thee a watchman (v. 17a).

Dwight L. Moody said, "A Christian is someone to whom God entrusts all his fellowmen." And William James affirmed that "The greatest use of life is to spend it for something that will outlast it."

A few of God's people have been caught up with that. The early disciples were. Looking at those men, as they were when Christ found them, who would believe that they would become and do what they became and did! Who would have dreamed that they would "turn the world upside down," and become, as they did become, and have remained in the thinking of the Christian world for two thousand years, "The glorious company of the apostles!" Just imagine that being said of vacillating Peter, of thunderous John, of silent Andrew, of doubting Thomas, and of those in that little band of whom the writers of the New Testament did not even feel led to list their names after Jesus called them.

But they came to feel that they were possessed by a superlative purpose and that resources were available for accomplishing that purpose—and nothing and no one could stop them! From their day to ours, here, there, yonder, a few men and women—never a large number in any one generation or in any one part of the world—have been so possessed and so assured and so supplied that the world has had to make way for them.

To see that phenomenon is one of the amazing experiences of life; few things so move the world to its depths. When such an individual or such a small group comes along, cynics, scoffers, nihilists, sophisticates, tired do-gooders, the hard and the crusty are ready, if not to cheer, at least to salute. This is true even in the entertainment field. Who would think that these tired, frustrated, modern audiences could be moved as they were by a song like "The Impossible Dream" from *The Man of La Mancha?* Yet, it brought crowds to their feet, often copious tears flowed, always there was a lump in the throat, as the song rolled over the audience, challenging and inspiring to a noble purpose.

"The Stub of an Old Checkbook"

Give, and it shall be given unto you (v. 38a).

When Thomas Carlyle was a small boy, a beggar came to the door. On an impulse the boy ran, broke his bank, and gave the beggar everything there was in it. Late in his life, looking back upon that incident, Carlyle declared that he had never before, nor since, known such sheer joy as was his in that moment of hilarious giving!

Many years ago I observed a young man, moved by a powerful missionary appeal, give his entire savings to the cause. The incident had a profound effect upon the youth, changing the course of his life for the better.

Few factors are more revealing than the pattern of a person's giving. If you can learn what a person spends his money for, you have one of the best indexes of the character and life of the person.

The biographer Philip Guedalla wrote that this factor gave him true insight into the life of the Duke of Wellington. The writer said there was no problem in learning what Wellington did, where he went, what he said, and who his friends were. All this was well documented. The real problem was to learn what kind of a man the "Iron Duke" really was. Then the biographer found the stub of Wellington's old checkbook. Eureka! He had found the real "Iron Duke."

> "Go break to the needy sweet charity's bread:
> For giving is living," the angel said.
> "And must I keep giving again and again?"
> My peevish and pitiless answer ran.
> "Oh no," said the angel, piercing me through,
> "Just give till the Master stops giving to you."
>
> —ANONYMOUS

"A Heart Fixed to Give"

Go, and do thou likewise (v. 37b).

Out in the desert the note was found, written with a lead pencil on a piece of brown wrapping paper. The note was stuck in a rusty baking powder can that had been tied with a piece of wire to an old pump. The words scribbled on the paper said:

Under the white rock I buried a bottle of water out of the sun, cork end up. There's enough water in it to prime this pump, but not if you drink some first. Pour about one-fourth and let 'er soak to wet the leather. Then pour the rest, medium fast and pump. You'll get water. The well never has run dry. Have faith. When you get watered up, fill the bottle and put it back like you found it for the next feller. Signed, Desert Pete

P.S. Don't go drinking up the water first. Prime the pump with it . . . I've given my last dime away a dozen times to prime the pump of my prayers and I've fed my last can of beans to a stranger while saying "Amen." It never fails to get me an answer. *You've got to git your heart fixed to give before you can be give to.*

"You've got to get your heart fixed to give before you can be give to." Yes! And, we have it on better authority than "Desert Pete," although I am slow to argue with experience. Still, there is a better authority. Listen: "For whosoever will save his life shall lose it; and whosoever will lose his life for my sake shall find it." "It is more blessed to give than to receive." "Give and it shall be given unto you, good measure, pressed down . . . and running over," and, "Give to him that asketh thee, and from him that would borrow of thee turn not thou away." Authoritative? Indeed! Jesus of Nazareth, our Lord and Master.

Of course, so many of his parables had this truth at the center: the rich man and Lazarus, the good Samaritan, the judgment, the fig tree, the talents, seed, and soil. Or think of the basis of our Lord's coming to earth. Paul said that he "emptied himself," held nothing back, gave it all, even his own life. And, when that was done, as if there was nothing more to give, went back to his Father!

"When I Get Around to It"

Repentance toward God, and faith toward our Lord Jesus Christ (v. 21b).

Paul preached that God calls on all people everywhere to repent. No person is excluded from that call. No geographical boundaries are exempt, and the time for repentance is now. The Bereans responded to that call, but the Athenians refused to do so. It is easy to believe that others should repent—Russia, Germany, Italy. We do not even object to repenting ourselves—at a later time. It is the "right here, right now" that we object to so strongly.

In *Uncle Tom's Cabin* the slave trader, Haley, confesses, "I al'ays meant to drive my trade so as to make money on't, fust and foremost, as much as any man; but, then, trade ain't everything, 'cause we's all got souls. I don't care who hears me say it, and I think a cussed sight on it so I may as well come out with it. I b'leve in religion, and one of these days, when I've got matters tight and snug, I calculates to tend to my soul and them ar matters."

But Paul says it is right here, right now that repentance is demanded. God demands repentance from everyone everywhere, but he does not require the same reaction to that repentance. Charles Spurgeon had a youth come to him following a sermon and ask in awe and wonder, "Do you mean to tell me that all I have to do to believe and be saved is to believe on the Lord Jesus Christ, and that can be done instantly? Why, my old daddy," exclaimed the youth, "was six months in awful trouble of soul and a part of the time he was so bad we had to keep him in a lunatic asylum!"

> There is one case of deathbed repentance recorded—that of the penitent thief, that none should despair; and only one that none may presume.
>
> —AUGUSTINE

"Let the Work Praise Itself"

He hath opened thine eyes . . . He is a prophet (v. 17b).

Abusinessman discharged one of his employees. "Where's Jim?" asked a friend. "Well, Jim doesn't work here anymore." "Have you gotten someone to fill the vacancy?" "Well, now, I'll just be frank with you, when Jim left he didn't leave any vacancy." Thoreau once asked an Irishman how many potatoes he could dig in a day. The man replied, "Well, I don't keep any account. I scratch away and let the day's work praise itself." Thoreau liked the answer.

When Wilberforce Whiteman was critically ill in Denver, his famous son, Paul the bandleader, hurried from New York to be by his father's side. The first thing the father said when he saw his son was reminiscent of Paul's pranks in former years. "Now what have you done?" asked his father.

Then the father began to speak of his favorite subject. "I shall tell you," he began, "why Toscanini is such a great conductor. It is because his orchestra never plays for Toscanini, nor does Toscanini reach out selfishly for the credit. First, Toscanini always conducts the music of Beethoven as if Beethoven himself were listening. And, second, Toscanini wants Beethoven to hear it done correctly."

> Honest toil is holy service
> Faithful work is praise and prayer.

Proverbs says of a faithful wife, "Give her of the fruit of her hands; And let her own works praise her in the gates." Jesus affirmed, "My Father worketh hitherto, and I work."

"A perpetual vacation," wrote George Bernard Shaw, "is a good working definition of hell. Revelation assures us that his saints 'serve him day and night.'"

"An Interposed Signal"

I was not disobedient unto the heavenly vision (v. 19).

On November 1, 1954, Alexander Rial Woods died at the age of seventy-four. He was the minister of St. Paul's White Chapel in the dockyard section of London's poverty-stricken East End. He had seen the congregation grow from seven to overflowing, with aisles crowded. The pastor lived the same poverty-stricken life that his flock lived. He seemed to speak their language and get through to their needs; they loved and trusted him.

But they knew little about their "poor man's parson" before he came to them. But, as death sealed his lips, it broke the seal on his past. The pastor had been Vice-Admiral Woods of the Royal Navy. He had received the coveted D.S.O. for his heroism with Admiral Jellicoe at the Battle of Jutland, the only major engagement between the English and German fleets during the First World War, fought on May 31, 1916.

In the midst of that battle, Vice-Admiral Woods received what he called, in military terminology, "an interposed signal which came from no earthly captain but from a higher command." He gave up his brilliant and promising naval career and entered a theological seminary. He was ordained and, at his own request, was sent to preach the gospel to the poor. And on November 1, 1954, thirty-eight years after hearing that "interposed signal," he died among the people who loved and followed him. He, with Paul, could say, "I was not disobedient unto that interposed signal."

Lord, when I look upon my own life, it seems Thou hast led me so carefully, so tenderly, Thou canst have attended to none else; but when I see how wonderfully Thou hast led the world and are leading it, I am amazed that Thou hast time to attend to such as I!

—AUGUSTINE

"The Window Sill of Heaven"

God is our refuge and strength, a very present help in trouble (v. 1).

It is as natural to seek the help of God in the great crisis experiences of life as it is to breathe. The form of approach may not be orthodox. Hear the sailors in Shakespeare's *The Tempest*, "All's lost! To prayers, to prayers! All's lost." And centuries before Shakespeare the psalmist wrote, "They reel to and fro, and stagger like a drunken man, and are at their wit's end. Then they cry unto the Lord" (107:27-28).

We also turn to the Lord in hours of gratitude. When you are on the receiving end of some kind and gracious deed on which you have made no deposit, you seek Someone to thank. It was before the days of free lunches for schoolchildren. A teacher, from her own initiative and resources, managed to get milk for the children in her class. The children began to show improvement; they were more alert, eyes were brighter; there was a different ring to their voices. Only one child, a small girl, showed no improvement. The teacher was concerned. One day she observed the little girl. After the bottles of milk had been given out, this little girl was seen to secretly put her bottle of milk under her coat and dart around the building to another classroom and give the milk to her younger brother.

During World War II five men were on a rubber raft in the Pacific. The raft would support only four. During the night one man voluntarily slipped off into the deep that the other four might live.

Lines around the eyes soften. There is a gentle tug at the heartstrings, and we say, "Aye, that is good; that is the way all life should be; that is the way life ought to be lived." And a "still small voice" answers, "It is the way life would be if you would only let the love of Christ constrain you."

What Prayer Is Not

Ye ask, and receive not, because ye ask amiss (v. 3a).

Prayer is primarily a relationship; its main purpose is not to get, but to be. From the marriage bond a person may get many things: good meals, a clean house, a generous checking account, and social and emotional security, but unless the relationship is good, "sure bad is our bargain!"

Christian prayer is not an information center, a daily broadcast to God in order to keep him informed of the needs of the world. One of the Alphonsos of Spain was greatly distressed, we are told, because he was not present at the creation of the world; he could have given God some good advice! The purpose of prayer is not to coerce God's will. It is not a substitute for work, either. One must do one's own homework.

There is a charming story of a little girl's prayer. Her mother heard the child pray, "Dear Lord, don't let the little birds get in Jimmy Brown's bird trap. Jimmy is a nice boy, but he does naughty things. He's built a mean old trap. Don't let the birds get in it. Thank you for hearing and answering my prayer, Amen." Her mother asked, "Dear, how can you be so sure that God will answer your prayer?" "Because, this afternoon he helped me 'bust' the trap." Cooperation!

Prayer, real prayer, is not autosuggestion, a mere talking to yourself, even though saying the right things to yourself is important. It is vital that we say positive rather than negative things to ourselves. But prayer is more than this. The saints keep on praying. Jesus taught that we "ought always to pray and not to faint" (Luke 18:3).

> This very remarkable man
> Commends a most practical plan:
>   You can do what you want
>   If you don't think you can't,
>   So don't think you can't think you can.

—ANONYMOUS

"God Healed Him"

The Lord gave Job twice as much as he had before (v. 10b).

We are told that the Lord turned the captivity of Job when he prayed for his friends and that the Lord gave Job twice as much as he had before. To some small degree, each of us has had similar experiences. We have prayed and have released from our captivity; we have prayed and have been given access to resources we never knew existed. Had Job known the fine words of Robert Browning—"Our times are in his hand . . . trust God; see all, nor be afraid!"

Beatrice Plumb wrote of being in the physician's church built by Canon Twell. She sat quietly and alone. Then she saw a man moving down one of the aisles to the chancel, there to kneel. She had never met the man, but she recognized him from pictures. He was a distinguished surgeon known for his "modern miracles." She saw the surgeon lift strong, slim hands in an attitude of prayer. For what could this modern knight of medicine be praying? A few days later she read that this doctor had successfully performed an operation which would go down in surgical annals as the first decisive victory over a dread physical disease before which earth's doctors had stood helpless. Beatrice Plumb remembered the words of the Canon Twell, "I dressed his wounds; God healed him."

There is much that we do not understand about prayer—why and how God hears and answers. It may be that it is more of a mystery than why God does *not* answer. We cannot understand either. Fortunately, we do not have to understand. It is essential that we cooperate with God in getting his will done on earth, in our own lives as well as those of others.

> Lord, what a change within us one short hour
> Spent in Thy presence will prevail to make!
> What heavy burdens from our bosoms take,
> What parched grounds refresh as with a shower!
>
> —RICHARD CHENEVIX TRENCH

November 7   Read John 1:43-46

On Taking Wagons Over Mountains

Come and see (v. 46b).

Andrew and Philip were not vanguard men; they seldom led the parade. Yet, there are lessons to be learned from these two men. Philip had a way of being present when big things happened! He did not push himself forward but he knew what was important. He also knew where it was taking place—Philip was there! Aubrey Smith once said that everytime Philip appeared he was concerned with great themes. It might have been sharing Christ with others, breaking the bread of life, finding God revealed in human life, or grasping the meaning of the cross. Philip was concerned with pivotal matters.

Philip believed that all one had to do to convince persons of the divinity and kingship of Jesus was to bring them in touch with the Master. He was not interested in arguing; he was perfectly willing for persons to make up their own minds once they stood face-to-face with Jesus. "Come and see" was his theme. Philip was like a good long-distance telephone operator, who gets your party on the line and then gets off the line, leaving it up to you and your party.

In 1834 Marcus Whitman, a medical missionary, rode horseback to Oregon. He was one of the first of the pioneers and one of the first to see the possibilities of the Pacific Northwest. Whitman returned to Washington and asked President Tyler for help to put families in the territory. We are told that the President listened, then shook his head. He said that while strong men might go over those mountains on foot or horseback, a settlement would require women and children. Women and children would require wagons and, said the President, "You can't take wagons over those mountains." Said Marcus Whitman, "Mr. President, I *have* taken a wagon over those mountains." "Then," said the president, "you may have the wagons and supplies." *Come and see.*

It is cruel to console another for a sorrow a man has not himself experienced.

—AUTHOR UNKNOWN

What Mary Did for Jesus

Can a woman forget her sucking child? (v. 15a).

Mary gave Jesus a home and a welcome. The first home was in her young body. Rosetti put it in beautiful words:

> So held she through her girlhood; as it were
> An angel-watered lily, that near God
> Grows and is quiet.

Modern psychology and worthy students of child guidance have made us aware of how important the home is to the growing child. God revealed this truth long before modern educators announced it. If there had been a better way for the Son of God to come into the world, the Father would have chosen it. Since there was no better means, God chose the way of the home. Knowing that God made this choice, let no mother ever feel that there is a greater or more important task than that of being a good mother and making a good home for a child.

Motherhood is a holy task. The marriage relationship was sanctified and purified through the fact that, by the will and grace of God, the woman who gave birth to Jesus became the mother of other sons and daughters. So, Mary gave Jesus a home with the human experiences which grow out of relationships with brothers and sisters. Mary kept the family together.

Mary gave Jesus love in the home. This, we may be sure, was easy at first. We may also be sure that later it was not so easy. Consider the event in the Temple when Jesus was twelve, the wedding at Cana, and the time when she and the family went to bring him home because the people were saying that Jesus was "beside himself." Yet, she gave love. And she encouraged trust, self-reliance, and a spirit of independence.

> He who gives a child a home
> Builds palaces in Kingdom come.

"Some Call It Autumn"

Thou crownest the year with thy goodness (v. 11a).

It was a great day for Moses, the children of Israel, and the world when, having led his sheep to the backside of the pasture at the foot of the mountain, he saw a bush that was ablaze with fire, yet was not consumed. Surely it was an autumn day! In October our hills, valleys, and country lanes are ablaze with color! Fiery reds, golden yellows, unfading evergreens, somber browns, rich orange, and tender pastels, all mingle in one gigantic panorama of canvas.

Take a tour. You can see a canvas a thousand miles long! Let human artists stand back when God begins to paint! Along the rivers, up and down the sides of the mountains, by the banks of the lakes, you will see the indescribable mixtures of gold and orange and crimson and saffron. Here and there the trees look as if their leaves have been touched with brilliance of fire!

In the morning light the forests will look as if they have been transfigured before the Lord, and in the evening they will glow as if the sunset has burst wide open and showered its splendor upon the leaves until the very glory of the Lord shines round about them.

Some of the highest mountainsides seem to be pouring, as T. DeWitt Talmadge once said, "cataracts of fire," and through the ravines can be seen the foaming streams plunging headlong to put out the conflagration! Then you know full well, that if God's urn of colors were not infinite, some of these vast stretches would exhaust his storehouse forever! Then you begin to grasp how Edna St. Vincent Millay must have felt when she wrote,

> O world, I cannot hold thee close enough!
> Thy winds, thy wide gray skies!
> Thy mists that roll and rise!
> . . . .
> My soul is all but out of me.[23]

As William H. Carruth has written:

> Some of us call it autumn
> And others call it God.

"'Minds Me of God"

The place whereon thou standest is holy ground (v. 5b).

Jesus asked that we "Consider the lilies of the field. . . . " Nature spoke to him of God. He never confused nature with God. He interpreted nature in the light of his more intimate knowledge of an experience with God. When Jesus did this, nature was as a garment that God wore. It reminded him of God.

Archibald Rutledge has a haunting and beautiful story that sounds this note. He said that he visited a lonely cabin in the North Carolina mountains, from which the owner had just been taken, accused of murder. He and a neighbor quarreled over a line fence and he had been "quicker on the draw" than the neighbor. The accused had borne a good reputation up to that time. Both men had seen service during the war. Rutledge was well-acquainted with both families.

As he went up the old gullied road toward the mountain home, he noticed that the rhododendrons were in blossom, surpassingly beautiful flowers! As he reached the cabin one of the man's sisters greeted him. Over the humble mantel he saw a crude little photograph of the brother in uniform; and beside it, in a small vase, was a sprig of rhododendron blossom. The visitor looked at the picture; then he said something casual about the flower. The sister said, "I don't know why but to have it there helps me. It 'minds me of God."[24]

And the angel of the Lord appeared to him in a flame of fire out of the midst of a bush: and he looked, and, behold, the bush burned with fire, and the bush was not consumed (Ex. 3:2).

November 11   Read Psalm 56:1-13

On Breaking the Years . . .

What time I am afraid, I will trust in thee (v. 3).

The fear of the future can rob us of living fully in the present; fear of poverty can cheat us of enjoying the good things in the present; fear for loss of health can keep us from taking chances that are necessary for full participation in the game of life; fear of death can make us cowards in the struggle with evil.

A man walks up to another and says, "Would you give me a match?" No response. He says again, "I say, friend, would you give me a match?" No response, not even the turning of the head. The first man is irritated and says, "Listen buddy, I asked you a civil question. If you don't have a light, you could say so. What's 'eating' you?"

The second man now turns his head and looks the questioner over carefully, then, says, with emphasis, "So, you want me to give you a light? I give you a light and you'll say, 'Thank you'; I'll say, 'Quite all right'; you will say, 'Nice day,' and I'll say, 'Yes, it is.' You'll say, 'Who do you think will win the game this afternoon?' I'll say, 'Not sure; what do you think?' And you'll say, 'By the way, my name is Tom Brown,' and I'll say, 'Glad to meet you, Tom; I'm Jim Smith. Why don't we have a cup of coffee together.' You will say, 'Fine, let's do that.' Now over that cup of coffee, I'll invite you to my house. I have a daughter. You'll meet my daughter, fall in love, and marry her; then you'll have a houseful of kids. You will get sick and die, and leave those kids for me to take care of. Now, buddy, I don't like kids, can't stand them! No! I'm not giving you a match!" And, the man stalks off.

We are afraid of the future, and that fear keeps us from making the most of the present. The years frighten us. But, we can handle, generally speaking, the hours. We have some control over the next hour of life: what we shall do, where we shall go, what we shall say. Let us take the hours as they strike and leave the years to God. And why not give the man a match?

322

"Life's Extras"

For the Lord is good (v. 5*a*).

A utumn is filled with "life's extras," as Archibald Rutledge called them. "Creation," said Rutledge, "supplies us with only two kinds of things: necessities and extras. Sunlight, air, water, food, shelter—these are among the bare necessities. With them we can exist. But moonlight and starlight are distinctly extras; so are music, the perfumes, flowers. The wind is perhaps a necessity; but the song that it croons through the morning pines is a different thing."[25]

It would have been possible for God to make a world without color. An eye could have been made without the marvelous intricacies of color discernment. The cones could have been left out of the eye, we presume; they are the nerve cells that let us see color. The rods allow us to detect the shapes of objects, the outline of the moving vehicle. Are not the rods necessities while cones are God's extras? The apple could have been as nourishing without the blush on its cheek. Birds could have flown and performed their utilitarian purpose without their marvelous coloration. Surely, surely, the world is filled with God's extras, especially at autumn time!

We shall not cease to be thankful for necessities—for Christ and his everlasting love, for the Holy Spirit with his gracious guidance, for the "Book divine" and its saving instructions, for church and home and loved ones, for work and its rewards, for friends and their loyalty. Aye, but in the amber months of autumn we shall be very thankful, too, for God's extras.

> Autumn in her scarlet cloak,
> Comes tumbling down the hills.
> . . . .
> An amber cup is in her hands
> From which the wonder spills.
>
> —CHARLES HANSON TOWNE

You Can't Go Home Again

When I was a child . . . when I became a man (v. 11).

Thomas Wolfe, novelist, grew up, and up and up in Asheville, North Carolina; he became a physical giant and a giant in the literary world. Asheville did not always appreciate Tom, and for good reason, the city felt. Tom believed that "fiction is fact selected and understood, fiction is fact arranged and charged with purpose. . . . A novelist may turn over half the people in a town to make a single figure in his novel."

So, Tom went on turning and looking and selecting and arranging. He opened closed doors, looked at family skeletons, got a good firm hold, shook them until the bones rattled with guilt and gaiety. He took large sections of hide off the community; the community returned the compliment by taking large sections of hide off Tom. So, for a time it was a hide for a hide and a snub for a snub.

After fame and fortune came his way, Tom returned to his home town, Asheville. But he found that it was not the same town he had left. Everything was changed. The streets, houses, hills, people were different, nothing was as he remembered it. He began to muse about that; as he mused the fires of creativity began to burn. Result, the fine novel, *You Can't Go Home Again*.

There he expounded his belief, which was his own experience, that you cannot go back to your childhood, your romantic love, your dreams of fame and glory, your ivory towers, old thought forms. The novelist thought the deepest and most profound truth he ever learned was, "You can't go home again."

The apostle Paul wrote, "When I was a child I spake as a child, I understood as a child, I thought as a child; but when I became a man, I put away childish things." "You can't go home again."

Unbelievable!

If ye have faith as a grain of mustard seed . . . (v. 20b).

In the September issue of *Reader's Digest* for 1973, the story of the Howard Christian Education Fund is told, briefly. The statistics read like fiction:

"Because the Howards have always chosen to remain at low-paying pastorates and schools where they've felt most needed, their combined yearly salaries (she has sometimes taught, too) have never exceeded $3,000. Yet, in 47 years they have assisted 1,692 students at 425 schools and colleges in 47 states and 92 foreign countries! They accomplished this amazing feat by personally raising and managing—in their spare time—a revolving aid fund which has totaled just over $2 million . . . Last year they gave Campbell College [now University] sufficient assets to endow a chair of religion—and they put up most of the money for two scholarship funds of $30,000 each, the income from which will assist outstanding high school students in two counties."

When I wrote that story and sent it to the *Reader's Digest,* they questioned my veracity. They did it in a nice way, but they let me know that I would have to furnish proof of my amazing statistics. So, I asked Dr. Howard to give me a personal statement. He did so and added that his files were open for inspection and all his auditor's reports were available. The *Digest* was not satisfied. Could they send a member of their staff to Buies Creek to interview Dr. Howard and me? It was arranged and their representative came and stayed with us for a week.

Toward the close of the week this seasoned journalist came to my office and asked if he might use my telephone to call the *Reader's Digest* home office. I asked if he would like for me to leave the office and was assured it was not necessary. In essence this is what I heard, "Yes, I'm at Campbell College in Buies Creek, North Carolina. I've been here all week. And, let me tell you, I've been at this business for thirty years but this is the (expletive deleted) thing I've ever come across; looks as if it's all true, too."

November 15   Read Psalm 112:6
"My Favorite Things"

The righteous shall be in everlasting remembrance (v. 6).

We have our favorite things. My favorite food is homemade ice cream; my favorite sport is baseball; my favorite vacation spot is the little village, high in the Blue Ridge Mountains of North Carolina, called Blowing Rock. Robert Browning is my favorite poet. Isaac Watts's "When I Survey the Wondrous Cross" is my favorite hymn. My favorite book, of course, is the Bible. But the Bible is many books and there are favorite passages and verses within the particular book within the Bible. What is your favorite passage?

For many it would be the first verse in the first book of the Bible, Genesis 1:1, "In the beginning God . . . " That does take care of a multitude of questions. And, in it you can hear the angel Gabriel's pronouncement in *Green Pastures*, "Gangway, Gangway for de Lawd God Jehovah!" Some would choose Deuteronomy 33:27, "The eternal God is thy refuge, and underneath are the everlasting arms." Psalm 23 would get the vote of many, for God is their "shepherd." Isaiah 40 and 53 would be high on the voting list for many.

And in the New Testament, what choices! Would it be the beautiful nativity story in Luke 2? The Sermon on the Mount, Matthew 5—7, is the favorite of millions. John 14:3 with its "many mansions" would certainly stand close to the top in votes. John 3:16 has been called, "The Little Bible." Paul's beautiful poem in 1 Corinthians 13 with its, "Though I speak with the tongues of men and of angels," is a passage that calls us again and again.

The children's hymn has it, "Holy Bible, Book divine, Precious treasure, thou art mine." It is holy; it is precious, and it is ours, all of it, not just one or more brief passages. The truth of the matter is this, our favorite passages change with the changing years, changing needs of life, changing insights given by God's Holy Spirit. "Let the redeemed of the Lord say so!"

"Living Letters"

We are more than conquerors through him that loved us (v. 37).

In writing of his personal reaction to translating the letters of Paul, J. B. Phillips said that he approached the task with the determination to maintain an emotional detachment. Yet, he found again and again that the material with which he was dealing was "strangely alive." He said that it spoke to his own condition in an "uncanny" way. Not just occasionally, but almost continually, he was aware of the "living quality" of those "strangely assorted books." It is unusual to hear such expressions from a strong Greek scholar! Just imagine what he felt when he came to translate Romans 8:31-39. It is reported that when Moffatt came to translate that passage that he sat for three weeks with cold towels about his head trying to turn that blazing Greek into English!

Of course, the passage is heady doctrine; it is frightfully theological. And that means it has at least one strike against it in getting our attention. The "average man in the street" couldn't care less about a theological approach. Like the lady who said of the Christmas carols, "They are so theological!"

Yet, a passage that has endured so long, been cherished by so many, and offers so much of what is so desperately needed in our time, deserves to be heard.

Dr. John Hutton, the English preacher, was beginning his sermon when he noticed that one of his parishioners was already settling down for a comfortable snooze. Dr. Hutton said, "I have always felt that if anyone can sleep while I am preaching he is entitled to do so; the blame is mine; I assume full responsibility. But a friend of mine this morning is taking an unfair advantage of me. He is going to sleep before I get started. No! No! That is wrong! We must start fair!" Well, I think Paul deserves the same "fair" treatment. Give him a chance!

"Superman!"

John did no miracle (v. 41b).

This yen for the wonder-worker is not new; it was as true in the first century as it is in the twentieth. The crowds milled about the Master. There was no time for him to eat or sleep. He said they came because of his miracles, his wonder-working power, in contrast to John the Baptist.

Some of us like Superman. That is true whether he is presented in a movie, a comic strip, a television program, a Nietzsche philosophic ideal, or in flesh and blood. It is the superperson who gets our attention: the most beautiful woman in America, the strongest man in the world, the richest person in the county, the greatest athlete in the conference, the best actress of the year, the best-selling author of the season; we follow these.

This is a disturbing thought. We are not wonder-workers, not many of us, certainly. We do not have the most beautiful faces, the strongest bodies, or the most brilliant minds. We do not live in the most expensive houses, drive the most costly cars, nor do we always reside in the most exclusive part of the city. We are not among the "ten best dressed women in America," nor are we listed among the five most eligible bachelors. The truth of the matter is, we are ordinary human beings.

We have normally functioning bodies; we have reasonably clear minds. We have homes, families, businesses, professions, jobs. We are normally reliable; we can be depended upon to do the decent thing, sometimes, even the heroic thing in a clinch. We love our families; we are decently patriotic; we give fair allegiance to Christ and his church. That is our pattern. Not superpersons, just normal human beings. Yet, we do have faith and we pray about our unbelief. We do want to be used of the Lord. Now, here is this man John, we are told that he was no superman, no wonder-worker. That is encouraging!

Unstoppable Faith

By faith they passed through the Red Sea as dry land (v. 29a).

John Steinbeck wrote a poignant story that he called *The Leader of the People*. It is the saga of an old man, who in his prime of life had led a wagon train across the desert all the way to the western coast. It was a thrilling experience. The Indians were unfriendly; every mile of the way was disputed ground. Once the redskins drove off the horses in the darkness of the night. Once the people got so hungry that they began to butcher their own work animals, and so would have eaten themselves into starvation.

The leader had to be on guard at all times. He had to think for the people; feel for the people; plan for the people; he had to act for the people. But the old man had been equal to the task. He never faltered. He led that wagon train safely, led it all the way across the plains right up to the ocean's edge, would have led it further had there been anywhere else to go. That day the old man ceased to live and began a mere existence. It had been a big job; he had done it well, but it ended too soon, and left him with nothing to do but to remember and talk.

And talk about his experiences he did, talked about it to everyone who would listen, told his stories of the crossing with boring repetition, always the same stories. The old man's tones would drop into its narrative groove, speed up for the attack, grow sad over the wounded, strike a dirge at the burials on the great plains.

There was one person who never grew tired of the old stories, Jody, the old man's grandson. The events seemed to speak to a great need in the boy. One day as the old man was coming to the end of his narrative, Jody looked up, smiled, and said, "Maybe I could lead the people someday?" His grandfather said, with sadness in his voice, "There's no place to go, Jody. There's the ocean to stop you." And the boy responded shyly, "In boats I might, sir."

November 19   Read 1 Corinthians 15:1-10
A Message of Good News

But by the grace of God I am what I am (v. 10a).

When James S. Pike was United States Minister to the Netherlands in 1863, he visited Thomas Carlyle. Pike came away from the visit shaking his head and saying that Carlyle seemed to believe there was a God, but that the devil was more than a match for him. Whatever may have been Carlyle's view, and Pike's words are not an adequate evaluation of the philosophy of the great Scot, certainly neither Jesus nor Paul had any such thought. They preached a message of good news!

The content of the New Testament word for *gospel*, the good news, is rich and full. In a world of lies, the gospel is the good news of truth; Paul would not yield to the Judaizers for he wanted the "truth of the gospel" to continue with the Galatians. In a world that has lost its nerve, the gospel is the good news of hope; Paul cautioned the Colossians not to turn from the "hope of the gospel" which had been preached unto others. In a world of threats and demands, the gospel is the good news of gift and promise; the Ephesians were reminded that they were partakers of God's promise in Christ by the gospel. In a world of strife, the gospel is the good news of peace. In a world of lost men and women, the gospel is the good news of salvation; the apostle reminded the Ephesians that they had trusted in the gospel of their salvation. In a world of skeptics the gospel comes as the good news of the risen Christ affirmed in the gospel Paul preached. The gospel is the good news of everlasting life!

The pagan gods were vengeful and vindictive and jealous. Much that the Jews had been taught of the God of the Old Testament had emphasized his wrath and anger. Jesus did not deny the holiness, righteousness, and judgment of God; he affirmed these, but he did preach the good news that God is a loving father.

Toyohiko Kagawa, great Japanese leader of two generations ago, related how a missionary helped him to understand the love of God. While he was sick and alone during his student days, a man knocked at his door. Kagawa told the visitor, "Do not come in. I have a contagious disease." But the missionary came in anyway, and said, "I have something more contagious than a disease. I have come with the love of God!"

330

"Our Faith Tremendous"

The kingdoms of this world are become the kingdoms of our Lord (v. 15b).

The great and the good and the helpful from all lands and all peoples and tongues and classes have come laying their trophies at his feet. Listen to F. W. Boreham, the Australian minister, on the sixtieth anniversary of his entrance into the ministry and ask if his words do not voice your own desire.

"From the day I was ordained to this, the one passionate desire of my heart has been to lead my hearers to Christ. I have never entered a pulpit without feeling that, if only the people could catch a vision of the Saviour, they would have no alternative but to lay their devotion at his feet. My soul has caught fire whenever I have exalted the cross. I have never in my life been so perfectly happy as when preaching on such texts as 'God so loved the world,' . . . 'The Son of Man is come to seek and to save that which was lost.' "[26]

Frequently, the way ahead seems long and the way is dark, so dark at times that it seems cats might run into each other! Will the way of Christ work? Eternity and time, history and experience, faith and life say yes. One other thing is equally sure—nothing else will work.

> What is the final ending?
> The issue, can we know?
>
> . . . .
>
> This is our faith tremendous,
> Our wild hope, who shall scorn,
> That in the name of Jesus
> The world shall be reborn.

—VACHEL LINDSAY

And, our prayer: Lord, we believe, help thou our unbelief!

Never Become Accustomed to Wrong

Your old men shall dream dreams, your young men shall see visions (v. 28*b*).

What the young in heart can see may be hid from the veteran. For sin is unique in this: the more a person experiences it, the less he really understands it. The young knight who has kept his body strong and his mind clear is far more sensitive to the dangers of drink than the drunk on skid row with bleary eyes and an appetite that makes him sell his soul for another drink. The virgin with sacred dreams of home and motherhood is far more shocked at the debasement of sex than the prostitute.

Let the old and the tired and the experienced compromiser smile his knowing smiles and in his worldly wisdom say to the young idealist, "Yes, I can understand how you feel; for when I was your age I felt just as you do." And to that the young idealist might reply, "Yes, and my greatest fear is that when I am old I will feel as you do now." Dorothy Parker has a penetrating poem called "The Veteran."

> When I was young and bold and strong,
> Oh, right was right, and wrong was wrong!
> My plume on high, my flag unfurled,
> I rode away to right the world.
> "Come out, you dogs, and fight!" said I,
> And wept there was but once to die.
>
> But I am old; and good and bad
> Are woven in a crazy plaid.
> I sit and say, "The world is so;
> And he is wise who lets it go.
> A battle lost, a battle won—
> The difference is small my son."
>
> Inertia rides and riddles me;
> The which is called Philosophy.[27]

The strength of our Saviour was that he never became accustomed to wrong.

—Archbishop Soderblom

"What I Am Grateful For"

Bless the Lord, O my soul: and all that is within me, bless his holy name (v. 1).

A very beautiful thing happened in one of the college departments of our church last Thanksgiving. When the name of the student speaker was announced for the morning there was an expression of approval and pleasure on the faces of the large student group. The speaker was, and is, one of the most respected and admired young women in the university or in our church. She came forward with her hand resting lightly upon the arm of a fine young man. When she was at the speaker's stand, and her escort had returned to his seat, she began to speak.

She said, "I have been asked to speak on the subject, 'What I am grateful for.' " With a smile in her voice as well as on her face she said, "I am grateful that I know you are not supposed to end a sentence with a preposition." The group enjoyed that, remembering certain professors! Then, the lovely young woman began her message. In essence, this is what she said:

"I am going to deal with the assigned subject by telling you my own story. When I was fourteen I began to have trouble with my sight. Our local doctors felt that I had a brain tumor. We went to the great city and I was examined by a well-known and famous surgeon. He confirmed the diagnosis of our own doctors and assured the family that I did have a brain tumor. He was quite frank with my parents, and with me. He told us that I would have to have an operation, that I could not live without it. He said the operation might result in the loss of my hearing, speech, mobility, thinking, or sight, but I could not live without the operation. The surgeon left us and my father led us in prayer. The operation was performed. You saw me walk; I heard you sing; I think coherently. True, I am blind; I cannot see your faces. And, yet, I see so much more than I ever saw with my natural sight. What am I grateful for? I am grateful for life and parents who know how to pray."

"I Thank My God for You!"

We are always thankful to God as we pray for you all (v. 2, Phillips).

Paul was a grateful soul! He was grateful to and for individuals within the churches. This comes out clearly in 1 Thessalonians, as well as his other epistles. If you look carefully at different translations, you can see how the apostle's heart was overflowing with thanks.

"We give thanks to God always for you all, constantly mentioning you in our prayers" (v. 2, RSV). "Remembering without ceasing your work of faith, and labor of love, and patience of hope in our Lord Jesus Christ" (v. 3). Your faith has meant solid achievement, your love has meant hard work, and the hope that you have in our Lord Jesus Christ means sheer dogged determination in the life that you live before God (v. 2-3, Phillips). "Your faith in God has become known everywhere" (v. 8, NIV). "Ye turned to God from idols to serve the living and true God" (v. 9). The message is often paraphrased: "God loves you." "God has selected you." "You are a breath of life to us." "We have longed more and more to see you." *We give thanks to God always for you.*

Imagine all of that being in one letter a former pastor wrote to you and others in the church! How would you like to be the kind of person, the kind of church member, who would cause a pastor to thank God everytime he thought of you? The love a pastor has for his people is a very special love and relationship. Probably it is impossible for anyone even to begin to understand if one has not experienced it. That loving relationship depends upon the lover and the beloved!

> Who hath not learned in hours of faith,
> The truth to flesh and sense unknown
> That Life is ever lord of Death,
> And Love can never lose its own!
>
> —JOHN GREENLEAF WHITTIER

A Farewell Banquet

And Levi made him a great feast in his own house (v. 29a).

Jesus was living in Capernaum. He had a neighbor by the name of Levi who was in the despised business of tax collecting. One day Jesus walked by the tax office and issued Levi a challenge, "Follow me," said Jesus. And, impossible as it may sound, Levi did just that. He left the tax office and became a follower of Jesus. A few nights later Levi gave a great banquet in honor of Jesus. That banquet is significant.

It is significant that Jesus was there! He was no killjoy; he was a radiant spirit; he loved dining and music; wherever he sat was the head of the table. The motive for the banquet is significant. It was to celebrate Levi's newfound freedom, to honor Jesus, to say farewell to old friends and, to announce his new life and work.

The conversation at that banquet was significant. In those Eastern homes uninvited guests were allowed to come and stand around. The scribes and Pharisees came and said to the disciples of Jesus—not enough courage to go to Jesus—"Why does your teacher eat with publicans and sinners?" The disciples had the kind of courage and relationship that caused them to tell Jesus. Then, Jesus answered openly, and we are glad that he did; in fact, we may be glad for the question.

Jesus said, in effect, "I eat with publicans and sinners for the same reason that a doctor goes to those who are sick; the well do not need him." When David Livingstone was asked why he was going as a medical missionary to Africa, he answered, "Because, God had an only Son and he gave him as a missionary physician." Again Jesus said, in essence: "You want to know why I eat with publicans and sinners? Why don't you read your Scriptures? You would know that God desires mercy and not sacrifice." Jesus went where they were that they might be where he was going—to his Father's house.

"A Sense of What Is Vital"

Enabling you to have a sense of what is vital (v. 9b, Moffatt).

How do we keep second-rate causes from taking front-rank positions in our lives? Now, that is a good question and a big problem. Moffatt translates Paul's prayer for his friends at Philippi to say, "It is my prayer that your love may be more and more rich in knowledge and all manner of insight, enabling you to have a sense of what is vital."

Our lives become cluttered, not necessarily with that which is bad and evil, but with that which is less than the best and short of what is vital. And, when our lives are full they are full, no matter of what. When all reservations have been taken on a plane then there is nothing to do but stand by.

And, does that not explain many failures? In our homes, for example. If forced to a careful analysis we would say that next to God in Christ our homes, companions, children, are the dearest and best things we have; yet, so often, our families are forced to take second, third, or fourth place in practice. Or, the student in school—he can't take everything; he can't go everywhere; he can't read everything; he can get only a certain number of hours in the day and night. What is vital? Two boys were debating what to do: "Heads we go to the picture show; tails we go to the grill; if it stands on edge we study." The same holds true in business and in the professions. We have to decide what is vital.

Jesus was insistent about priorities. He indicated that if we gained the whole world but lost our own souls, it would mean the worst. He said that we should seek first the kingdom of God; that was first; that was vital. He said that we must not love father or mother or wife or children more than we loved him. There we have the matter of priorities again.

What are the five most important things in your life? Write them down.

"God's Glory in the Morning"

And in the morning, then ye shall see the glory of the Lord (v. 7a).

James Stewart of Scotland has taken the above words out of context and applied them to different "morning experiences," and, as anyone who knows Dr. Stewart would expect, he gives a helpful and exciting discussion.

The days of the week, every day, that dawn comes with a freshness that may reveal the glory of the Lord. The psalmist must have felt that when he sang, "This is the day the Lord hath made!" Once Miss Barth Berry of Berry school fame was deeply discouraged. A friend and neighbor, a plain man of the hills, said, "Miss Martha, I don't see why you are so worried; tomorrow ain't been teched yet."

There is the Lord's Day in particular. As locks on a river make it possible for upstream boats to rise and move off at a different elevation, so weary souls move into the locks of the Lord's Day, feel his presence, hear his voice, and move off to their responsibilities on a different elevation.

Dr. Stewart speaks of the mornings of childhood. Every child should have the heritage of good mornings, when everything is new and fresh from the hand of God. Wordsworth wrote about it, "There was a time," he recalled, "when meadow, grove, and stream, . . . and every common sight, . . . did seem Apparelled in celestial light,—The glory and the freshness of a dream."

And the morning of Christ's coming to the human soul—we have words and phrases for that. "Born again," "Babes in Christ," "Behold I make all things new," "New creation in Christ." These mornings when Christ comes to us, as he came to tired fishermen on the sea of Galilee; the weary labors of the long night are forgotten and the feast is spread, a feast that he, himself prepares. Then, we "see God's glory in the morning!"

"Personal Delivery"

But go your way, tell . . . (v. 7a).

The tomb is empty; the news must be told! The imperative springs from the indicative. God rolls away the stone; we tell what he has done. It has been said that the high meaning of the resurrection never gets into a person until it gets in his feet. The empty tomb starts the disciples running! *Go, tell,* these two words require the total person.

On September 16, 1961, Bernard J. Connolly of Oakland, California, left San Francisco International Airport on his vacation. It was a unique vacation to last three months. In his possession, this neighbor of mine had 250,000 letters to be delivered in thirteen countries of the Far East. In 1960, Connolly had delivered letters to people in twelve European nations. Most of the letters in 1961 were from children in America to children in the Far Eastern countries; a few letters were to officials of those countries; thousands of the letters were from store clerks in the San Francisco Bay area to store clerks in, say, Tokyo. Lions International helped finance the trip. Connolly put in quite a bit of his own money, and he had some private donations.

The idea behind the trip? Hear the letter carrier's explanation, "Well, it sounds corny, but I think this is the best way to tell America's story abroad. This is a people-to-people-program."

"Go, . . . tell," said Jesus. Make it a person-to-person-program.

> We've a story to tell to the nations,
> That shall turn their hearts to the right,
> A story of truth and mercy,
> A story of peace and light.

> For the darkness shall turn to dawning,
> And the dawning to noon-day bright,
> And Christ's great kingdom shall come on earth,
> The kingdom of love and light.

> —H. ERNEST NICHOL

"Burn That Book"

Ye have made it a den of thieves (v. 17b).

Often it is not that people do not understand Christ and therefore oppose and reject him. They oppose and reject him because they *do understand* him. Mark Twain was at least honest. He observed that it was not those parts of the Bible which he could not understand that worried him; it was those parts that he did understand.

We oppose Christ because of our pride. This is the sin that caused Adam's fall. Adam and Eve were unwilling to yield God the place in their lives that he demanded. The children of Adam and Eve have never gotten away from the sin of their parents. It is not that we are unwilling for God to have a place, it is that we are unwilling for God to have the absolute place. It is still true, "He must be Lord of all or he will not be Lord at all."

We oppose Christ on the basis of selfishness. We not only want to control our lives, we want to live them in our own way. I once talked to a husband and wife about the meaning of the word *agape*, Christian love. In this love one is not motivated by the worth of the object or the attractiveness of the object, but rather by the need of the object, the person. The wife said, "Then that means that he [her husband] should think of my needs and not his desires."

We oppose Christ because his way is hard and steep. Kïerkegaard, the Danish theologian, is reported to have said:

> Let us collect all the New Testaments that are in existence. Let us carry them out to an open place or upon a mountain, and then, while we all kneel down, let someone address God in this fashion: "Take this book back again; we men, such as we are now, are no good at dealing with a thing like this. It only makes us unhappy." My proposal is that like the inhabitants of Gadara we beseech Christ to "depart out of our coast."

> *But, Lord, to whom shall we go? thou hast the words of eternal life (John 6:68).*

"Plod and Plough"

Whosoever of you will be the chiefest, shall be servant of all (v. 44).

Seers, poets, saints, and philosophers all recognize the rightness and the truthfulness of the emphasis that Jesus made on the greatness of service. Charles Dickens said that no one is useless if he lightens the burdens of another; Frederick W. Robertson affirmed that it is not the possession of extraordinary gifts that makes for extraordinary usefulness, but the dedication of what gifts one has to the service of God; Paul Moody believed that the measure of man is not the number of servants that he has, but the number of people he serves; William Wordsworth wrote, "The best portion of a good man's life is his little, nameless, unremembered acts of kindness and of love." And Ralph Waldo Emerson, "Give me some great task, ye gods, and I will show you my spirit!/'No, no,' says the good heaven, 'Plod and plough.'"

Those who have the ability to see acknowledge that service is the badge of true greatness. It is one thing, however, to see this and acknowledge it intellectually; it is something else again to practice and realize it in one's own life. James and John were disciples of Jesus; they seem to have been among those who were closest to the Master. Yet, the standard of greatness used by James and John was about the same as the one used by pagans.

They asked for location and proximity. If they could just be in the right place, with the right people, they would have greatness. And, we? If we can live in the right neighborhood, work at the right place, have the right title, serve on the right committees, if our pictures can appear with the proper dignitaries, etc.

Jesus comes and says that we have it all wrong. The great are those who serve; and he is greatest who serves the most. In the eyes of the Master, "The useful and the beautiful are never separated."

Everyone Is in Debt

Owe no man any thing, but to love one another (v. 8).

Everyone is in debt. The books may be balanced and the account marked, "paid in full." But morally, intellectually, culturally, spiritually? Ah, there's the rub! But, a word of encouragement: he who is aware of and grateful for a favor has made the first installment on its repayment. So, I am on my way toward getting out of debt!

Years ago I decided that one day in the year, Thanksgiving Day, was not enough for the full expression of thanks. So, I set aside the full month of November for this project. I wrote at least one letter of thanks each day during the entire month; if I skipped a day, the next day I wrote two letters.

I proved to my own satisfaction that a letter of thanks each day will keep the blues away! I remembered persons who had been especially kind to me and my family during the past year: the individual who had given me a book, the couple who had sent flowers on our anniversary, families who had invited us into their home for a meal, the men who had whisked me away on an overnight fishing trip, or had mailed football tickets on the fifty yard line. Of course, I had written notes of thanks immediately upon receiving these favors; but this was an extra thank you. Notes of thanks went to the milkman, the postman, the service station attendant, the waitress at our favorite restaurant, the checkout girls at the supermarket, the barber, the doctor.

One year I majored on sending letters of thanks to persons in the civic, political, legal, and entertainment life of our city, they had made my city a better place to live. I told them so. The mayor, fire chief, police captain, judge of the juvenile court, and bank officials were just a few whom I remembered.

God has two dwellings; one in heaven, and the other in meek and thankful hearts.

—Izaak Walton

"I Had Forgotten the Scar"

I bear in my body the marks of the Lord Jesus (v. 17b).

We are made to smile as someone reminds us for the "umpteenth" time of the man saying to the office seeker, "Yes, but what have you done for me recently?"

We have good forgetters; we tend to forget past favors and sacrifices made on our behalf, or from which we have gleaned benefit.

After the War Between the States, General John B. Gordon became a candidate for the United States Senate. Candidates were then elected by the state legislatures. For some unknown reason an old war comrade of General Gordon's, serving in the legislature, disliked the general, and intended to vote against him. When the old soldier's name was called, he stood, fully intending to cast his vote against General Gordon. Suddenly his eyes fell on the ugly scar on the general's face. For a moment the man hesitated and then, in deep emotion, said, "I cannot vote against him; I had forgotten the scar."

Interesting that while we tend to forget the scars born by others, on our own behalf, the scars may be all that we do remember. A person of ninety whose hands tremble, whose fingers are unsure when holding a coffee cup, whose shaking makes wiggly lines with the pen, may be very much aware of those "scars" but forget all that they represent. How faithfully the hands have prepared the food, made the little clothes, swept and dusted and cleaned, written letters of love and encouragement, touched the face of her beloved in the dark night. With adequate memory of what the "scars" stand for, perhaps the "scars" could be forgotten, or turned into cause for gratitude?

But Thomas . . . was not with them when Jesus came. The other disciples therefore said unto him, We have seen the Lord. But he said unto them, Except I shall see in his hands the print of the nails, and put my finger into the print of the nails, and thrust my hand into his side, I will not believe (John 20:24-25).

What Are You Muttering?

O how I love thy law! it is my meditation all the day (v. 97).

At the heart and center of the man blessed of God is the man's attitude toward the "law of the Lord." He loves it, delights in it, meditates upon it. That is interesting. Many study the law of the Lord, preach and teach it, try to obey it, rebel against it, but love it, delight in it, meditate upon it. We are more like the little boy who, when told, "You will take your medicine and like it," said, "All right, I have to take it; but I don't have to like it, do I?"

Here is a person who rejoices and takes delight in the law of the Lord. The law of the Lord meant more than the Ten Commandments. It meant the Pentateuch, the first five books of the Bible; for us, it means the Bible. The law has to do with the creation, the preservation, and the providence of God. It has to do with God in the past, present, and future.

The person who loves and delights in the law of the Lord *meditates* upon it. The word originally meant to sing or murmur or mumble. It carries the picture of a man humming, murmuring, at his work. Others cannot hear what he is saying but it is a theme that he returns to again and again whenever he is not forced to give attention to other things.

In Goethe's *Egmont,* Jetter, a tailor, complains that the spies of the Inquisition listen for every unguarded word. He says that if these spies take a fancy, they will push into his house while he is seated at his workbench humming a psalm and thinking nothing of it, humming it just because "I've got it in my throat," then right away he is a heretic and sent off to jail.

If an enemy were to listen carefully to our "mumblings" what would he hear?

"I Get the Green Light"

He is my refuge and my fortress: my God; in him will I trust (v. 2).

This ninety-first Psalm is a favorite of many. It sings its way into our souls; it waves the banner of hope over the citadels of doubt. Yet, in the midst of it all, we wonder if the assurances and promises are true. If these wonderful words are not literally true in the physical sense and the material sense, just how, and in what way, are they true?

One of the most appealing characters in popular fiction was Lloyd Douglas's Dean Harcourt in the novel *Green Light*. The dean was almost a hopeless cripple. He had to have braces, canes, crutches, assistants to support him as he moved heavily and painfully about the cathedral. Yet, he was an inspiring character. Life and strength seemed to flow from him into the morally weak, the mentally tired, and the spiritually defeated. Seldom did the dean speak of his own condition and resources.

There was one outstanding exception. It was during his conference with Dr. Newell Paige. With a tremendous burden, with a blank wall staring him in the face, Dr. Paige was facing the dean. The dean was trying to give him back his hope and purpose for living, trying to convince him that understanding of the skill in dealing with life were available. Dr. Paige rose to leave the dean's office and the crippled man spoke:

> Before you leave I have something further to say to you. I want you to know that I am not a stranger to the problem of frustration. It has not been my custom to speak of my own dilemmas, but you have a right to benefit by my experience. . . .
>
> For your comfort, my son, let me tell you that I have laid hold upon a truth powerful enough to sustain me until I die! I know that, in spite of all the painful circumstances I have met, *my course is upward!* . . . I have suffered—but I know that I am Destiny's darling! . . . *You* have suffered—but *you, too, can carry on through!* . . . Take it from me! I know! . . . I have been delayed—long—long—long—but—at length—I get the GREEN LIGHT![28]

344

"Path of Duty—Way to Glory"

What shall I do, Lord? (v. 10a).

L ord, what wilt thou have me do?" That knowledge will come
gradually; it cannot be revealed for a lifetime in an instant. But the
way to the ultimate answer is to deal with the instant command. The
Lord said to Paul, "Take the next step, 'Arise, and go into the city.'"
That next step is the key to everything. As the journey of a thousand
miles begins with the first step, so the obedience of a lifetime begins
with the next step. "Arise, and go into the city."

Once a woman called on Phillips Brooks, the great New England
preacher, telling him she had just returned from the Orient with a new
religion. She was sure her new religion would transform the world and
leave Christianity far behind. Brooks asked, "How did you get it
through customs?" "Why, Dr. Brooks," the lady replied, "you do not
understand. This is a new religion. The customs officials have no
interest in such things." "Oh, I see," replied the beloved minister, "your
religion has no duty connected to it!"

The religion of the Lord Jesus Christ has a heavy duty attached to it;
Paul knew that. And, if you and I do not know it, we have not followed
the way of the cross. Inscribed on the statue of General Robert E. Lee,
in the Hall of Fame are his own words:

> Duty is the sublimest word in our language.
> Do your duty in all things.
> You cannot do more;
> You should never wish to do less.

In *Ode on the Death of the Duke of Wellington,* Tennyson wrote:

> Not once or twice in our fair island story
> The path of duty was the way to glory:
> He, that ever following her commands,
> On with toil of heart and knees and hands,
> Thro' the long gorge to the far light has won
> His path upward, and prevail'd,
> Shall find the toppling crags of duty scaled
> Are close upon the shining table-lands
> To which our God Himself is moon and sun.

Deal with the Present Opportunity

The Lord said unto him, Go, return on thy way (v. 15b).

The beloved C. Roy Angell used to tell the old story about how a great hotel came into being. Into a small, third-class hotel, in the city of Philadelphia there came one night two tired, elderly people. Going to the night clerk the husband said, "Please, don't tell me you have no room. My wife and I have been all over the city looking for a place to stay. We did not know about the big conventions that are meeting in the city this weekend. The hotels where we usually stay are all full; we are dead tired, and it is after midnight. Please don't tell us you have nowhere for us to sleep."

The clerk looked at them for a moment and then said, "There is not a vacant room in the hotel, except my own. I work at night and sleep in the daytime. It is not as nice as the other rooms, but it is clean and I'll be happy for you to be my guests for the night." The wife said, "God bless you, young man!"

The next morning at the breakfast table, the couple sent the waiter to tell the clerk they would like to see him. The night clerk came into the dining room, recognized the couple, and said, "I do hope you had a good night's rest." Then he had a surprise.

The husband said, "You are too fine a hotelman to stay in a hotel this size. How would you like for me to build a big, beautiful, luxury hotel in the city of New York and make you general manager?" The clerk was stunned. Was something wrong with the couple he had let stay in his room? But, finally he stammered that it would be great! Then the man introduced himself.

"I am John Jacob Astor." So, the Waldorf-Astoria Hotel was built, and the night clerk became the best-known hotelman in the world.

Cast thy bread upon the waters: for thou shalt find it after many days (Eccl. 11:1).

"In What Language?"

They rehearsed all that God had done with them (v. 27b).

rnest Dimnet, the French writer, was almost perfectly bilingual. He wrote far more in English than he did in French, his native tongue. He was once asked if he dreamed in English or French. He wrote, "We think and dream in pictures rather than in words; the real question is, in what language do you take notes?" Good question that! Life is hard and easy, up and down; we face joy and sorrow, success and failure. "In what language do you take notes?"

In the thirteenth and fourteenth chapters of Acts is recorded the first missionary journey of Paul and Barnabas. When they returned they called the church together and presented their report. Listen, "They rehearsed all the things that God had done with them, and that he had opened the door of faith unto the Gentiles." That report might have been different and still been factual. Listen to how it might have been.

> Brethren, when we left you we went to Paphos. There we had a terrible battle with the devil in the form of a magician. It was terrible, just terrible! From Paphos we went to Antioch. There we had the whole town out listening to us; it looked as if we would have a great revival. But some jealous Jews contradicted everything we said; they turned the women of the town against us; that was just too much. It was bad, brethren, very bad! Then we went to Iconium. There we were on the verge of success; Jews and Greeks believed our message. But a big crowd of ruffians stirred up the heathen and poisoned their minds. The officials of the city entered in league with these hoodlums to stone us. We learned about the plot and escaped with our lives. It was terrible, just terrible! But, we were not quitters, no sir! We went to Lystra. And, hear this, the people there thought we were gods; right, thought we were gods. But a group of those no-good thugs from Antioch, Pisidia, and Iconium came all the way to Lystra and stirred up the crowd so that they stoned Paul until they thought he was dead. It was bad, very bad.

> Now, brethren, we are sorry to give you such a dismal report but that is the way it was. Bad, very, very bad.

That would have been a factual report. But what did they report? "They rehearsed all the things that God had done with them, and how he had opened the door of faith unto the Gentiles." That is how they took notes!

December 7   Read Luke 9:23-27
"Divine Mathematics"

But whosoever will lose his life for my sake, the same shall save it (v. 24b).

It has been suggested that one difficulty about children getting help with their lessons at home is that the teachers soon learn how dumb the parents are! But the truth of the matter is that any disciple of Jesus who takes a course in divine mathematics will be amazed at how different the course is from mathematics as the marketplace teaches. For example, in divine mathematics:

To add you have to subtract. That is, in order to get you have to give. Now that is a new pitch! (Mark 10:43-45).

To be first you have to be last. In order to stand at the head of the class you have to go to the foot (Mark 9:35).

To be wise you have to be foolish. The world teaches that to get ahead you have to use people; Christ says to get ahead you have to serve people, to the world that is foolishness (1 Cor. 1:21-24).

To be strong you have to become weak. One thing that is deadly to any athletic team is overconfidence. Weakness causes you to seek help. Paul said, "When I am weak, then I am strong" (2 Cor. 12:9-10).

In order to live you have to die (Col. 3:3).

The H. Allen Smiths were in London. They asked an American lady who had lived in the city for a long time what she considered the most impressive thing London offered. The lady thought for a moment and then said, "Wait for a good, thick fog, then board a certain bus after dark, and ride through mists as thick as cream soup until the conductor sings out, 'World's End! Salvation next door.' That cry signals the arrival of the bus at the crossroads where stands a pub called 'World's End.' Adjoining it is a Salvation Army hall."

On Shirking Active Duty

But their nobles put not their necks to the work of their Lord (v. 5).

The Jews were in captivity; Jerusalem had been destroyed. Some rebuilding had been done but much remained to be done, especially the walls, gates, and towers. One of the exiles by the name of Nehemiah had risen to a high and important position. He asked the king for permission to return and rebuild the walls of Jerusalem. His request was granted and he returned. He investigated thoroughly, surveyed carefully, got his information, and went to the people with the suggestion that they immediately begin to rebuild. The people responded positively. The way the work was carried out is suggestive of deeper building than the physical walls of a destroyed city.

The work was related to the worker. You find the words, "Jedaiah . . . repaired opposite his house." "Benjamin and Hasshub repaired opposite their houses" (v. 11, 23, RSV). So, there was a personal stake in the matter: his own home and family were involved; personal responsibility.

But the work was united, too. Most of the verses in the third chapter begin with the words, "And next unto him," "After him." We have individual responsibilities; we must assume those responsibilities. But, there are responsibilities that have to be faced jointly. Some of the work of the Lord can only be done in cooperation with our fellows.

There were those who shirked their responsibilities, personal and joint responsibilities. And, strangely enough, these were the nobles, "their nobles put not their necks to the work" (v. 5). Strange? Nobles should act nobly; they were privileged, they should have defended those privileges. They had been given much, they should have served much. Yet, is it not true, that frequently, the geniuses, five-talented persons, do not enter into the service of the Lord? WHY?

Little Sanctuaries

I will be to them as a little sanctuary (v. 16b).

There are dry and arid places in everyone's life. Every life has its high and shining hours, the soul-shaping experiences, the hours and experiences when we saw life clearly, knew its purposes, and were sure there would always be adequate resources at our fingertips. The Bible knows about that.

The Jews had been carried into captivity; they were far from home and the blessings of sacred places. They remembered the high hours of worship in their lovely Temple. The Jews who remained in their native land looked down upon those who had been carried away. God sent his servant Ezekiel to the exiles with this message, "I will be to them as a little sanctuary."

So, in effect the message was that though they were away from home, were pilgrims and strangers, though they missed the familiar and sacred places of worship, God would come to them and be as "a little sanctuary." If you cannot get to the great Temple, you can find your God in the small places and experiences of life. If you cannot go to the holy place, God will come and make your place holy.

Every soul needs the "Temple" experience, needs the high and holy hours, the soul-shaping and molding experiences. But there is need for "a little sanctuary" along the road of life, too. And if you are a child of God, you have "a little sanctuary." They are different for different people; one thing, person, place, activity becomes the "sanctuary" for one, other experiences for another. This is true too, our lives are rich, deep, and significant according to the number and quality of these little sanctuaries. A flier, forced down in the African desert, testified, "I was saved by a vision of my wife's eyes under the halo of her hat."

"Running"

There came one running (v. 17).

He was a young man with courage, with eagerness, with ideals, with humility, with religion, and with dissatisfaction. He had much but he wanted more. Yet, he was unwilling to pay the price for that "something more." He went away sorrowful. Think of what he missed.

He missed a great friendship. Think of being a close friend of Jesus! In friendship with Jesus men and women find the freshness of the dawn, the strength of the everlasting hills, the tang of the salty sea, and the red, rich blood of courage. He missed all that. A British poet writing of the man who had meant most to him, admitted that his own life had been tame and colorless. But there were two glories that could never be taken from him, "For I was Shakespeare's countryman,/And wert not thou my friend?"

He missed a fantastic adventure! When he saw Jesus and that little band of disciples disappear down the road, how could he know that they were walking into the middle of the greatest adventure the world has ever known? He could have been a part of that!

> Some men die by shrapnel,
> And some go down in flames,
> But most men perish inch by inch,
> Who play at little games.

He might have won a nation to Christ, written a Gospel, had churches named for him, been known in Christian records as a saint! Instead he stayed put, hugging his riches.

He missed a great salvation, for without Christ the man was lost. A wonderful friend of mine tells how he called on a cruel agnostic who took pride in exposing the ignorance of "simple preachers." In his library he was shown book after book that he, the preacher, had never read. Finally there was a moment of silence. My preacher friend inquired of the brilliant agnostic, "Now, may I read to you from the one book I have?" He read, "He was wounded for our transgressions; he was bruised." "And," reported my friend, "that brilliant man just fell on his face and got religion."

The Obligation Remains

I am debtor both to the Greeks, and to the Barbarians (v. 14a).

Some years ago my family and I visited Concord, Massachusetts. On a red-letter day, I went down to Walden Pond and found the spot where Henry David Thoreau built his small cabin. In his famous book, *Walden,* Thoreau says that there were three chairs in his cabin, "one for solitude, two for friendship, three for society." He who would be true to Christ must have these three chairs. In the deep solitude of his own soul he must accept or reject Christ. His close family, friends, and neighbors must be influenced by the gospel. But society at large, the "whole world," must also hear of the living Christ.

Carl Sandburg said that the War Between the States was fought over a verb. In addressing a school body in New York City on April 6, 1959, he referred to Governor Faubus and the tense racial situation in Little Rock, Arkansas. Sandburg said that Mr. Faubus would not understand much that Lincoln said. For example, he did not understand that that fearful four-year bloodbath of the 1860s had one curious result. Before that conflict, the Department of State in its treaties with foreign nations wrote, "The United States *are,*" but after the war it was written, "The United States *is.*" The war was fought over a verb.

In like manner, the church of Jesus Christ moves out into the battle of life for one purpose; to lead all those who know Christ to share the good news with all those who know him not. The end result will be: "The kingdoms of this world are become the kingdoms of our Lord, and of his Christ." No longer two kingdoms but one kingdom and, therefore, to be written *is.*

The late Bishop Gerald Kennedy once commented that he was the only Methodist bishop to flunk a college course in Bible. When he was elected a bishop, he had a letter from his old professor congratulating him, but adding: "You still owe me a paper on Jeremiah." The obligation remains.

Ready to Go Anywhere

Go ye therefore, and teach all nations (v. 19a).

No chapters in the annals of heroism are more thrilling than those which tell of men who have gladly claimed the privilege and joyfully discharged the duty of telling the good news to others. None excelled the circuit-riding preachers of our own western frontier. Bernard Weisberger has said of these:

> [They were] ready to go anywhere, at any time, where sinners were in need of the saving word. No settlement was too rundown, too remote for them. They roughed it along the trails in snow and rain, taking their chances on bears, wolves, cutthroats and Indians. They put up where they could find local hospitality, which usually meant cornbread and pork and a spot for sleeping on the dirt floor by the fire. They spent a good part of their lives hungry, wet, cold, verminous and saddlesore; and if they did not die young of consumption, they could expect an old age of rheumatism and dyspepsia. But they went almost literally everywhere.[29]

Luke says that when Mary and Joseph presented the child Jesus in the Temple for dedication, a just and devout man named Simeon was there "waiting for the consolation of Israel." Not only was Simeon waiting, but all Israel and the whole world were waiting. The world is still waiting in all those places and parts where God's love has not been declared and believed, the good news of the consolation for all men. For the gospel of Christ is "the power of God unto salvation to every one that believeth."

> Christ for the world we sing;
> The world to Christ we bring,
> With loving zeal;
> The poor, and them that mourn,
> The faint and over-borne,
> Sinsick and sorrow-worn,
> Whom Christ doth heal.
>
> —S. Wolcott

Leadership and Followship

I will make you fishers of men (v. 19b).

During the "silent years" in Nazareth, Jesus had faithfully served and patiently waited. At his baptism he had committed himself and received his Father's approval. In the wilderness of temptation he had forged his ways and means. Immediately following the temptation experiences, he had announced himself and his program. It was now time to select and mobilize his men.

A leader may be committed himself, committed to the right ideas and to the right person; his area of operations may be decided upon; the time of his action may be pinpointed; but he must still rely upon his personnel. He must have around him those on whom he can rely, people who will accept and carry out his orders and his plans.

Douglas Blatherwick records an incident that took place years ago at a great concert given by the Halle Orchestra under the skilled direction of Sir John Barbirolli. The hall was packed; every seat was taken. As the crowd was dispersing, a church member spotted his minister and said, "Tell me, when are we going to have an auditorium packed on a Sunday evening as this place is packed this evening?" The minister answered, "When, like Sir John Barbirolli, I have under me eighty trained and disciplined men." But leadership and "followship" are essential.

Christ alone can save the world—he cannot save the world alone. God has so ordained that we are essential to that great undertaking. Breathtaking in its implications! That the Holy God would allow us to be partners with his Son in bringing the world home to him! Fearful thought, that there are those who will never come home to God unless you and I invite them.

And the Spirit and the bride say, Come. And let him that heareth say, Come (Rev. 22:17a).

On the Hills of Morning

The young man saith unto him (v. 20a).

The job a person has to do determines the kind of personnel he chooses to do the job. Look at the Master's men. When Jesus walked by the seashore and called James and John, they left their father, Zebedee, and the boat and followed Jesus. That is significant. Jesus got two men; one man was left. Did James and John come because Jesus called them, and did Zebedee remain because he was not called? Could there be more involved than that? Is it not likely that Jesus did not call Zebedee because he would not have come had he been called!

"Age," says Walter Russell Bowie, "did not follow him as readily as youth. There was something about him that drew the eager and adventurous, and left settled and conservative people shaking their heads." It is an old story. Terah died in Haran; Abram, his son, moved out, following the voice of God, and went into a land he knew not of. In the first Christian sermon following the ascension of Jesus, Peter talked about "young men" seeing visions.

"Christianity began as young people's movement," said James S. Stewart. "Most of the apostles were probably still in their twenties when they went out after Jesus." For proof of that, remember when Paul wrote, almost a generation later, he said that of the five hundred to whom Christ appeared, most of them were still alive. Does it not suggest that the spiritual appeal of Jesus was mainly to the young? Again and again, Jesus addressed his disciples as "children," or "my dear children," or, as Moffatt and Phillips translate the word, "lads." When the Christians drew the likeness of Jesus on the walls of the catacombs, they drew him "as a young shepherd out on the hills of the morning."

> Lift high the cross of Christ!
> Tread where His feet have trod;
> Be loyal to the King of kings;
> March on, O youth of God!
>
> —WILLIAM P. MERRILL

The Lord Knows Your Size

They turned back and tempted God, and limited the Holy One of Israel (v. 41).

In the oft-quoted words of Paul we are assured that "in everything God works for good with those who love him, who are called according to his purpose" (Rom. 8:28, RSV). That is not to say that everything is good, or that everything is as God desires it. If you are lost, that is not as God desires it! It does affirm that nothing is beyond the power of God, the providence of God, the working of God.

The providence of God, however, does not depend upon God alone. He and he alone can bring his will to pass, but he does not bring his will to pass alone. He uses his children; he calls for their cooperation. The assurance of God's providence does not release us from responsibility and diligent work. God's loving will and providence includes our help. Without our faith and work we can "limit the Holy One of Israel."

When Paul understood that "in everything God works for good with those who love him, who are called according to his purpose," Paul did not cease his effort. He worked more diligently because of that assurance of the working of God for good. Think of the results. Paul was able to use the resources of the pagan Roman Empire to help him spread the gospel! He and God were able to use Rome for good!

Many interesting stories are told about the quaint English preacher, Billy Bray. One day a lady came and said that she would like to give him some of her husband's good suits but she did not know if they would fit the preacher. Billy Bray asked, "Did God tell you to give me the suits?" "Well," said the lady, "yes, I think the Lord led me to offer the suits to you." Said the preacher, "Then don't worry about the fit; God knows my size." Yes, he does.

The Menninger Story

They that are whole need not a physician; but they that are sick (v. 31b).

In *The Menninger Story*, Walker Winslow tells about the dedication of a new hospital in Topeka, Kansas, to house the world-famous Menninger Clinic. The old doctor who had pioneered in the famous institution was ninety years old, and on his birthday he was asked to lay the cornerstone for the new hospital that was to bear his name. Outstanding citizens from Topeka and from over the nation were present. Many of the best medical minds of the world were present.

When the time came for him to speak, Dr. Karl A. Menninger stood. He was tall and straight, and his looks belied his ninety years. He gazed out upon the great throng of people. Later he said that he had known at the time that the throng expected him to give his medical credo, and he had prepared such a statement. When the moment came, however, he could speak only from his heart, and this is what he said:

> From the very beginning, God's hand has been guiding this, and it is fitting to invoke His blessings on what we are going to do. We believe that He put it into our hearts to build this hospital for the art of healing men.

After a moment of silence he bowed his head and prayed,

> Almighty God, Father of all Mercies and God of all comfort, look upon us with favor as we dedicate this building to that end. Bless all who come here sick and troubled. And bless, we pray, all who labor here to relieve affliction. Direct us, we beseech Thee with thankful hearts, in thy way of righteousness and peace, and to Thee be glory and praise, now and forevermore. Amen.[30]

And Luke the physician has this to say of the Great Physician:

> *Then Jesus answering said unto them, Go your way, and tell John what things you have seen and heard; how that the blind see, the lame walk, the lepers are cleansed, the deaf hear, the dead are raised, to the poor the gospel is preached (Luke 7:22).*

A Bigger Job

And greater works than these shall he do (v. 12c).

Included in the call of Jesus to those men who became his disciples was the promise of success. He said to them, "I will make you." He had confidence in his students to learn and in his own ability to teach. Both were necessary. Thinking of those students, as they were when Jesus called them and what they had to learn before they could measure up to his standards for them, one has a fresh view of the optimism of Jesus! It was no easy task to which he set himself, for he would accept no shortcuts in teaching and training.

In the days when men went to sea in wooden ships, an inexperienced youth visited a hiring hall in London hoping to get a job as a seaman. The first question asked was, "Have you ever gone round the Horn?" In those days shipping companies wanted experienced men who had made one or more trips around Cape Horn. The youth replied that he had never been around the Horn. "Then," said the agent, "you will have to come with me into the back room." There in the middle of the floor lay the horn of a steer. The agent said, "Now, young man, just walk slowly around that horn there on the floor; walk slowly." The would-be sailor did as he was told. "You can now qualify for the job," said the agent, "you have been around the Horn."

While Jesus would accept no shortcuts in the field of teaching and training, he did indicate to his men that their former experience as fishermen would be useful to them. He promised, "I will make you fishers of men." They knew fishing of a sort, but if they would follow him, he would teach them to do some real fishing. The difference between the barefoot boy on the creek bank catching minnows with a reed pole and a bent pin and the skilled sportsman reeling in a giant blue marlin from the Gulf Stream is just a suggestion of the difference between what the disciples had been doing and what Jesus could teach them to do. A bigger job!

Read 2 Corinthians 3:1-3 — December 18

Does God Take a Vacation?

Ye are our epistle written in our hearts (v. 2a).

One Christmas my wife and I became dangerously bold; we did not send Christmas cards, not one, and that does take courage! Instead, as we received cards from friends far and near, we filed the cards carefully. With this file we placed our own Christmas card mailing list, which we normally used with great diligence. Then, beginning January 1, using the file of cards and our own list, we began writing "Christmas letters," at least one each day.

We completed that project the following November. There were days when we did not get to write a letter; there were days when we wrote as many as six letters. Each day as we selected the card or name, we had, through memory and imagination, a visit in absentia with that friend. We tried to write warmly, with enthusiasm and gratitude. We tried to tuck a piece of our best selves in each envelope.

It proved to be a rewarding departure from the usual Christmas card syndrome. It brought some of the best of Christmas into our daily rounds—imagine having Christmas in July and August, even every day of the year! It peopled this joyous experience with friends whom we cherished, bringing the two, Christmas and friends, together. Incidentally, or possibly not so incidentally, this plan spread the cost of postage over the months. Too, we learned that a good sheet of writing paper and envelope are less expensive than an attractive Christmas card! As the slogan puts it: "Try it; you'll like it!"

Timmie's letter to God:

Dear Mr. God: We are going on vacation so we won't be in church Sunday. I hope you will and I hope you will be there when we get back. When do you take your vacation? Good-bye until after vacation.

Your friend,
Timmie

359

December 19   **Read Matthew 11:25-30**
God's RSVP

Come unto me all ye that labour and are heavy laden (v. 28a).

It is said that Francis E. Clark, founder of the Christian Endeavor Society, had the word *welcome* carved on the beams of his front porch in seventeen different languages. Those who have taken time to count say that the word *come*, some form of the word, appears six hundred times in the Bible. God's problem is akin to the parents of large families, how does he get his children to come home for Christmas! Think of the invitations he has sent to his children.

"Thou shalt call his name Jesus: for he shall save his people from their sins"; *Home for Christmas!* "They shall call his name Emmanuel, which being interpreted is, God with us"; *Home for Christmas!* "For God so loved the world, that he gave . . . " *Home for Christmas !* "But when the fulness of the time was come, God sent forth his Son"; *Home for Christmas.* "God was in Christ, reconciling the world unto himself"; *Home for Christmas!* "The Spirit and the bride say, Come. And let him that is athirst come. And whosoever will, let him take the water of life freely." Come! *Home for Christmas!*

That is what Christmas is all about, in its deepest meaning. This is why Christ has come. He came as God's warm, urgent, loving invitation, wrapped in human flesh, inviting us, one and all, to come home for Christmas.

The prophet saw this centuries ago; Handel's *Messiah* has made it familiar to us: "Comfort ye, comfort ye my people, saith your God. Speak ye comfortably to Jerusalem, and cry unto her, that her warfare is accomplished, that her iniquity is pardoned: for she hath received of the Lord's hand double for all her sins" (Isa. 40:1-2).

The hinge of history is on the door of a Bethlehem stable.

—RALPH SOCKMAN

360

"A Madhouse?"

They presented unto him gifts (v. 11b).

It was one of the last days of the frantic Christmas rush and a saleswoman in one of the large department stores was serving her last customer. As the shopper gave the name and address for the sending of the purchase, the clerk gave an exhausted sigh and said, "It's a madhouse, isn't it?" "No," replied the customer, "It's a very nice private home."

To turn "madhouses" into "nice private homes" is a worthy project, especially at Christmastime. One way to do that is to send the right kind of Christmas letters and gifts.

Ralph Waldo Emerson gave valuable suggestions in one of his essays, "Gifts." He said there were three kinds of gifts. First, there were gifts of necessity; these are the easiest to give. When a man is hungry, you give him bread; when he is barefoot you give him shoes. Second, there are gifts that are associated with the person receiving the gift; a book for the scholar, a picture for the artist, a delicate piece of china for the collector.

Finally, and best of all, there are the gifts associated with the giver, something that comes from his own life, talent, or work. So, the shepherd might give a lamb; the farmer might give grain.

Of course, the mind and heart will not stay on material things at this point. Gifts associated with the giver, the Giver? This beams in on the deep meaning of Christmas. For when God "sent forth his Son," he was giving a gift "associated with himself." And when we think of the most treasured gift that we may give to him at Christmas, or on any day of the year, it is a gift of self. And, when we give this gift, we know that we are giving the highest and the best, because we are giving as God gave!

"I Wonder as I Wander"

*Believe on the Lord Jesus Christ, and thou shalt be saved,
and thy house (v. 31a).*

"The Word was made flesh." Jesus was a man, but it was the *Word*
that became flesh. He was divine. The disciples and his early
followers came to see that as one of the clearest stars in their sky!
"Believe on the Lord Jesus Christ . . . " "He that believeth on the Son
hath everlasting life."

How he could be fully God and fully man we do not know. The best
minds have tried to explain it; they have done so only in part. A
musician visiting in one of our small North Carolina towns in the
mountains heard a young mountain girl singing an old ballad. He
asked her to sing it over for him; he rearranged it and gave us the
lovely Christmas message:

> I wonder as I wander, out under the sky,
> How Jesus our Saviour did come forth to die,
> For poor ornery people like you and like I
> I wonder as I wander, out under the sky.[31]

—John Jacob Niles

We do wonder, whether in church, lecture hall or "out under the
sky." We shall know fully only when we know as we are known. Still
could we agree on the following?

I believe that in and through Christ, God has given you and me a
perfect example. I believe that in and through Christ, God has spoken
a word of victory for you and me. I do believe that in and through
Christ, God has shown the terribleness of sin. I believe that in Christ,
God has revealed his own love and suffering. I believe that through
Christ, God's love and God's grace and God's power and God's
presence are made available to you and to me. And, further, I believe
that in and through Christ, God has done something that changes my
status before God. This we do believe!

"Though Nobly Born"

They that gladly received his word were baptized (v. 41a).

One day I walked in the cemetery of old St. John's Church in Richmond, Virginia; there I read epitaphs on tombstones, ancient and moss-covered. There I read the following:

> To the mother of Edgar Allen Poe, Elizabeth Arnold, born in England, 1787, died in Richmond, 1811, buried here. The actor of talent is poor of heart indeed if he does not look with contempt upon mediocrity, even in a king. The writer is himself the son of an actress, has invariably made it his boast, and no earl was ever prouder of his earldom, than he of his descent from a woman, who though nobly born, hesitated not to consign to the drama her brief career of genius and of beauty.

I tediously deciphered those words from a moss-covered, simple slab on a Lord's Day morning many years ago. But I believe I have never seen, heard, or thought of them from that day to this but that the life and death of Christ has come to my mind. For Christ, though nobly born, hesitated not to consign to the church his brief career of genius and of beauty. "I will build my church," he said. The apostle Paul wrote, "Christ loved the church, and gave himself for it."

The truth should inspire and rejoice our hearts! It should assure and reassure us. It lets us know that we are in no small task when we give ourselves to the building of the kingdom through the churches of our Lord. Victory, not defeat, is ahead for the church that is founded on Christ, the "solid Rock."

Recently a father took his young son to church. The boy entered enthusiastically into the singing. The hymn was, "Rise up O men of God!/Have done with lesser things." The father listened closely to his son's singing and heard: "Wise up, O men of God!" The father decided it was not a bad interpretation!

"Home for Christmas"

Return unto thy own house (v. 39*a*).

Lloyd C. Douglas wrote a little book he called *Home for Christmas*. It is about the Clayton tribe, five children, three girls, and two boys. They grew up in an old farmhouse with its hardships and simple pleasures. Long ago they left the old place and became prosperous American citizens. The two boys, Jim and Fred, had made their mark. The two older girls had "married well." Nan, the youngest girl had not married. It was her idea that the five Claytons return to the old farmhouse for Christmas, just the five of them, living as they had when they were children. The project sounded a bit alarming for the older brothers and sisters, settled in their comforts, but they loved Nan and wanted to humor her. So, families were banished and the five Claytons gathered. What follows makes a lovely story filled with humor, tender nostalgia, and two delightful love stories.

Jim and Fred kill the pig and make the sausage; the girls bake the cakes and pies, roast the nuts, pop the corn, and hang the greens. The boys bring a huge tree from the forest. Neighbors are invited to the home for Christmas Eve.

The event is presided over by "Miss Packer," a retired teacher who has taught about everyone in the community, including all the Claytons. It is a delightful and delicious time, a time of happy memories. The evening comes to a close with "Packy" calling on Jim Clayton to "say a few words." Jim is surprised and unprepared; he cannot laugh this off. He stood, looked at the group, and smiled, then shifted from foot to foot. He reminded the group of the simple faith, loved and cherished by their parents. He said that if all the composers of all time were gathered it would be the unanimous opinion that the song chanted above the hills of Bethlehem had moved mankind to its best endeavor; while the star they heard about as children had given men and women their most luminous ideas and hopes. "Home for Christmas," home to God, is a good idea.[32]

On Missing Christmas

The people which sat in darkness saw a great light (v. 16a).

Some years ago a ship approached the international dateline just before midnight on Christmas Eve. The captain of the ship announced to the passengers that they would, in all probability, miss Christmas Day entirely. For as the international date line is crossed, either twenty-four hours are lost or gained, depending on which direction your ship is going. This ship would lose twenty-four hours and miss Christmas!

What a frightful possibility! What if the whole world were to miss Christmas, had never known Christmas! What if the Son of God had not been born in Bethlehem of Judea! But "God sent forth his Son" (Gal. 4:4).

The wise man said, "To every thing there is a season, and a time to every purpose under the heavens" (Eccl. 3:1). There is a proper rendezvous between man and the occasion. It is a pathetic sight to see a man arrive before his time! He comes with a message that will be welcomed and hailed tomorrow; today he is considered an idle dreamer. Or, one comes too late; the occasion has fled. There was a time when he would have had an audience but now the world has moved on and he is trying to rally forces that have dispersed. And, with Thomas Wolfe he learns that he can't "go home again."

A few years before Jesus was born the Latin poet Virgil wrote:

> The last great age, foretold in sacred rhymes,
> Renews its finished course; Saturnian times
> Roll round again; and mighty years, begun
> From their first orb, in radiant circles run.
> The base, degenerate iron offspring ends,
> A golden progeny from heaven descends.

December 25   Read Luke 2:15-20
God and Simple People

They came with haste and found . . . (v. 16a).

Christmas is good news about God and simple people. Why did God choose the plain, the simple, and the humble? Was it because their ears were open?

What would have been the reaction of Caesar that first Christmas night if the angels had come to him instead of to the shepherds? What if it had been announced to him that a peasant woman was giving birth to a son in one of his smallest and most despised provinces and that he had better forget whatever he was doing and hurry there to give his allegiance? Christmas is good news about God and the day of small things. Great events frequently spring from small beginnings.

Imagine the modern world stripped of all the blessed ministries that date from that event! Pull down the churches and chapels; obliterate the best of art, sculpture, and music; blast the institutions of healing and mercy; wipe out most of the volunteer service to others that has no thought of reward. Pull woman from her pedestal; take the child from "the center" and "expose" it again. That is just a beginning.

In his flesh Jesus was a Jew, but he came to all people. He was born in Palestine, but the whole world is his field. He spoke Aramaic and Hebrew, possibly Greek, but all people hear in their own tongues. He wore the garments of the East, but he is recognized in all forms of dress.

This is good news, but it is frequently disturbing news! Did you see the cartoon of the man being fitted for new glasses? He was saying to the doctor, "I'd like to see a little less clearly, please."

It is good to be children sometimes, and never better than at Christmas, when its mighty Founder was a child himself.

—CHARLES DICKENS

366

"He Loved Me So Much"

I live by the faith of the Son of God, who loved me . . . (v. 20b).

The churches and the community need to cooperate in many matters. If the world is in the church, and it is, the churches need to be in the world, though not "of it." We must keep the church windows open toward Jerusalem, otherwise we are lame like the beggar at the pool; but unless the churches keep their windows open to the street they deny their Lord who said to the disciples of the multitudes, "They need not depart; you give them to eat."

The only safe thing for the individual and the churches is to see that all of life is committed to the living Christ who loved the individual and the churches and gave himself for both. Dr. William Barclay gives a poignant story in this field. The story deals with an experience that Sir George Adam Smith, the great Old Testament scholar, once had. In his travels Dr. Smith found himself sitting by a young man who was going out to the mission field. The young man was tall and handsome, winsome and attractive, brilliant and gifted. As they talked, Dr. Smith soon found that the young man was on his way to a post in a certain part of Africa that Dr. Smith knew well as a deadly place for the white man; the climate and disease were simply more than the body of a white man could withstand. He knew there were no medicines or inoculations available for protection. Hence, at that time, a white man's life was measured in terms of months, not of years.

It seemed such a waste. Though Dr. Smith was a committed Christian he tried to reason with the young man. Could he not invest his life elsewhere and for a longer period of time, where the accumulated service would be greater? But the young man was adamant. To the needy but dangerous territory he would go.

The train came to the station where Dr. Smith was to depart; the young missionary was to continue his journey. The older man still tried to reason with the younger man. As the train left the station, the young man was in the door, and he said to Dr. Smith: "He loved me so much and gave himself for me—can I hold anything back?"

Wingless Victory

But when the fulness of the time was come, God sent forth his Son" (v. 4a).

In his play, *The Wingless Victory,* Maxwell Anderson says a sharp and penetrating word about Christianity's place in an evil world. He locates his play in Salem, Massachusetts. Nathaniel has been away for many years. He returns with a Malay princess as his wife. This lovely young woman has been attracted to the life and teachings of Jesus. But the people of Salem are prejudiced. They will have none of her. The pressure is so great that even her husband weakens. The princess knows that she must leave the community alone, save for her children and faithful servant. She boards the ship, resolved to die. She turns back to the pagan gods she knew as a child, and talks to them in disturbing words, giving her thoughts about this "Christ of peace." She says the world is not ready for him yet; it may be ready in a hundred thousand years but it has to drink of blood and tears for a long time to come. The world is not yet ready for the Christ; his time has not come.

The apostle Paul would have disagreed. He thought the time had come. That it was in the "fulness of the time" that God sent forth his Son. It is true, and Paul knew that the world was not ready to accept the "Prince of peace" without a struggle.

Yet, it was just the sin and the struggle that brought Christ. If there had been no wickedness, if the world had been ready to receive him, what would have been his mission? For it was to save that he came. Let evil rebel and shout; let the devil sound "like a peg-legged man on a tin roof having a fit," it is still true that "every knee shall bow and every tongue shall confess."

The Lure of Life's Leftovers

There was taken up of fragments that remained (v. 17).

Frequently our major tasks and desires fail, fall far short of fulfillment; then, when much of time, resources, and life are gone, we have to take the leftovers and try to do something worthwhile with them. Those leftover fragments after the five thousand had been fed are suggestive. *Sunshine* magazine years ago published the following statement.

Take a Real Man . . .
Cripple him and you have a Sir Walter Raleigh.
Bury him in the snows of Valley Forge and you have a Washington.
Have him born in abject poverty and you have a Lincoln.
Throw every obstacle in his path and you have a Booker T. Washington.
Load him with bitter racial prejudice and you have a Disraeli.
Stab him with rheumatic pains until for years he cannot sleep without
    drugs and you have a Steinmetz.
Make him a second fiddler in an obscure South American orchestra and
    you have a Toscanini.
Real men accept hardship as a challenge.

—AUTHOR UNKNOWN

How can these leftovers be taken and be made to pay dividends, not just for the great and the mighty but for you and for me, everyday folk? If you read biographies carefully, you will probably come up with suggestions close to the following:

1. Don't blame God for your failure.
2. Be slow to blame others for your failure.
3. Do the best you can with what you have at hand.
4. Know when to quit; have the courage to admit failure.
5. Live one day at the time.
6. Trust God for what you cannot do yourself.

Remember the old spiritual that talks about taking our burden to the Lord and leaving it there? Saying if our bodies suffer pain and health we can't regain, and our souls are almost sinking in despair, that we are to remember Jesus knows how we feel, just take the burdens to the Lord and leave them there.

"Let Us Go On"

Let us go on unto perfection [maturity] (v. 1b).

There is a story of the two men talking about a new preacher that had come to the local church. "How do you like him?" one inquired. "Like him fine, especially his praying; I tell you he is a praying man." "You mean he prays better than your last preacher did?" "Why man, this preacher asks the Lord for things our other preacher didn't know the Lord had!"

The writer of the Book of Hebrews challenged his readers to claim from the Lord new and advanced blessings. He was an apostle of progress. He was disturbed over the fact that his readers were not growing in the Christian life; they were content to remain in the kindergarten class of Christianity. "Let us go on to maturity," he cries. "Let us leave the elementary doctrines."

From alphabet to words, from words to sentences, from sentences to paragraphs, to chapters to books. Blossoms are for the production of fruit. The architect has his plans; the builder says, "Let us go on." Then the plumbers, the electricians, and the decorators come and say, "Let us go on." It is no reflection upon the architect, the brick masons, carpenters, etc. Each expects another to carry the work forward.

It is disturbing to see an intelligent, competent man or woman stay in the same class year after year after year, never putting into practice what has been taught. For surely by this time many should be teaching. "For unto whomsoever much is given, of him shall be much required." The writer of Hebrews says, "Let us go on."

The little boy was from a home of poverty; he had always had to share his glass of milk with brothers and sisters. At camp he was given a full glass of milk. "How deep may I drink?" he asked. With choked voice, the counselor said, "Just as deep as you can." "Let us go on" into new depths, just as deep as we can.

"Time to Remember"

I kept back nothing that was profitable unto you (v. 20a).

Time to Remember is the title of Lloyd C. Douglas's autobiography. There are times when it is natural to evaluate one's record in Christian service—beginning of a new year, an anniversary, election to a new place of service or, on being reassigned to an old responsibility.

Paul had reached a "time to remember" in his service; his term of service at Ephesus was over. How had he served? What did he remember? First, it is good to remember that you have been humble in service. Paul said he had served "with all humility of mind."

Second, compassion and earnestness should mark our service. It is possible to be too objective in our service; Paul served with tears. Third, it is good to remember that we have always been faithful in service. It is not easy to so live and serve that you can say that nothing is kept back from the people that was for their welfare. A desire for approval and harmony can easily cause us to "trim our sails" to compromise.

Fourth, it is good to remember that our teaching and living have revealed courage. Paul could say that he had declared the "whole counsel of God." What a claim! Woodrow Wilson once said, "I had rather be defeated in a cause that will ultimately triumph than to triumph in a cause that will ultimately be defeated."

Fifth, Paul lived independently. He paid his freight. One should pay for one's ticket on the train of life. Looking back over his term of service in Ephesus, Paul remembered these five things.

> Memory is a treasurer to whom you must give funds, if you would draw the assistance you need.
>
> —NICHOLAS ROWE

"Life's Uncut Pages"

All that I have is thine (v. 31b).

On the last day of the year we stand between the years. The old Greeks dedicated the time to Janus, the god that looked both ways. So, we look back; we look forward. Let us give thought to the older brother in the parable that Jesus told, the parable that is usually thought of as the parable of the prodigal son, the younger son in the story. In looking back over the past year, there is so much that has not been done. As someone has said, there are many "uncut pages." Have you ever bought a book and found that several of the pages were folded but not cut apart? So you were not able to read those pages without cutting them. The older son certainly left many uncut pages.

He left uncut the pages of *gratitude*. He reminded his father of all the work that he, the son, had done, how he had kept the father's commands. He could remember only the things his father had *not* done for him.

He left uncut the pages of *humility*. In the first sentence (v. 29) when the boy spoke to his father he mentions *himself* five times! It has been said that in reality this is a parable of *three* sons: prodigal son—prodigal in body, at home in heart; older son—prodigal in heart, at home in body; Son of God—gave heart and body for home and family.

He left uncut the pages of *love*: love for father, love for brother; he only cut the pages of love for himself. He did not like his father; he hated his brother; he pitied himself. He never called the younger son, "My brother," it was always, "thy son."

He left uncut the pages of *joy*. Not liking his father, hating his brother, feeling sorry for himself, of course he did not know joy. When we sprinkle the perfume of joy on others we always get a bit on ourselves!

HAPPY NEW YEAR!

Notes

1. Reprinted from *Poems* by George Santayana. Copyright 1923 by Charles Scribner's Sons; 1951 by George Santayana. Used by permission of the publishers.

2. From Kirby Page, *Living Joyously* (New York: Holt, Rinehart & Winston, 1950), p. 248.

3. Leslie D. Weatherhead, *How Can I Find God?* (New York: Fleming H. Revell, 1934), p. 126.

4. G. K. Chesterton, *The Autobiography of G. K. Chesterton* (New York: Sheed & Ward, 1937), p. 167.

5. From "Teach Me to Pray." Words by Albert S. Reitz. Copyright 1925 A. S. Reitz. Renewal 1953 by Broadman Press. All rights reserved.

6. From "God, Give Us Christian Homes," copyright 1949, Broadman Press. All rights reserved.

7. W. Macneile Dixon, *The Human Situation* (New York: St. Martin's Press, 1954), pp. 415-16.

8. Quoted in Roland H. Bainton, *Here I Stand* (New York: Abingdon-Cokesbury, 1950), pp. 233-34.

9. C. S. Lewis, *The Screwtape Letters* (New York: Macmillan and Company, 1943), p. 47.

10. Lloyd C. Douglas, *The Robe* (New York: Pocket Books, 1969), p. 293.

11. Quoted in *San Francisco Chronicle*, Jan. 25, 1965. Pages, 1,7. Used by permission.

12. Douglas, *The Robe*, pp. 123-24.

13. Morris L. West, *The Shoes of the Fisherman* (New York: William Morrow & Company, 1963), p. 231.

14. A. M. Chirgwin, *The Bible and World Evangelism* (New York: Friendship Press, 1954), p. 30.

15. William Saroyan, *The Human Comedy* (New York: Harcourt, Brace & Co., 1944), pp. 34-35.

16. Quoted in Leslie D. Weatherhead, *A Private House of Prayer* (Nashville: Abingdon Press, 1959), p. 28.

17. From "Judean Hills" by William L. Stidger. Used by permission Rodeheaver-Hall-Mack.

18. Ian Burnett, *Lord of All Life* (New York: Rinehart & Company, 1952), pp. 12-13.

19. Used by permission *Christian Century*.

20. Benjamin P. Browne, *The Writer's Conference Comes to You* (Valley Forge, PA: Judson Press, 1956), p. 21.

21. Used by permission of Mrs. Louise H. Sclove, New York City.

22. Graham Greene, *The Heart of the Matter* (New York: Viking Press, 1962).

23. From Edna St. Vincent Millay, "God's World," *Collected Poems* © Copyright Norma Millay Ellis. All rights reserved.

24. Archibald Rutledge, *Life's Extras* (New York: Fleming H. Revell, Co., 1946), pp. 10-11.

25. Ibid., p. 6.

26. T. Howard Crago, *The Story of F. W. Boreham* (London: Marshall, Morgan, & Scott, 1961), p. 237.

27. Dorothy Parker, *Not So Deep as a Well* (New York: Viking Press, 1955), p. 52. Used by permission.

28. Lloyd C. Douglas, *Green Light* (Boston: Houghton Mifflin Co., 1935), pp. 182-83.

29. From Bernard Weisberger, *They Gathered at the River* (Boston: Little, Brown & Co., 1958), p. 45.

30. Walker Winslow, *The Menninger Story* (Garden City, NY: Doubleday Publishers, 1956), p. 24.

31. Copyright 1934 by G. Schirmer, Inc., New York, NY. Used by permission.

32. From Lloyd C. Douglas, *Home for Christmas* (New York: Grosset & Dunlap, 1937).

Original Sources

J. Winston Pearce has based the majority of these daily devotions all or in part on his previously published books. The following list of sources first names the original work, then the dates of the devotions based on it, and by each date the pages found in the original book—for instance: April 11 (139-141).

Based on *A Window on the Mountain,* © Copyright 1968. Broadman Press, Nashville, TN. All rights reserved: January 7 (vii.-viii.), 8 (ix.), 9 (1-2), 20 (5); May 15 (2-3), 23 (7-8), 25 (7-8), 31 (65-66); June 9 (69), 10 (84-85), 11 (31-32), 12 (24-25); July 3 (62-63), 4 (143-144); August 1 (61-62); September 24 (30-31), 25 (32-33), 26 (38-39), 29 (138-139); October 1 (16-17), 2 (144-145), 3 (124-125), 4 (67-68), 5 (36-37), 6 (33-34), 7 (28-29), 8 (27-28), 9 (25-26); November 9 (92-94).

Based on *The Window Sill of Heaven,* © Copyright 1958. Broadman Press, Nashville, TN. All rights reserved: February 8 (77), 10 (48-50), 11 (1-3), 14 (19-20); March 28 (109-110), 29 (107), 30 (123-124), 31 (129-131); April 7 (60-61), 8 (70-71), 11 (139-141), 12 (135-137), 13 (132-133); May 11 (113, 121-122); June 1 (22-23), 3 (7); July 17 (78-79), 18 (57-58), 22 (149-154), 23 (141-142), 24 (146); November 2 (65-67), 3 (66-67), 4 (6), 6 (9-10), 10 (101-102), 11 (75-76), 12 (95-96), 13 (46-47).

Based on *I Believe,* © Copyright 1954. Broadman Press, Nashville, TN. All rights reserved: January 24 (32,112-114), 25 (99ff), 26 (96-98), 27 (92-94), 28 (11-12), 30 (49-52), 31 (60-61); April 22 (100-103), 23 (103-105), 24 (106-109); May 6 (75-77), 7 (77-80), 8 (80-81); June 2 (17-18), 27 (21-22), 28 (84-85); September 1 (118), 2 (117), 3 (116-117), 4 (115-116), 6 (7-9), 21 (22-25); December 21 (25-30), 22 (59-60), 24 (42-44).

Based on *The Light on the Lord's Face,* © Copyright 1970. Broadman Press, Nashville, TN. All rights reserved: January 1 (103-104), 11 (24-25), 12 (26-27), 13 (29-30); February 24 (125-126), 25 (107-108), 26 (75-76); March 24 (125-126), 25 (124-125), 26 (111-112), 27 (18-19); April 5 (80-81), 14 (85), 15 (71-72), 16 (83-84), 20 (118-120); May 2 (14-15), 3 (13-14), 4 (10-11), 5 (11-12); June 14 (22-24), 15 (28-29), 16 (31-33), 17 (51-52), 18 (54-55); July 25 (70-71), 26 (87-88), 27 (94-95), 28 (97-101), 29 (69-74); August 15 (109-110), 20 (59-60), 23 (73), 24 (74); October 25 (67-68), 26 (35-42), 27 (35), 28 (41-42), 29 (16-17), 31 (86-81); November 15 (43-44), 16 (44-45), 17 (53-54), 18 (61-62), 19 (96-97), 23 (93-94), 26 (116-117).

Based on *Say It With Letters,* © Copyright 1981. Broadman Press, Nashville, TN. All rights reserved: May 1 (7-8), 29 (15-17); June 4 (40-41); July 1 (55-56), 2 (73-74), 8 (46-47); August 8

(97-98); November 30 (30-31); December 18 (41-42), 20 (38-39).

Index of Persons

375

Index of Topics

Index of Special Days